D1553640

BUYING MILITARY TRAN$FORMATION

BUYING MILITARY
TRAN$FORMATION

Technological Innovation and the Defense Industry

Peter Dombrowski and Eugene Gholz

COLUMBIA UNIVERSITY PRESS NEW YORK

Columbia University Press
Publishers Since 1893
New York, Chichester, West Sussex

Library of Congress Cataloging-in-Publication Data

Dombrowski, Peter J.
Buying military transformation: technological innovation and the defense industry /
Peter Dombrowski and Eugene Gholz
p. cm.
Includes bibliographical references and index.
ISBN 978-0-231-13570-2 (cloth : alk. paper)—
ISBN 978-0-231-50965-7 (e book)
1. United States—Procurement. 2. Military art and science—
Technological innovations—United States. 3. Military art and science—
Computer networks—United States. 4. United States—Armed Forces—
Reorganization. 5. Defense industries—United States.
6. Information technology—United States.
I. Gholz, Eugene, 1971– II. Title.
UC263.D66 2006
355.6'2120973—dc22   2006009067

Columbia University Press books are printed on
permanent and durable acid-free paper

Printed in the United States of America

c 10 9 8 7 6 5 4 3 2

References to Internet Web Sites (URLs) were accurate
at the time of writing. Neither the author nor Columbia
University Press is responsible for Web sites that may
have expired or changed since the book was prepared

To Ann and Johanna

P.D.

and to Jenny

E.G.

CONTENTS

PREFACE   IX

ACKNOWLEDGMENTS   XV

CHAPTER ONE Buying Transformation   **1**

CHAPTER TWO Implementing Military Innovation   **16**

CHAPTER THREE Small Ships   **34**

CHAPTER FOUR Unmanned Aerial Vehicles   **59**

CHAPTER FIVE Communications   **84**

CHAPTER SIX Systems Integration and Public-Private Partnership   **111**

CHAPTER SEVEN Military Innovation and the Defense Industry   **136**

NOTES   **149**

INDEX   **185**

In the 1990s, American political and military leaders watched the world around them changing: computers and communications innovations revolutionized all areas of civilian and commercial life for the Information Age. Generals, admirals, and civilians in the Office of the Secretary of Defense grew anxious. Decades earlier, when they had entered military service, most took pride in military equipment that was at the cutting edge of technology. As the World Wide Web, cellular telephones, and Playstations beckoned from the civilian world, military technologies looked increasingly obsolete. By the late 1990s most military leaders were committed to applying comparable information technology to military tasks.

"Military transformation" is now at the top of the American defense policy agenda. In the 2000 election campaign, President Bush promised a more humble foreign policy that would eschew humanitarian operations, nation-building exercises, and other activities that might distract the nation from America's main challenge: preparing to defend against new threats and to exploit new opportunities in the coming century. The president's stated goal was to revolutionize the U.S. military by introducing Information Age computing and telecommunications technologies to the "legacy force" that had fought the Cold War with Industrial

Age equipment. According to transformation proponents, the information technology will vastly increase American military effectiveness and efficiency. For the first nine months of 2001, military transformation is exactly what Secretary of Defense Donald Rumsfeld focused on.

With the September 11 attacks, priorities shifted to prosecuting a war on terror and removing foreign regimes thought to provide safe haven for terrorists or to harbor ambitions to produce weapons of mass destruction. But even with the increased pace of operations, the administration believes that military transformation—the process of drawing information technology into the military sphere and adapting the military's organization and culture to capitalize on the new network technology—will make a vital contribution both to the long-term security of the United States and to achieving the near-term goal of winning the Global War on Terror.

On October 29, 2001, Secretary Rumsfeld created the Pentagon's Office of Force Transformation. Establishing an office takes a good deal of preparation, and this initiative had been in the works even before September 11. Reporting directly to the secretary, the new office became the coordinating point and the advocate for transformation in the defense policy process. As the office noted in the forward to its report, *Elements of Defense Transformation*:

> During those extraordinarily difficult days, it was easy to think of the future of transformation in the Department as a narrow consequence of 9/11. [But] it has become increasingly clear that defense transformation is not simply a response to global terrorism. While the events of September 11th triggered a 'system perturbation' … profound change was already occurring in that system. Thus, the establishment of the Office of Force Transformation signified not just a reaction to terrorism, but rather Secretary Rumsfeld's overall commitment to the process of transformation within the Department.[1]

But transformation advocates quickly capitalized on the new salience of national security threats to the public agenda: the ongoing operations in Iraq and Afghanistan showcase transformational weapons and highlight the benefits of the new style of operations that rely on networks.

The Office of Force Transformation set about creating official definitions of military transformation, sponsoring experiments and simulations to define the new military doctrine that would explain to soldiers and

seamen how to fight in a "network-centric" environment, and interfac-
ing with the acquisition process that was developing and procuring the
equipment for the military's future. For example, they explained, "the
concepts of NCW [Network-Centric Warfare] and our steadily improving network-centric capabilities are transforming how we fight. Thus,
NCW is at the very center of force transformation."[2] Each of the military
services has adopted this network-centric vision as part of its service-
specific transformation planning, and the vision also permeates efforts
to increase the level of cooperation among the services.

The vital first step, then, is to improve military networking technologies and to design weapons systems to take advantage of the new capabilities. Over and over, military and civilian leaders have stressed that
transformation is more than a technological or acquisition project; to
date, the majority of the transformation effort has sought to figure out
how a networked force will fight in the future. "The implementation
of NCW is first of all about human behavior as opposed to information
technology. While 'network' is a noun, 'to network' is a verb."[3] But new
behaviors will be possible only if the network itself exists; network-centric warfare cannot work without a network. The military must replace
its legacy equipment, in which each piece was designed to fight on its
own or with limited voice radio and data communications on the battlefield, with new, network-centric technology.

> In essence, [Network-Centric Warfare] translates information advan-
> tage into combat power by effectively linking friendly forces within
> the battlespace, providing a much improved shared awareness of the
> situation, enabling more rapid and effective decision making at all lev-
> els of military operations, and thereby allowing for increased speed of
> execution. This "network" is underpinned by information technology
> systems, but is exploited by the Soldiers, Sailors, Airmen, and Marines
> that use the network and, at the same time, are part of it.[4]

The next logical question, then, is how best to acquire the military's
network equipment. Transformation advocates themselves have argued
that the military services would benefit from higher rates of technological innovation and greater efficiency if they reduce their reliance
on traditional suppliers and switch to new, network-oriented firms—
perhaps even the very firms that drove the transformation of the civilian
economy. After all, the names of new information-technology companies

became household words during the transition to the civilian Information Age. In the commercial world, just-in-time logistics, lean manufacturing, flat organizations, and a host of other developments enabled by the information revolution have made retail giants like Wal-Mart the darlings of Wall Street. At the same time traditional firms like Sears have struggled to remake themselves, and Kmart went bankrupt. If Cisco Systems makes vital networking equipment for Wal-Mart, perhaps Cisco can and should make similar equipment for the military. Yet, even if commercial equipment cannot be used directly in the military context, it seems reasonable to replace the established defense firms, which are skilled in developing and manufacturing non-networked, traditional military equipment, with more dynamic, information-technology specialists with new core competencies.

Visionaries of military transformation—people like retired Vice Admiral Arthur Cebrowski, until recently the director of the Office of Force Transformation—draw an explicit analogy between Wal-Mart's success as a "category killer" company and their goals for the future of American military power. A key part of the Wal-Mart story is that computer networks link the scanners that replaced cash registers to the firm's inventory management system: stores can be resupplied faster and more accurately, reducing distribution costs and speeding reaction to trends in consumer tastes. Perhaps the combat performance of soldiers on the front lines could similarly be improved if they were linked to depots and ammunition dumps. Moreover, information technology has helped chains to adapt their different stores to local tastes. The military might benefit from similar decentralization to deal with tactical complexity.[5]

Our book analyzes in detail the widespread claim that military transformation requires a revolutionary approach to the defense industrial base. In particular, we examine the quest for military innovation and the conventional wisdom that firms outside the established defense industry can provide the systems necessary for twenty-first century combat. We develop and apply a new theory of military innovation, building on insights from the literature on business innovation and the political economy of the relationship between the military and the defense industry. We conclude, contrary to the expectations of transformation theorists, many military officers, and most high-ranking officials within the Department of Defense, that transformative weapons and supporting technologies will come, with a few noteworthy exceptions, from the same firms that have been supplying the nation's military needs since the end of the Second World War.

This finding is important because military transformation presents a tremendous challenge to military organizations and offers the possibility of a dramatic increase in military power, vital to U.S. national security. Given the hard work required to invent new military concepts and to overcome institutional resistance to major cultural change, it is fortunate that transformation advocates need not attempt to transform business–government relations at the same time they change the military itself. In short, if we are correct, military transformation is more likely to succeed than it would be if it were necessary to fight the political battles required to dismantle the existing defense industrial base.

Of course, the policy debates about transformation continue. Some missteps and mistakes are almost inevitable, and in fact they are part of the transformation process itself. No one can know in advance the exact trajectory of technological progress, and no one can predict the best way to use new technologies until real troops have an opportunity to experiment with them in the field. But political and military leaders could certainly make the process much more difficult and more expensive than it needs to be, especially by neglecting analyses like the one presented in this book. Billions of dollars of national security investment are at stake—more than $200 billion in the next decade, according to one estimate.[6] Even if the military were ultimately to succeed in exploiting information technology developed and acquired from new suppliers, the extra effort and political controversy would surely divert resources that could be better spent and delay the transformation, needlessly squandering opportunities to help the American military.

The world of information technology offers many options to the military—many good ideas and perhaps even more bad ones. Congress and the military services are already making hard choices regarding the specific weapons systems and technologies that the United States will buy, and the American taxpayers will not be willing to fund every possible plan. In the spring of 2005, the U.S. Navy was forced to scale back one of its most innovative shipbuilding programs, an advanced destroyer known as the DD(X), in the face of expected budgetary shortfalls. Finding the best industry partners to work on transformation with America's military and political leadership is vital to the success of transformation, which is itself a key part of the U.S. national security strategy.

The national security policy debates about transformation reflect underlying changes in the global economy—the shift from the Industrial Age to the Information Age—and in the international security environment. These debates need to be integrated with political choices about America's strategies for dealing with the world and about the role of defense in the economy at home. Our research links U.S. strategic preferences, defense policies and politics, and the technological innovations necessary to protect America's national security in the coming decades.

Buying Military Transformation has its origins in a project begun nearly seven years ago. The then-President of the Naval War College, Vice Admiral Arthur K. Cebrowski, asked for a study of the role of the defense industry in supporting transformation and, in particular, network-centric warfare. The project team—Andrew Ross, Peter Dombrowski, and Eugene Gholz—published a *Newport Paper* from the Naval War College Press and a short article in *Orbis* that focused on the Navy and a few key industrial sectors. We hope that those publications were directly useful to those in the Navy who supported the initial project. Vice Admiral Cebrowski and Alberto Coll, the Dean of Naval Warfare Studies at the War College, stimulated our thinking and provided essential institutional support for our research. We owe them a great debt of gratitude.

After those initial publications, we decided to expand the project into a book, which could provide broader lessons about the theory of military innovation and about the relationship between "Revolutions in Military Affairs" and changes in the civilian economy and society. Andrew Ross stepped aside to pursue a separate project on military transformation. While he surely would not agree with all of our analysis in this book, his contributions to the earlier project continued to influence our thinking about transformation, and we appreciate his continuing willingness to discuss many topics about the military and industry.

For the book, we added a considerable amount of new empirical material, collected through many interviews and informal discussions with military and civilian experts. We incurred numerous debts to the hundreds of industry and government officials we interviewed and to the dozens of scholars with whom we discussed aspects of this project. Catherine Kelleher, Michael Desch, and Harvey Sapolsky deserve particular thanks for reading long drafts. And we would be especially remiss if we did not thank our respective spouses and families for their support and patience during our many trips, long phone conversations, and late night writing sessions.

BUYING MILITARY TRAN$FORMATION

CHAPTER ONE

BUYING TRANSFORMATION

Even before the shock of September 11, the United States national security establishment was planning major changes for the nation's armed services. After the collapse of the Soviet Union, American defense planners had the opportunity to develop doctrine and establish equipment requirements in response to technological opportunities rather than strategic threats. Information technology had changed the American economy and society, while computer network connections deepened links between local and global economic events. Advocates of military transformation consciously used that civilian transformation as a model for their vision of the future American military.[1] In their view, investment in enhanced network infrastructure accompanied by changes in strategy, doctrine, and tactics would allow the U.S. military to leap ahead of potential adversaries and guard against asymmetric threats to America's military dominance. In short, a window of opportunity opened for the United States in the 1990s to secure military primacy far into the future.[2]

This book analyzes the role of the defense industry in implementing America's ongoing revolution in military affairs (RMA).[3] Without industry's development and production of a host of new equipment, military transformation will not be possible. Moreover, transformation promises to challenge the structure and performance of the defense industry, as new technology is developed and new military systems are acquired. In this book, the focus on the connections between advocates' new ideas about military doctrine, the practical need to convince political leaders to spend money, and industry's business strategies to manage technological change yields a new theory and prescriptions for facilitating military transformation.

Scholars have long recognized three important components of innovations: conception (invention), proposal, and implementation.[4] Much previous work on military innovation emphasizes conception (the sources of new military doctrines) and the proposal process (the roles of military and civilian leaders in promoting new ideas). Our theory pushes the state of the art in innovation studies by explaining the process of implementation. In the military context, we explain something about the demand for invention and a good deal about how inventions are applied through a practical, political-economy process.

Our analysis runs contrary to the conventional wisdom about military transformation and the future of the defense industry. The links between the RMA and broader economic and technological changes naturally suggest to transformation advocates that the United States cannot rely on the existing defense industrial base to supply transformational equipment.[5] Traditional defense suppliers have not emphasized networking in their products, and transformation advocates fear that they have neither the skills nor the inclination to change. More important, the whole idea behind transformation is to import information technology successes from the civilian world into the military context. Surprisingly, though, despite the obvious technical capabilities of commercial information-technology firms, our case studies show that current defense-oriented suppliers are likely to dominate the future defense market. In fact, the established suppliers are especially likely to maintain their position in the segments of the defense industry that rely most intensively on information technology. If any defense firms are vulnerable to new competition as a result of the RMA, it will be the suppliers of large, defense-unique platforms like naval surface combatants. Even those "old economy" companies have an important role to play in the political-economy coalition needed to implement transformation. And the importance of the political-economy foundations of military innovation implies certain policy and organizational choices for the military services and the acquisition community that might help smooth the transformation process in the face of political opposition, budgetary constraints, and pressures for technological overreach.

This chapter explains the origins of the new American military doctrine of network-centric warfare (NCW), which attempts to capitalize on the information-technology revolution in military affairs. The idea for network-centric warfare has evolved from a particular view of the RMA, specifically that economic and social revolutions in response to information technology have preceded the military adaptation to the Information Age. This chapter applies well-known theories of military doctrinal innovation to explain American military and civilian leaders' attraction to NCW. It also describes the core tenets of network-centric warfare—vital background for later chapters' detailed look at the technological requirements of key types of next-generation military equipment and the relationships among the military, the Congress, and the defense industry that will actually govern the implementation of military innovation.

THE ORIGINS OF THE RMA

The conventional wisdom among military strategists is that the character of warfare is changing, although the nature, scope and implications of the changes remain hotly contested.[6] "New wars" featuring the active engagement of non-state actors, including terrorists and private military firms, may soon be the norm.[7] Other analysts have learned from the absence of great-power conflict and the large number of complex humanitarian emergencies in the 1990s that operations other than war will define the most important military tasks in the future.[8] Finally, some American strategists fear a revival of more traditional great-power competition as a result of the emergence of China, which might attempt to gain control of Taiwan or resource-rich territory using conventional forces.[9] Despite vast differences in their detailed interpretations, experts widely agree that the United States and other nations will face a new international security environment that presents new military challenges in the coming years.

Scholarly research into revolutions in military affairs provides intellectual depth for these concerns—in some cases explaining that new technology will enable a new way of war, and in other cases arguing that the United States must capitalize on new technology to be ready for new missions.[10] Many researchers have drawn on the historical record, linking countries' leadership in the international system and their ability to exercise military power to their use of whatever contemporary technology was on the cutting edge. For example, in the late nineteenth century, the Industrial Revolution spawned a mode of warfare that depended on raising, equipping, and maintaining mass armies, communicating via telegraph, moving troops and equipment on railway systems, and controlling the seas with dreadnaught battleships.[11] In a similar fashion, modern analysts believe that the dawn of the Information Age will not only revolutionize civilian life but also drastically alter the way in which humans fight wars. An information technology revolution in military affairs (IT-RMA) would emphasize the contributions of data and analysis to the effectiveness of future warfighters and their weapons; it would focus less on "mass" and more on the role of knowledge in making weapons more accurate and deadly. And if the analogy to past revolutions in military affairs holds true, the American grand strategy of primacy will succeed only if the military adapts to the RMA; otherwise, the hegemonic position of the United States will be overthrown.

Because these scholars' ideas have been incorporated into the current American policy debate, the United States is developing a new military doctrine. These scholars start with two key propositions: (1) that the world and, in particular, the United States is experiencing a period of rapid socioeconomic change, and (2) that broad socioeconomic shifts often cause revolutions in military affairs.

The first proposition is relatively uncontroversial. Technologists, investors, social theorists, political scientists, economists, and other analysts have all noted the vast transformation. The strongest academic descriptions refer to the emergence of a postindustrial or a networked society, and by most accounts the United States is in the vanguard of the transition.[12] The industrial economy upon which that United States built its preeminent international position has given way to a postindustrial service economy. Today's high-growth economic sectors include telecommunications, informatics, computers, and biotechnology, while traditional smokestack and metal-bending industries have largely disappeared or migrated offshore. Scholars disagree strongly about the cause of the transition, but America's entrepreneurial culture and large investments in education, especially at the university level, are among the key factors widely cited. The recent invention of the Internet in a society poised to take advantage of open access to information has quickened the pace of socioeconomic change.

Moreover, deregulation and the emergence of more competitive domestic and international markets have changed the way firms do business. Competition exerts relentless pressure on firms to cut costs, capitalize on growth opportunities, and innovate with cost-saving processes and new products. Firms in the relatively labor-scarce United States outsource more expensive, labor-intensive processes offshore at the same time they work to develop and maintain intellectual capital that both generates the "next new thing" and remains available for licensing and further innovation.[13] Inexpensive, fast, reliable communications networks enable the new way of doing business—and also new ways of organizing firms, governments, non-state actors and social movements.[14]

"New economy" theorists, writing at the height of the "Dotcom" bubble of the late 1990s, claimed that the successes in the information technology sector would undermine generally accepted economic "laws:"

> Communication is the foundation of society, of our culture, of our humanity, of our own individual identity, and of all economic systems. This is why networks are such a big deal. Communication is so close to culture and society itself that the effects of technologizing it are beyond the scale of a mere industrial-sector cycle. Communication, and its ally computers, is a special case in economic history. Not because it happens to be the fashionable leading business sector of our day, but because its cultural, technological, and conceptual impacts reverberate at the root of our lives.[15]

Although the subsequent collapse of the overvalued high technology sector demonstrated the continued importance of economic fundamentals, the reverberations of new-economy thinking continue. The key to the so-called information revolution is the rapid and ubiquitous spread of new technologies into industries and spheres of life not necessarily envisioned by the technologies' original inventors. Computers, for example, have evolved from room-sized machines for large-scale number crunching (for example, to design nuclear weapons and process tax returns) to today's palmtops, and tiny microprocessors and memory chips are now embedded in everything from coffee makers to automobiles.

As information technology migrated to unexpected consumer products, military analysts began to wonder if the Information Age could run full circle. After all, military demand had been instrumental in the early development of the computer industry, but the booming commercial markets had left military-specific applications behind.[16] However, with the spread of the network society, perhaps the military needed to change its conception of how to operate, relying less on industrial-era technologies and more on emerging information technologies.

This line of thinking is the modern version of the second proposition—that broad socioeconomic changes have revolutionary consequences for the military. For many contemporary strategic and military analysts, it simply follows intuitively that the ways that states fight and prepare for war should change if global society undergoes a revolution in technology and organization. Nations and militaries seeking strategic advantage should race to adopt or adapt inventions that change civilian economies.[17] Dominant military capabilities should always derive from the leading industries of the age.[18] Famous futurists like Alvin and Heidi Toffler have often been quoted to this effect: "A military revolution, in its fullest sense, occurs only when a new civilization arises to challenge the old, when an entire society transforms itself, forcing its armed forces to change at every level simultaneously—from technology and culture to organization, strategy, tactics, training, doctrine, and logistics."[19] According to RMA thinking, in the postmodern age military doctrine should follow the best practices of the emerging information society—conceptual, organizational, and technological.

AMERICAN MILITARY TRANSFORMATION

The absence of catastrophic threats to U.S. national security in the immediate post–Cold War period was less important to military transformation advocates than the possibility that technological modernization could yield a more capable, less expensive force to fight future wars. In effect, it was argued that the systematic introduction of Information-Age technologies would help the military services overcome several of their most pressing problems: the need to maintain force structure (next-generation platforms would be cheaper and therefore more numerous), to reduce casualties of both American soldiers and civilian noncombatants (weapons could be fired at greater distances with more accuracy from stealthier platforms), and to operate with fewer officers and enlisted personnel (automation would reduce the demand for soldiers and sailors and force fewer of them into dangerous situations). When the time came to justify the expenditures necessary to achieve transformation objectives, threats could either be manufactured—perhaps the United States should invest in advance of the possible emergence of a peer competitor—or, failing that, the threat-based planning approach itself could be replaced.[20]

Contemporary military transformation—understood as the "act of creating and harnessing a revolution in military affairs"—cannot emerge spontaneously.[21] It must be encouraged, nurtured, and promoted by civilian and military leaders who are well placed to influence national strategy, military doctrine, and the various implementation processes by which the armed forces are trained, organized, and equipped. A strong case can be made that the process of military change began in the late 1970s and that it will continue on for another decade or more, if the U.S. military is to become a fully network-centric force.[22] The victories in the Persian Gulf War, Kosovo, Afghanistan, and Iraq drew on the results of choices made nearly thirty years ago. Not only did the previous generations of leaders fund the research, development, and procurement programs that produced precision-guided munitions, stealth technologies, and the vast communications infrastructure enjoyed by the military today, but they also experimented with and refined doctrine. Air-Land Battle Doctrine and other steps paved the way for new network-centric concepts. Today, the United States is poised to complete the military revolution: the experiments and increments of technological progress have culminated in a complete doctrine that could reorganize strategic, operational, and tactical thinking across the entire breadth of the U.S. military services—if the last transformational steps are fully implemented.

The information revolution allegedly has myriad implications for the next generation of American military forces. Air Force, Army, Navy and Marine combat units are to become less "heavy," more information intensive, and more expeditionary than in the past. The ability to process information faster and to respond to tactical intelligence with greater accuracy and fewer delays will increase lethality, even as American weapons become "lighter." Already, precision-guided weapons that can hit targets over the horizon are exploiting more accurate targeting and intelligence systems, and advocates of the IT-RMA expect this technological trajectory to have increasingly powerful political and strategic effects. The future U.S. military will fire fewer rounds, but those rounds will be more effective because they will hit what they are supposed to hit. Most, but not all, of these changes rely on the gradual incorporation of advanced information technologies that mirror commercial innovations into military systems and weapons.

To military officers who every day operate weapons systems with information technology components that would be considered several generations out of date in commercial products, the possibility of introducing more modern equipment holds great promise. There is ample anecdotal evidence of technological opportunism. Vice Admiral (ret.) Arthur Cebrowski, the first head of the Pentagon's Office of Force Transformation, frequently gave speeches about transformation in which he admired the rapid investment cycle that Silicon Valley firms use to develop new products. He often referred to "Moore's Law" that governs the incredibly high rate of advance in computer processing power. When he was President of the Naval War College, he circulated books among staff and students that purported to explain the origins and implications of the Information Age—books like Kevin Kelly's *New Rules for the New Economy: 10 Radical Strategies for a Connected World.*[23] In some of the pioneering efforts to define NCW, Admiral Cebrowski and his co-authors drew on business examples, including Wal-mart's successful retailing strategies and the trading practices of securities firms.[24] Transformation advocates readily convinced the rest of the military that a Brave New World was at hand, and they labored to figure out how information technologies should be adapted to warfare. Network-centric warfare doctrine emerged from their intellectual struggle.

Even in the post 9/11 world that has shifted attention to operations in Afghanistan and Iraq and to fighting terrorism, the rhetoric of "revolution" and "transformation" remains pervasive among military analysts and planners. Top-level statements by the Joint Chiefs of Staff, by the leaders of the individual services, and by civilian politicians and Pentagon appointees routinely endorse network-centric concepts. For example, *Joint Vision 2020*, the overarching statement of the Joint Chief of Staff's vision of future military operations, foresees the U.S. armed forces dominating the full spectrum of military operations from low-intensity conflicts to major theater wars by exploiting information superiority.[25] The Army's transformation project, billed as the most significant change for the service since World War I, is supposed to deliver an "Objective Force" that will be responsive, deployable, agile, versatile, lethal, survivable, and sustainable using the network-intensive Future Combat System.[26] Similarly, the Air Force promises to control and exploit both air and space, "to find, fix, assess, track, target, and engage any object of military significance on or above the surface of the Earth in near real time."[27] The Navy coined the phrase "network-centric warfare," and it remains the touchstone for the transformation of the Navy,[28] but NCW concepts are no longer specific to a single service.[29] NCW has infected the presentation of U.S. military transformation writ large. As one observer noted, "NCW forms a central part of the [Bush] Administration's plans for defense transformation."[30]

NETWORK-CENTRIC WARFARE

The idea of network-centric warfare is to exploit technologies to "shift from platform-centric operations to Network-Centric Operations."[31] Networks harness the power of geographically dispersed nodes (whether personal computers, delivery trucks, or warships) by linking them together into networks (such as the World Wide Web) that allow for the extremely rapid, high-volume transmission of digitized data (probably multimedia data). Networking has the potential to increase exponentially the capabilities of individual nodes or groups of nodes and to facilitate the efficient use of resources. When networked, individual nodes gain access not only to their own organic capabilities but also, more importantly, to capabilities distributed across the network. The loss of a networked node need not be crippling; in a robust network, a lost node's functions will be assumed by other nodes. Since networked nodes can share information efficiently, they can be designed as simple, low-cost adjuncts to the network itself. Not all nodes, though, are created equal. Some are more complex and therefore more expensive than others. The point is that networked nodes should be simpler and lower in cost than stand-alone nodes.

Early research into network-centric warfare identified four key supporting concepts: information and knowledge advantage, effects-based operations, assured access, and forward sea-based forces.[32] First, NCW will rely greatly on the development of a large number of capable sensors that can be deployed to the battlespace and connected to the military network—the sources of information and knowledge advantage.[33] Netted sensors should provide commanders with "unmatched awareness of the battlespace."[34] That situational awareness should be displayed in a "common operational picture" (COP), which should be visible to all friendly forces through their connections to the network.

Sharing such detailed information should help warfighters to obtain several of the main advantages of network-centric warfare. The network should help "lift the fog of war," reducing the danger that the enemy will be able to achieve tactical surprise against friendly forces, reducing the likelihood of a friendly-fire incident, and simplifying the task of command and control.[35] As long as each friendly unit understands its commander's general intent, it should be able to apply a set of rules (doctrine, tactics, techniques, and procedures that every soldier would learn in training) to the situation that it sees in the COP. The result would be "self-synchronization" of friendly activities, reducing the need to take the time for complex orders to pass down the chain of command—and the risk of confusion.[36] Self-synchronization should also allow small-unit commanders to take more individual initiative; many studies of military effectiveness argue that small-unit initiative is a key trait that determines which of two forces will win a battle.[37]

Information advantage and self-synchronization in theory will also enable the use of "swarming" tactics. Friendly forces will maneuver to attack the enemy from all sides. Instead of gathering friendly units into a concentrated formation to go on the attack, commanders of network-enabled forces will tell their units to concentrate their fires on a particular location: munitions will converge on the enemy rather than massed forces that could be vulnerable to a counterattack or an area-effects weapon (a big bomb). The result will be greater tactical stability—each American unit will be able to apply tremendous, network-derived combat power against the enemy, but the enemy will have little ability to reduce American combat power by incapacitating or destroying a single American unit.[38]

The second pillar, effects-based operations, seeks to exploit a detailed understanding of the enemy forces to find and destroy the Clausewitzian "center of gravity" or the "critical node" that allows the enemy to fight. The network is a crucial tool to find the adversary's points of vulnerability. Warfighters can use the network to reach back to extensive databases about the enemy; the network should also allow commanders to share and debate ideas with each other and with experts far from the forward line of troops. The goal of effects-based operations is to erode the enemy's will to resist rather than to kill and destroy as much of the enemy as possible. Attrition was the hallmark of the old style of warfare; in theory, information technology will enable an alternative. Precision-guided munitions in conjunction with advanced intelligence, surveillance, and reconnaissance capabilities will allow targets to be hit with greater economy, and the ability to hit many targets simultaneously rather than sequentially might greatly increase the possibility of inflicting disproportionate effects, particularly psychological effects, on the adversary. Effects-based operations suggest a way in which tactical operations can achieve strategic objectives.

The third and fourth pillars of NCW show the concept's naval origins: assured access and forward-deployed sea forces. "Assured access" refers to the ability of the U.S. armed forces to gain entry to both overseas infrastructure, such as ports and airfields, and the battle space itself—even when a capable and hostile adversary confronts the lead American elements.[39] No sanctuary is to be ceded to the adversary. It is the job of the Navy and the Marine Corps to enable and ensure access for follow-on forces from the Air Force and the Army—the heavier forces necessary to fight and win major regional contingencies. The Navy accomplishes this through the combat capabilities inherent in its ships on station at sea during peacetime. Since sea-based forces "do not rely on permissive access to foreign shore installations that may be withdrawn or curtailed," they "furnish an assured infrastructure for additional joint forces."[40]

The two naval components of the original NCW vision, however, have direct analogs in subsequent joint and service interpretations of network-centric warfare. Air Force transformation plans highlight the development of expeditionary forces able to operate from austere bases and strike from vast distances with stealthy aircraft like the B-2 and F-22. Expeditionary Air Force units will help ensure access by, among other things, suppressing or destroying enemy air defenses or mobile anti-ship cruise missile batteries. The Army has also shown a great deal of interest in forward sea-basing and fast sealift. In the future, land bases may not be readily available. Further, the prospects for shipping large combat units are limited by the speed at which modern conflicts develop, so the Army is developing smaller, less heavily armed, highly networked units that they expect to be able to deploy much faster than the legacy force. All four services have thus joined the Navy in ensuring access to areas in conflict and ensuring that some assets are capable of forward deployment.[41]

Robust interpretations of NCW also feature smaller, lighter, faster, less complex, and less expensive nodes that will present adversaries with fewer high-value targets. The new nodes will be purpose built to facilitate self-synchronization, swarming tactics, and tactical stability. Network-centric platforms may include small ships, fast sealift, unmanned vehicles for intelligence-gathering, unmanned vehicles for launching attacks on highly defended targets, new satellites, and a host of other platforms. In each case, complexity is to reside in the web rather than in the node; the expensive, multipurpose platforms that populate the traditional, "legacy" force will over time be displaced by less expensive, single-purpose ones. In today's military, networking capabilities reside in heavy, expensive systems that can be installed only on large platforms. In the future network-centric military, plans call for nodes of all types— from individual soldiers to unmanned vehicles—to be able to plug in, and each node's capabilities will be tailored to the network requirements from the node's earliest conception. The American military is on the cusp of acquiring the systems to implement this full vision of network-centric warfare.

Explaining Innovation in Military Doctrine

The theories of military innovation circulating in the security studies community have generally sought to explain the origin of doctrinal visions. How were entrepreneurs like Vice Admiral Cebrowski able to develop their ideas into a comprehensive package of concepts for importing the civilian information revolution into the military sphere? Military analysts continue to debate the mechanisms. Three prominent theories, developed by Barry Posen, Stephen Rosen, and Owen Coté, each contribute to explaining the emergence of the NCW consensus.[42]

Barry Posen argues that most innovation in military doctrine stems from the actions of civilian politicians. In response to the changing goals of the state or to changes in the international political-military environment, civilian leaders revisit the country's grand strategy. In a time of high external threat, when civilian leaders choose a new grand strategy, they can intervene to disrupt the standard operating procedures by which the military services would otherwise continue to invest in training and equipment that serve the old grand-strategic goals.[43] In the context of the contemporary transformation debate, the Bush administration's commitment to changing the face of the American military as well as Secretary of Defense Donald Rumsfeld's very public efforts to reassert the primacy of the civilian Office of the Secretary of Defense over the uniformed military showcase the role of civilian intervention.[44] On the other hand, the absence of a traditional security threat to the United States from a "peer competitor" might allow the civilian national security agenda to be dominated by pork-barrel concerns that will not drive the services toward long-term doctrinal innovation. The short-term pressures of the war on terrorism may consume the civilian (and military) leadership, and prospects for military doctrinal innovation may fade. Pressures for technological innovation in the defense industry would then recede as well.[45]

In contrast to Posen's emphasis on external pressures, Stephen Rosen explains military innovation by focusing on the internal dynamics of military organizations. Rosen argues that peacetime military innovations depend on visionary officers who work steadily to solve problems with existing strategic and operational concepts that they identify through their expertise and operational experience. Military innovation succeeds when high-ranking visionaries protect creative junior officers from political threats and when those junior officers can gain promotion on the basis of their innovative ideas.[46] Vice Admiral Cebrowski's vital role in developing the core concepts of network-centric warfare looks like an example of Rosen's innovation mechanism at work. Furthermore, the establishment of the Navy Warfare Development Command and the new emphasis on experimentation at Joint Forces Command provide "organizational homes" for thinking about network-centric warfare.[47] Finally, when Admiral Vern Clarke was Chief of Naval Operations, he used his position to protect the NCW vision—specifically by pushing hard to accelerate procurement of small naval combatants so that they will be locked into the fleet before anything can weaken the NCW consensus.[48] On the other hand, the increasing involvement of commanders of the unified regional and functional combatant commands in preparing service acquisition plans and budget proposals is introducing an institutional bias toward current operational concerns rather than toward long-term doctrine development and future modernization.[49] According to Rosen's logic, this trend presents a threat to military transformation.

Owen Coté traces military innovation to inter- and intraservice rivalry for roles and missions; his theory envisions civilian leaders adjudicating that competition.[50] Leaders of warfighting communities—such as, in the Navy, surface warfare officers, submariners, and aviators, and in the wider interservice context, Army and Marine infantry officers—gain professional status when they can offer the president the best solutions to particular strategic or operational problems. Each community can even gain status by taking a leadership role in promoting a particular joint solution, although there may obviously be a natural bias in favor of service-dominated concepts. Each community can also offer its military judgment to discredit competing proposals, and each can draw technical advisors into the process to support its own proposals or to undercut alternatives. According to Coté's theory, the best innovative doctrines are adopted through the traditional American process of open debate.[51] In this view, Defense Secretary Rumsfeld's decision to ask Vice Admiral Cebrowski to retire from the Navy in the summer of 2001 so that Cebrowski could serve as the first director of the Pentagon's Office of Force Transformation can be seen as an endorsement of the network-centric warfare vision by the civilian leadership.[52] Full implementation of the vision, however, will still require a sustained commitment of resources from political leaders. The Office of Force Transformation also must maintain its role in the development of the Future Years Defense Plan, the Defense Planning Guidance, and the Transformation Planning Guidance—the documents that the American military uses to plan its technology development objectives and acquisition spending.

The purpose of our book is not to advance a new theory of doctrinal innovation, much less to resolve the long-standing disputes between these prominent contenders. Instead, we intend to extend the analysis of military innovation to the next step, implementation. Although Posen, Rosen, and Coté each offer a perspective on the source of creative ideas about how the military will fight, none shows how doctrine is translated into demand pull for new military equipment.

IMPLEMENTING MILITARY INNOVATION

Our book contributes a new theory to explain the implementation of military innovation. It explains how the military can stimulate technological progress to fulfill the strategic, operational, and tactical promise of new doctrine. Specifically, a scaled-down version of the innovative doctrine of network-centric warfare may work with existing platforms and networks. But the military is unlikely to realize the full benefits of information technology unless new systems are designed from the bottom up for a network-centric military rather than a platform-centric military.[53] New weapons and systems to implement transformation are on the drawing board. Many have already started through the Pentagon's acquisition process, but few have passed out of the early design phases.

How those projects are managed in the next few years will determine the extent to which military transformation is successfully implemented.

In chapter 2, we draw on the literatures on commercial innovation and defense acquisition to develop a theory of technological innovation for the military. The core of the theory integrates the political environment facing military consumers and private-sector suppliers, the relationship between warfighters and the industrialists whose companies design and build their equipment, and the characteristics of transformational technologies themselves.

Chapters 3 through 5 present case studies of sectors of the defense industry as they respond to the pull of military demand for technological innovation. The chapters deal with shipbuilding, unmanned aerial vehicles, and communications, respectively. Each chapter explains the situation in a part of the defense industry in light of pressures for military innovation, showing how our theory applies and also how technologies and business prospects are developing and will develop over the medium term.

Chapters 6 and 7 assess the prospects for sufficient technological progress to implement network-centric warfare in the United States. Chapter 6 analyzes the assumption that an entire complicated web of platforms and networks can be integrated and optimized into a functioning whole. Large technology-management projects, especially those embedded in the political environment of government procurement, face special organizational hurdles. We thus examine the performance metrics associated with systems integration and the various types of organizations that might provide the government with sufficient expertise to develop the proverbial "system of systems" for network-centric warfare. Chapter 7 concludes by summarizing our case-specific findings about the defense industry and American military transformation, elaborating the contribution of our theoretical approach to scholarship on military innovation, and recommending policy approaches to ensure that the relationship between the military, the political leadership, and the U.S. defense industry succeeds during the remaining decades of transformation.

CHAPTER TWO

IMPLEMENTING MILITARY INNOVATION

The United States has now adopted a military doctrine of network-centric warfare. For roughly five years, Department of Defense planners have sought to implement the NCW vision through organizational, personnel, and even cultural changes. But in the end, for the doctrine to fulfill its promise, new technologies must be developed as well.[1] Communications systems and networks must provide warfighters and their support systems more accurate data, both at the front and at bases far from the forward lines. Over time, platforms from ships to aircraft to unmanned vehicles must be designed to take advantage of the connectivity offered by improved networking. While many scholars and policy analysts have studied the problem of military innovation, no one, as of yet, has offered a convincing account of how weapons innovation derives from doctrinal change.

This chapter introduces our theory of military innovation. Some important military innovations—organizational and doctrinal innovations—mainly change the way that military units train and fight. However, other innovations, including present-day transformation efforts, require the military to acquire new equipment, relying on the performance of the defense industrial base. We focus on the critical relationship between the military and the defense industry, which provides essential political support to the military's investment program and facilitates the development of new technologies tailored to the military's needs.

Most previous studies of military innovation have addressed situations in which militaries need to change their doctrine to capitalize on the capabilities provided by new equipment that has already been developed. For example, the pre–World War II constraint on the ability of armies to execute rapid breakthrough-and-exploitation operations was due less to the limited technical capabilities of tanks than to the armies' confusion about how to deploy tanks to maximize their effectiveness. The mainstream French military leadership generally had the wrong idea about how to use tanks and motorized infantry for combined arms offensives, while the German development of *Blitzkrieg* doctrine transformed offensive operations. The explicit reason that Barry Posen studied doctrinal innovation in *The Sources of Military Doctrine* was his dissatisfaction with technological explanations of the German success fighting the French in 1940.[2] The principal World War II belligerents had comparable numbers of tanks of comparable quality; doctrine is what separated their military effectiveness. Many subsequent studies have argued with Posen's explanation of why different countries choose different doctrines, but few have questioned the focus on doctrine and organization in studies of military innovation and military effectiveness.[3]

Today's discussions of the information technology revolution in military affairs (IT-RMA), however, rest on a yet-to-be-acquired technological foundation. The military has myriad communications systems dedicated to specific missions and specific types of forces, but it does not have anything that looks like the Internet adapted for combat. New radios and vastly more data processing, storage, and display capabilities will have to be acquired and distributed down to the small-unit level in order to make the transformation vision a reality. Transformation apostles report that individual soldiers and commanders are eager to train and fight applying the doctrinal vision,[4] but little of the military equipment that underpins the transformed force exists yet. A communications network overlays existing military equipment, allowing units to coordinate with each other and sometimes even to talk to forces from other military services, but little of the existing equipment was designed to rely on network connectivity for its core functionality.

One key goal of military transformation is to capitalize on the individual initiative of small-unit commanders, which requires giving those commanders access to sufficient information not only to make tactically optimal choices based on local information but also operationally optimal choices based on collaboration with other friendly forces. Individual initiative and aggressiveness—tactical decentralization—is an entrenched hallmark of military effectiveness, but large-scale military operations, especially joint operations that involve many different platforms and multiple military services, are still centrally coordinated, because equipment cannot yet distribute essential details in a timely fashion and cannot enable sufficient command and control in response to information.[5] The vision of self-synchronization and massing fires rather than forces awaits technological innovation.[6] Instead of having equipment without a vision of how to use it—the problem that confronted generals before World War II—the U.S. military now has a vision of how it wants to fight without the equipment that it needs to carry out operations.

The military has an idea of what it wants to buy, but it needs to assemble a coalition of supporters to convince the political leaders, who control the budget, to buy transformational equipment. That political coalition needs to exploit the lobbying power of the defense industry. At the same time, the military has to work with suppliers who are comfortable with the terms and conditions of working for the government, who are able to translate the language in which the military describes its doctrinal vision into technical requirements for systems engineering, and who are trusted by the military to temper optimistic hopes with technological realism without undercutting the military's key objectives. Strong political support both within the military and from key legislators has long been a prerequisite for technological innovation in the U.S. military.[7]

Finally, the contractors cannot be chosen just for their political skills and trusted relationship to the military: they must also have the right business processes and technical skills to develop the particular products that the military wants. Clayton Christensen introduced a distinction between "sustaining" and "disruptive" technological innovations—that is, whether they improve performance measured in traditional ways or require new, unfamiliar metrics.[8] Christensen showed that innovations that demand sustaining technological development can be relatively easily obtained from the established suppliers. In the military context, then, those firms that already have strong ties to the military services (and the levers of political power) should be a good source of sustaining innovations. According to our theory, the military can exploit the political strengths and organizational understanding of established defense firms to buy new systems built on sustaining innovations. On the other hand, military innovations that demand disruptive technological development face difficult political and organizational hurdles. We argue that the new firms primed to offer products derived from disruptive innovations are less likely to relate smoothly to the military customer and to have enough political influence.

In sum, our theory describes key characteristics of the customer-supplier relationship and how that relationship interacts with the technical requirements of transformation. A more general form of the theory could also be used to explain other cases (besides the ongoing U.S. military transformation) in which the key constraint on military innovation has been the development and procurement of equipment rather than the adaptation of military doctrine to capitalize on new equipment that has already been acquired.

THE POLITICAL COALITION: THE MILITARY SERVICES AND THE DEFENSE INDUSTRY

Defense acquisition is a unique environment that blends military analysis, political pressure, and technological invention. During the Cold War, the defense acquisition budget rose and fell through several cycles, but real spending stayed high compared to pre–World War II peacetime levels, even during Cold War spending troughs.[9] The opportunity to earn a share of that bounty attracted private firms into the defense business, where only arsenals had produced in previous interwar periods. The American military also supported the shift to a private defense industrial base, as public arsenals gained the reputation for being unresponsive to military needs and for being unable to attract the top scientists and engineers to defense work.[10] The private firms worked closely with their military customers to respond to the Soviet threat and to persuade Congress that new military systems were crucial to the nation's defense.

The partnership convinced legislators by combining appeals to the military's expert judgment of the international threat with the industry's savvy lobbying strategies.[11] They called for aggressive technological innovation to counter the Soviet armed forces' numerical advantage: arguments about military effectiveness dominated debates over national-security strategy, and successful defense firms responded by acquiescing to the military's preferred definition of the requirements for new equipment.[12] Since the end of the Cold War, the relative weight of the influence of firms' lobbying and the military's professional response to the threat environment has reversed (lobbying is now much more important than it used to be). But even with the new balance of influences on acquisition decision-making, business choices to invest in military innovation still are channeled by military and political forces rather than directly responding to traditional financial calculations.[13] From an analytical perspective, the result is that the major theories of innovation developed in business schools and economics departments, which depend on the profit motive to explain the actions of scientists, entrepreneurs, and customers, cannot be applied directly to the military community.

Business-school models of innovation address two main concerns, neither of which is very relevant to the defense industry. First, the theories try to help entrepreneurs find customers for their inventions.[14] But there is only one customer, the government, for new military equipment, although that customer has several branches: the military services and their various subcommunities like aviators and submariners. The branches do not necessarily coordinate their equipment investments, but they share the same concerns with national security and military operations. Innovative military equipment will always have to be marketed to one of a limited number of clearly identifiable buyers. Defense firms make their living by developing close relationships with that well-known list.[15]

The other great concern of business theories of innovation deals with the source of the resources needed for research and development (R&D). In the "normal" business environment, companies invest in order to reduce their production costs or to enter new markets in which they can charge monopoly prices for proprietary products.[16] Many theories of innovation focus on how entrepreneurs can raise the money to fund their research and development—for example, through access to venture capital funds—or whether sectors of the economy with few firms invest more in research and development, because they expect to earn above-normal returns, or less in R&D, because they are complacent, protected by the lack of market competition.[17] Normal companies base their investment plans on economic criteria.

In the military context, however, R&D funding comes from the defense budget, so defense investment depends on political calculations. Most of the money comes in the form of R&D contracts: the government pays the industry to work on developing specific weapons systems or equipment. The industry may earn a small profit for doing the work, but it does not need to generate a "normal rate of return on investment," because it is spending the government's money rather than money that it obtained on its own from shareholders or lenders.[18] When firms are spending the government's money rather than their own, the profit motive does not provide the traditional incentive to innovate.

Nor would the profit motive stimulate much military innovation through a second, smaller stream of defense technology investment, the "independent research and development" (IR&D) account. IR&D is a special payment from the government to contractors manufacturing the current generation of equipment with the explicit requirement that the money be spent to develop future technologies—analogous to a commercial firm's use of a share of its current profits to invest in the future of its business. Because defense firms know that any product that they develop with IR&D money must eventually be sold to the military on a production contract, the goals of IR&D investment are usually closely aligned with the announced goals of the military's direct research and development contracts.

Additionally, defense firms hesitate to spend their own money (profits) on R&D investment for two reasons. In most cases, defense firms cannot hope to earn very high profits from production after successful private R&D investment because the government buyers impose profit caps. The firms therefore cannot earn exceptional profits from proprietary technologies that would compensate them for the technological risk and the upfront cost of capital.[19] Even more important, the military customers' interest in controlling the characteristics of the weapons that they buy often leads them to reject systems proffered by contractors when government-determined requirements did not define the original product specifications. Equipment can influence the services' organizational cultures, so military leaders jealously guard the requirements-definition process.[20] The industry generally knows its customer well enough to respond to customer preferences rather than to try to "shape" the market with its own investment. The occasional firm that forgets this rule usually loses money—for example, the U.S. Air Force never bought Northrop's privately developed F-5 fighter or its derivatives.[21] Such examples have taught the defense industry that R&D funds should come from the military services.

Business-school theories that hope to predict profitable avenues for investment are of little use to strategic planners in the defense industry.

Any theory of technological innovation in military equipment needs to begin with an explanation of the political decisions about R&D investment priorities: how do the military services convince Congress to part with taxpayers' money?

When the threat level is high, Congress tends to defer to the military's professional expertise.[22] In the American system of checks and balances, Congress weighs the military's natural desire to provide as much protection as possible from every threat against the resource demands of the other parts of government (education and welfare, for example).[23] When the nation is under serious external threat, no politician wants to face the argument that he undercut the military's ability to provide for the common defense by ignoring expert military advice. Political leaders sometimes choose between competing proposals when each is backed by a particular military service or community, but it is very difficult for civilians to reject military recommendations without cover of expert testimony.[24] As a result, military leaders strive for consensus and avoid public disagreements whenever possible: a unified front protects their budget requests from political "interference."[25] Widespread respect for military professionalism usually allows military leaders with ideas for technological innovations to invest in implementing their visions. At the margin, industry's lobbying helps the defense budget thrive in Congressional logrolls. But the primary task for a defense firm is to convince military leaders that it understands the requirements for new defense systems and that it has the technical capability to develop the innovative equipment.

However, when threats are less immediate or visible, Congressional leaders are less likely to defer to the military's professional judgment. Domestic policy priorities and political expediency weigh more heavily in the appropriators' calculus. Relatively small research funding requests are still unlikely to receive much scrutiny, but major development initiatives can be controversial. On the one hand, American political leaders are generally fascinated by technology,[26] so requests for funds to promote military technological innovation are often met with favor. Specific ideas like the IT-RMA can capture the imagination of political leaders in the same way that they appeal to military leaders. But on the other hand, unless an innovation promises to respond to a specific strategic problem, legislators will also ask how it will affect the interests of key constituents in their Congressional districts.[27] Innovations that might undermine programs to manufacture the current generation of technology will have to promise compensation to the established defense firms. Under those circumstances, including in today's post–Cold War environment, the military depends on the political power of the contractors to fund its priorities through the "pork barrel."[28]

Knowing that their future funding depends on their lobbying skill, defense firms hire armies of lobbyists.[29] They provide background information to friendly legislators whose staff members do not have the time or the resources to do as complete a job through their own research and analysis, and they fund expensive public relations campaigns to support the military programs linked to their businesses.[30] Firms in the defense industry are happy to cooperate with the military services' defense budget requests, as long as the defense budget proposal promises to buy the firms' major products. To maintain funding, new projects and investments in technological innovation often add onto the defense budget base from previous years.[31] New programs can be funded only if they have enough political support to convince Congress to shift funds from non-defense areas of government spending, to raise taxes, or (most likely) to expand the federal budget deficit. Consequently, military leaders seeking technological innovation need powerful political partners. The first step in our theory of military innovation answers this demand for political support. Firms that want a share of the R&D budget need to choose their business development strategy based on political considerations rather than the economic calculations of theories of innovation developed to explain cases outside the defense environment. A suitable political strategy should lead to successful allocation of defense spending for innovation, and absence of the political strategy should lead to failure.

CUSTOMER-SUPPLIER RELATIONSHIPS: UNDERSTANDING AND TRUST

The need for political cooperation does not by itself explain the close relationship between the military services and their established suppliers in the defense industry. Why do the military services seek their political support from defense firms rather than from firms outside the defense industry that might have equal levels of political influence with the Congress? Over time, defense firms have developed particular insight into the military services' goals and the ways that military leaders think. They assiduously cultivate this insight by hiring former officers, devoting overhead to monitoring developments in the Pentagon and in the field, and funding a wide range of activities that encourage a blurring of military–civilian boundaries. The firms' performance on past projects has also earned them a measure of the military leaders' trust.[32]

Most American businesses would have great difficulty becoming military suppliers, because the factors that drive military acquisition decisions are unfamiliar to most business executives. In the commercial world, entrepreneurs and business development experts generally understand their customers' product development, manufacturing, and marketing strategies. Customers are usually interested in the same things that drive suppliers' decision-making: minimizing costs and maximizing profits. Customers make the same sort of decisions about product development and marketing that their suppliers do. The only thing that separates them is their place in the "value chain."[33] For the defense industry, however, the customers' operational concerns depend on military concepts that are alien to most technological entrepreneurs and businessmen. While the normal relationship between an innovative supplier and a customer must combine shared understanding of technical needs and capabilities with shared understanding of value added and economic constraints, the defense market imposes the additional demand for the supplier to share the customers' understanding of military operations.

The full-time job of the established defense firms' business development offices is to monitor and understand the firms' military customers, just as the firms' Washington lobbying offices follow the twists and turns of Congressional support for defense programs. The military has a bewildering array of organizations involved in planning, technology development, and acquisition, and the defense community is famous for its jargon and acronym-ridden communications. Specialists are needed to figure out what the various organizations' products mean and to separate the draft documents that will have lasting influence from the bulk of the reports that are ephemeral or insignificant. Over time, members of the defense firms' business-development staffs develop the ability to judge. Boeing, for example, had a grasp of network-centric logic before most military organizations, not to mention a business plan to take advantage of the emerging opportunities in systems integration and space-based communications.[34]

Meanwhile, each defense firm also hires countless retired military officers as consultants and employees to gain the benefits of their experience and of their friendly contacts with those officers who remain on active duty.[35] Those contacts are especially important during times of doctrinal ferment, when written documents and briefings on how to define requirements have not yet been finalized. The visionaries driving the military innovation and the soldiers and civil servants charged with implementing that vision need to trust the potential equipment suppliers enough to share early drafts and discussion papers about evolving ideas for new military tactics and operational art. Trusted defense firms can even informally (or formally) advise writers of military doctrine on technological, economic, and industrial-base constraints on doctrinal innovation. In a few cases, retired military officers employed by the defense industry— those particularly friendly with or trusted by their former service's leadership or with particularly relevant active-duty experience—have even advised on the military aspects of doctrinal innovation.[36]

Defense firms also hire former civilian acquisition officials as part of their quest to understand the government's decision-making. Analysts have noticed a "revolving door" in which political appointees in the Defense Department are often drawn from corporate ranks and then return to the defense industry after a short period of public service. The prospect of a lucrative private-sector job waiting for a civilian government employee might introduce bias into his decisions, if he were given sufficient discretion to act on such personal influences, and the revolving door certainly introduces the appearance of bias that can create political problems for defense investment.[37] But "clean government" crusaders have imposed heavy regulation on defense acquisition to constrain decision-makers.[38] Defense reformers vigorously dispute whether or not that regulation works to prevent corruption, but the regulation certainly has the effect of creating a barrier to entry that keeps nonspecialist firms out of the defense business.[39] Established defense suppliers learn to operate relatively efficiently in the face of intrusive regulatory constraints. One of the hallmarks of a defense firm is its ability to maintain a close relationship to its military customers, allowing the firm to understand and accommodate the customers' special concerns, while navigating the intrusive political and regulatory pressures of federal acquisition rules.[40]

The final component of the trusted relationship between the military services and the established defense industry concerns the reaction to program failures. Few development projects meet all of the official requirements set out in the original contract.[41] Very often, the resulting equipment turns out to be very capable anyway, and military officers can often adapt it to achieve the purposes that doctrine-writers had in mind when the project was begun.[42] But the acquisition bureaucracy nevertheless asks the reasonable question, "did the project fail to reach its upfront goals for bad reasons (e.g., because the contractor did not try hard enough or because the contractor deceptively over-promised in its submissions during the competitive development phase of the program), or did the project fail because of real technical constraints despite the best efforts of talented, hard-working engineers?" If there is reason to believe that a project failed for the former reasons, military leaders worry about the political ramifications of the scandal for the sustainability of defense investment. Established firms can find that essential military support can evaporate quickly when their actions raise feelings of betrayal among the military leadership.[43] On the other hand, military leaders help defend their contractors from criticism when projects fail for the latter reasons, especially if the military can find ways to achieve their operational goals with the actual equipment delivered by the contractor. The trusted customer–supplier relationship between the military services and the established defense industry can help ensure a smooth investment path supporting technological innovation.

The second step in our theory of military innovation explains the dependence of the military on a certain subset of the American economy, the defense industry. If defense firms maintain a trusted relationship with their buyers, hire the right people, and learn to understand the specialized operational environment in which the military uses the firms' products, then they can contribute to military innovation. Conversely, failure to account for these organizational politics is likely to block military innovation.

TECHNICAL CHARACTERISTICS: SUSTAINING AND DISRUPTIVE INNOVATION

The close relationship between the military services and the defense industry facilitates the political maneuvering to obtain the resources to invest in innovative projects. The relationship also explains the process by which goals are set and communicated to the defense industry's engineers who will actually work on the projects. It does not, however, explain whether the projects' technical requirements will connect well to the defense contractors' business decision-making processes and their technical capabilities to create the products that the military wants.

Some projects call for what Clayton Christensen has called "sustaining" innovations, while others call for "disruptive" innovations.[44] Christensen's key theoretical claim, bolstered by a broad array of evidence in his books and articles, is that established suppliers usually succeed at sustaining innovation but fail at disruptive innovation, which, in the military context, implies that suppliers with close relationships to the military services will be most able to offer innovative products with sustaining characteristics. New suppliers that can develop products based on disruptive innovations lack the political connections and trusted ties to the military services that are essential for military innovation.

Boiled down to its essence, Christensen's definition of a sustaining innovation is one that builds on familiar product-quality metrics: "What all sustaining technologies have in common is that they improve the performance of established products, along the dimensions of performance that mainstream customers in major markets have historically valued."[45] Sustaining innovations, no matter how complex, technically radical, or resource intensive, almost never drive established firms out of business; instead, they tend to reinforce the success of current suppliers. Expert technical and financial advisers in established firms' strategic planning departments predict that sustaining innovations will prove feasible, and they understand how to update business plans to capitalize on the new technology. Hence the established firms take the steps necessary to develop sustaining innovations.

According to Christensen, sustaining innovation reinforces time-honored customer-supplier connections. Customers and suppliers can cooperate on systems definition and engineering to develop the new products.[46] We apply this framework to the military context, and our theory predicts that when the military's requirements demand sustaining innovation, the process of working with established members of the defense industrial base should be straightforward.

Christensen contrasts sustaining innovations with his definition of disruptive innovations. These technological advances initially perform less well than legacy systems, when their performance is measured by traditional standards. Established firms' strategic planning departments tend to recognize the inferior performance and to reject the proposals to invest in disruptive innovations; alternatively, strategic planners may force the new technology into a traditional line of business, where it is destined to fail in the marketplace.[47] According to Christensen, disruptive innovations can flourish only when they are managed by nontraditional organizations, in which case they can find customers in fringe market niches, where their performance is measured by new metrics. Building on experience gained in the fringe market, disruptive products improve on traditional measures of performance, overtaking the old market-leading product and eventually driving the established suppliers out of business in mainstream markets.[48] In his books and articles, Christensen shows this dynamic in several important industries including those that produce construction equipment and computer data storage devices.

Of course, if an established firm's strategic planning department could predict the rapid improvement in the disruptive product's performance, then the established firm would happily invest in the new technology despite its initial inferiority. Unfortunately, it is especially difficult to predict improvements upon previously unrecognized product attributes. Business strategists fear that new technologies will develop into "bad performers" in the long run rather than revolutionary products that fundamentally change the market.[49] That fear explains why successful firms miss opportunities for disruptive innovations that are well within their technical capabilities.

Christensen's definition of disruptive innovation must be applied with care to the defense sector. The military environment differs from the usual situation in which a mainstream customer decides whether to accept or reject an innovation offered by an upstart supplier. In the defense sector, there are few buyers, suppliers are totally dependent and reactive, and the demand for military innovation originates with the military customer. As a result, even disruptive innovation is unlikely to fail for the reason Christensen identifies—that is, because the product cannot find buyers. The problem for disruptive innovations in the military environment is that nontraditional firms, whose strategic planning departments might be interested in the disruptive technologies, lack the comfortable customer–supplier relationships required to understand the military's requirements definition. Moreover, those established firms with the political capital required to convince Congress to give them resources to develop the disruptive technology are the same firms whose strategic planning departments are likely to advise their lobbyists against spending political capital in pursuit of the disruptive projects.

Disruptive innovations in the military environment require organizational adaptation to blend the relationship and political advantages of working with established prime contractors and the technical and business process advantages of working with startup firms. Traditional

defense contractors can partner with startups—either through joint
ventures or by buying the startups outright—to enable the newcomers
to translate the language of military operations into technological and
industrial requirements and to provide the newcomers with political
heft.[50] However, innovations that require established firms and entrepreneurs to work together will surely be more difficult to manage than
straightforward sustaining innovations. Cultural misunderstandings may
inhibit cooperation between the partners, or the large acquirer may end
up imposing its sustaining strategic planning process or its design-team
philosophy on the smaller firm.

The third step in our theory of military innovation incorporates
Christensen's categories of technological change. If the military's doctrinal plans call for sustaining innovation, established suppliers should
be able to follow the requirements generation process, help lobby for the
funds to invest in R&D, and develop the needed equipment. If, on the
other hand, the military's doctrinal plans call for disruptive innovation,
the acquisition community is likely to struggle to explain the requirements to potential new suppliers, the new suppliers are unlikely to have
sufficient political power and savvy to obtain adequate R&D spending,
and the military's plan for technological innovation may fail.

Technological Innovation and Network-centric Warfare

One major component of military transformation is producing a new
set of equipment requirements. In sum, our theory suggests that developing the technology to implement the envisioned military innovation
will require firms to respond to the new requirements, and to add their
engineering capabilities and their political strength to the military's
authoritative interpretation of the international environment. The combination of technical research and development, political support, and
military analysis should position the United States to respond to any
emerging threats and/or to take advantage of opportunities in international affairs.

Combining lessons from the business and military analysis literatures
on innovation gives us a framework for determining which types of
firms—established defense contractors, leading commercial information
technology firms, or small startup ventures—will populate each sector

of the future defense industry. The distinction between sustaining and disruptive innovation has significant implications for military transformation generally and for the transition to network-centric warfare specifically. First, NCW's requirements for sustaining and disruptive innovation will determine whether established, traditional defense suppliers or nontraditional suppliers, particularly commercial IT firms and startups, are best positioned to support military transformation. Since the requirement for sustaining and disruptive innovation appears to vary across sectors of the defense industry (shipbuilding, tactical aircraft, missiles, etc.), the opportunities for nontraditional suppliers will vary across sectors as well. Second, because the services' technical and acquisition organizations—the defense industry's key customers—will exert a tremendous influence on the trajectory of technological change in the defense sector, the management of the customer-supplier relationship throughout the systems-development process will be central to efforts to prepare the defense industry to implement transformation.

Proponents of network-centric warfare recognize that their vision requires a range of doctrinal, organizational, and technological changes within the military. When he was President of the Naval War College, Vice Admiral Arthur Cebrowski traveled across the country playing the pied piper for his vision of NCW, and he became concerned early on that industry would not produce the cutting-edge technologies that he believed were necessary for its implementation.[51] As he reported to the authors, in his visits to firms like Northrop Grumman and Raytheon and to government organizations like the Defense Advanced Research Projects Agency and the Space and Naval Warfare Systems Center—San Diego he had been struck by how poorly their managers understood the concepts of NCW.

Vice Admiral Cebrowski's instinct about the importance of the defense industry for providing the technologies essential to his vision was on target. His instinctive response was less accurate. He and many like-minded analysts argued that military transformation must be accompanied by the transformation of the U.S. defense industry.[52] NCW proponents argued that the United States no longer needs a defense sector per se; instead, they felt that the military should purchase equipment, software, and services from leading commercial technology companies. More specifically, since information technology was at the core of the RMA they were trying to promote, they suggested that the government should rely less on defense-specific firms and more on commercial vendors that changed the business world in the 1990s: Microsoft, Sun, Cisco Systems, and the like. With the success of these firms came enormous financial rewards and a sense that at least one large and growing segment of American industry would once again dominate the globe. The military naturally wanted to derive its next doctrine, operational concepts, and technologies from these winner industries rather than the hide-bound firms from which it had traditionally bought products.

Today, one legacy of this view can be found in a series of reports from the office of the Deputy Under Secretary of Defense (Industrial Policy).[53] Under Suzanne Patrick's leadership, DUSD (IP) interpreted its job, in part at least, as identifying nontraditional suppliers and "emerging defense suppliers that could grow up to be tomorrow's giants."[54] These "smaller innovative, emerging suppliers" would be able to "solve difficult defense problems."[55]

As we shall demonstrate in the following case studies on small ships, unmanned aerial vehicles, communications systems, and ultimately systems integration, the early suppositions of Vice Admiral Cebrowski and his supporters about replacing the defense industry were largely wrong. Once the major players in the defense industry figured out the principles of NCW, they responded quickly and accurately to the demand for both sustaining and disruptive technologies. They have begun to work closely with Congress, specific military customers and other firms, both traditional and nontraditional, to produce network-centric equipment, software, and services.

In fairness to Vice Admiral Cebrowski, who we are using as representative of a wide range of officers and civilian proponents of NCW, his initial instincts about what needed to be done were a product of the times and, perhaps most important, the intellectual origins of the NCW vision. When the admiral and others first became interested in the problem of innovation and the defense industry's ability to meet the needs of transformation, the defense industry was in the depths of a slump. Defense industry analysts bemoaned the poor performance of defense firms in the stock market compared to the high rates of return earned by Silicon Valley firms. Defense budgets seemed likely to drop or at best stagnate, and rumors of major program cancellations swirled at industry conferences. Calls for more innovation, more spending on research and development, and more willingness to risk existing programs were met with disbelief.

If this was the atmosphere in which Vice Admiral Cebrowski and others first turned their attention to industry, it was not long lived. At the macro level, the Internet boom went bust. At the micro level, the domestic politics of defense industrial production, the self-interest of defense firms, and the specific technologies required to implement NCW led to a more nuanced view of transformation. As we shall see in the coming chapters, industry's role in this big military innovation varies by the specific sector of the defense industry and with firms' relationships with both the military and Congress.

Choosing Case Studies

Proponents of network-centric warfare divide the world into nodes and networks. Roughly speaking, nodes correspond to what have traditionally been referred to as weapons platforms—ships, aircraft, satellites, and vehicles of various sorts. Networks refer broadly to the various ways in which platforms connect with one another to share data and information. In selecting our cases, we chose equipment and services from both the node and network sides of network-centric warfare. First, we chose a classic "node," ships. At the beginning of the debates about transformation, the shipbuilding sector was thought to be on the verge of a huge shakeout, and visionaries proposed new classes of small warships ranging from surface ships designed to operate in the littoral to small-deck carriers intended to host a few short takeoff and landing aircraft. Second, we chose to study the firms that make unmanned aerial vehicles (UAVs). UAVs may serve both as nodes and key links in networks: on one hand, they can serve as platforms when they host weapons or sensors; on the other, many NCW concepts of operations now envision using UAVs to relay data gathered by other platforms (nodes). Third, we chose to study the suppliers of new communications and information technologies, the military version of the industry that stimulated the entire idea of network-centric warfare. Visionaries expect major innovation in military communications—that is, the development of a true network—so we naturally chose to study business–government relations in the military communications sector.

In the concluding section of the book, specifically chapter 6, we introduce what amounts to a fourth case, systems integration (SI). Systems integration is neither network nor node, but it is an essential process, carried out by specialty firms, that helps define and create the entire network-centric system of systems. SI is perhaps the most important and understudied element of network-centric transformation, because systems integrators will make fundamental choices about the very nature of the network and the nodes that populate it. Some entity, public or private, will need to make basic decisions about system architecture and to analyze alternative approaches (for example, deciding whether a platform should perform a particular task or whether it should call on other nodes in the network to provide the capability in question). Systems integrators will develop and enforce the rules and standards for the network-centric operational environment—if the appropriate synergy of political support, military trust, and industrial-technological capability comes together to enable transformation's military innovation.

CHAPTER THREE

SMALL SHIPS

During the Reagan-era naval buildup, the U.S. Navy briefly approached and quickly fell back from its headline goal of a 600-ship fleet. The large force was designed to implement the so-called Maritime Strategy and to maintain U.S. naval supremacy on the high seas against both the blue-water Soviet navy and regional naval powers.[1] Even before the Navy approached its numerical objective, however, it became apparent that prospective procurement budgets would not be sufficient to build enough new ships to sustain a fleet of that size. Wear and tear and ships' finite natural service lives guaranteed that the Navy would shrink without a procurement surge some thirty years after the Reagan buildup. By the late 1990s the number of U.S. naval ships had declined to its current level of approximately 300 vessels through scheduled decommissioning, early retirements, and lower levels of acquisition spending.[2]

The lack of a clearly defined mission for the U.S. Navy in 1990s and early 2000s exacerbated the budget pressure.[3] In the post–Cold War era, the great raison d'être for the Navy, meeting the Soviet naval challenge, evaporated. Efforts to devise new maritime strategies succeeded in justifying the existence of the Navy, but they failed in the sense that the new naval roles and missions did little to protect force structure. Even maintaining forward presence, the perennial justification for maintaining a large fleet, foundered, because it became clear that presence did not produce quantifiable much less auditable foreign or security policy benefits.

The invention of network-centric warfare in the late 1990s and its subsequent adoption as the conventional wisdom about fighting future wars helped the Navy justify its remaining forces. Almost hidden amidst the conceptual jargon, NCW gave the Navy key roles in ensuring access to contested regions of the globe and maintaining a global presence through sea basing. It also posed a tremendous challenge to the traditional way in which the Navy fights, trains, and equips its forces. By emphasizing the need for smaller, lighter, and faster "nodes," NCW challenged the Navy to reverse a trend that had lasted through generations of ship designs that favored larger, massively complex, multipurpose ships. Intentionally or not, this change introduced a potential solution to the Navy's force-structure problem: the smaller, lighter, faster ships would operate in groups (known as swarms), so the Navy would necessarily have to buy notional NCW ships in greater quantities. NCW's combination of new warfighting concepts and its focus on operations close to shore meant that the Navy would plan less for air-to-air and ship-to-ship combat on the high seas and more for projecting military power ashore.

THE ROLES OF SMALL SHIPS IN NETWORK-CENTRIC WARFARE

Network-centric warfare proponents argue that the Navy needs to purchase larger numbers of smaller, faster, stealthier ships, each of which requires a smaller crew than current ships. In short, NCW calls for ships that look and perform differently from those in today's fleet. Advocates believe that larger numbers of such ships promise both tactical and strategic benefits. Given the continued strategic requirement for expeditionary forces, next-generation warships must operate close to shore in the littoral and must be prepared to fight against regional adversaries practicing access-denial strategies. Next-generation warships might also be modular: ship designs should allow the Navy to deploy different mission packages on the same basic platforms, from antisubmarine warfare (ASW) suites to deep-strike configurations, depending on the requirements of the mission at hand. Visionaries discussed the need for a variety of new naval vessels, including patrol craft-like "STREETFIGHTERS,"[4] fast sealift for both intra- and inter-theater mobility, and small aircraft carriers.

The Navy has numerous shipbuilding programs underway, including a new class of aircraft carriers (CNX), a new class of amphibious ships (LPD-17), a new type of cruise missile-shooting submarine (SSGN), and the DD(X) family of ships that includes cruisers, destroyers, and a new class of vessels called littoral combat ships (LCS).[5] This chapter will not discuss all of these programs; instead, we focus on the platform that best exemplifies the transformation model—smaller, faster, and lighter. We thus concentrate on the LCS. Other potentially transformational shipbuilding programs discussed by NCW proponents have not progressed as far in the acquisition process. So-called "small deck" aircraft carriers exist mainly in the dreams of the most extreme advocates of NCW,[6] and the fast transport ships that have received a great deal of attention in recent years remain relatively low-level experimental programs.[7] Specifically, ships such as the High Speed Vessel (HSV) are experimental test beds, leased from shipbuilders rather than purpose-built specifically to meet naval requirements. The LCS, by contrast, is a stand-alone, design-to-production program of record.[8] It is part of the DD(X) "family," because it will complement "but . . . not replace, the capabilities of DD(X) and CG(X)," a new destroyer and cruiser, respectively, as part of a "netted force."[9]

Littoral Combat Ships fit most closely with the vision of NCW transformation in part because, as then-Vice Admiral Mullen argued,

> They are less expensive so you can put these out in numbers and they are modular [in their mission systems]. In one area I could load up the ASW module on a handful of these and really go and attack that problem along with the rest of the architecture. If I have a mine problem, it's the same thing. So that will be a major mover for us in terms of not just getting into the ring, but staying in the ring. They [LCSs] have got to be fast, lethal, stealthy, and they have to be there in numbers. . . . LCS is not defined by size yet[,] . . . but it needs to be able to pack some punch and it needs to be able to stay.[10]

Vice Admiral Mullen's characterization of LCS illustrates the performance metrics that NCW advocates hope to apply to most future ship acquisition.[11]

As a program on the leading edge of military transformation, the LCS is just starting to make a transition from the drawing board to prototype production, making the LCS' progress an important harbinger of the results of efforts to implement NCW. As of late 2005, "Flight 0" of the LCS program, the first of two planned flights of LCS variants, is under construction. Construction on a second version of the ship, designated Flight 1, is scheduled to begin in Fiscal Year 2008, although the Navy has signaled that the Flight 0 design may meet its requirements well enough so that, rather than paying to develop an improved "Flight 1" design, it may instead simply purchase additional Flight 0 ships. [12] Two teams of firms—one headed by General Dynamics Bath Ironworks and the other led by Lockheed Martin Maritime Systems—were each awarded contracts for detailed design of a Flight 0 ship. Each team includes a small shipbuilder that promises to bring innovative concepts to the competition: General Dynamics is working with Austal USA, a subsidiary of an Australian shipbuilder, and Lockheed Martin is working with Bollinger Shipyards and Marinette Marine, neither of which has recently built a major combatant for the U.S. Navy. The first LCS, christened the USS *Freedom*, is being built by the team led by Lockheed Martin. If all goes according to schedule, the first Flight 0 LCS will enter the Fleet in 2007. [13]

In this chapter, we explain the challenges and opportunities for military innovation in the shipbuilding sector by considering the performance metrics associated with NCW-inspired ships, the relationship between the Navy and shipbuilding firms, and the politics of naval procurement. The performance characteristics of NCW platforms may require some disruptive innovations along with some sustaining ones; consequently, the industrial landscape of the shipbuilding sector may well be the part of the defense industrial base that is most changed by military transformation. [14] However, the need for a close relationship between buyers with professional military expertise and sellers with technological expertise will work against this change. The importance of tacit understanding between customers and suppliers at a time when requirements are in flux is likely to preserve the platform-integration business for the established "Big Six" military-oriented shipyards. Moreover, greater cooperation with the Big Six will also help the Navy to craft a political strategy to support the innovations it requires. Transformation plans that emphasize too many disruptive innovations and seek to replace all of the established suppliers with new entrants would undermine the key constituencies that can convince Congress to fund programs required for military innovation.

THE SHIPBUILDING SECTOR

On initial consideration, shipbuilding, one of the oldest industries in the world, is a prime example of an "old-economy" industry that should be eclipsed in the postindustrial age. But initial impressions are often off the mark. Shipbuilding may well be an example of the emerging "new old economy," where traditional extractive and metal-bending industries are reinvigorated by information technologies.[15] With the introduction of new design and production processes, old-economy industrial sectors outside the defense industry have begun to offer broad arrays of near-custom products manufactured using techniques that spread fixed costs more widely and hence reduce consumer prices.

Yet the impact of "new old-economy" dynamics may be more limited in the U.S. military shipbuilding industry than in other old-economy industrial sectors. Naval shipbuilders are constrained from making the technological investments necessary to benefit from the new old-economy dynamic. Naval shipbuilders rely on their military customer to fund investment in cutting-edge production technologies, but those investments are typically closely tied to "stovepiped" program offices, whose accounting rules make it difficult to share process improvement across products. And in the face of the pre-transformation trend in which the Navy planned to buy smaller numbers of complex, multimission ships, shipbuilders had little hope of realizing returns on up-front technological investments during long, high-volume production runs. In one shipyard, for example, a robotic welder that was purchased as part of a move to more flexible, automated production is almost never used; the cost of programming the machine for specific parts has proven prohibitive, because it would be used only on "onesies and twosies."[16]

Under the right circumstances, however, transformation could yet reinvigorate the naval shipyards. Expansion of the fleet to include more, smaller ships would help justify the information-technology investments that would enable shipbuilders to capture the advantages of flexible design and manufacturing. Transformation plans have already attracted investment interest from shipbuilders and local politicians in the states where the yards are located.[17]

The landscape of the naval shipbuilding sector reflects the broader defense industrial landscape. Naval shipbuilding has experienced considerable consolidation since the end of the Cold War. Until 1995, six separate firms owned the Big Six shipyards—Avondale, Bath Ironworks, Electric Boat, Ingalls, NASSCO, and Newport News Shipyards. But by 2001, a wave of acquisitions had created a duopoly, with Ingalls, Avondale, and Newport News owned by Northrop Grumman, and Electric Boat, Bath, and NASSCO owned by General Dynamics.[18]

Shipbuilders have been even less likely to close production lines than other defense firms. Instead, facilities have been downsized, workforces have been reduced, and production schedules have been stretched out to keep yards open and operating even during the lean times. Powerful politicians seeking to protect jobs and strategists foreseeing the need someday to rapidly meet emerging naval challenges combined to sustain shipyards even as low-rate production raised costs. Significant overcapacity burdens the naval shipbuilding industry. Despite the propensity to keep shipyards open, the declining number of military ships built each year and the paucity of commercial work has resulted in the decline of naval shipbuilding.

Many second-tier shipyards, whether building for the Navy or for the commercial sector, are at least as unhealthy as the Big Six. Most American shipyards not involved in naval work rely heavily on commercial orders that would not exist without the Jones Act, which mandates that U.S. coastal trade be carried in American-built ships.[19] High labor costs, the need for recapitalization, the indifference of financial markets, and heavy government subsidies to overseas competitors plague the American industry. This weakness makes it difficult to imagine that shipyards outside the Big Six will enter the naval market in response to transformation, except as partners with the major shipyards or other large defense contractors.

The prospects for innovation in the shipbuilding industry, however, are not as bleak as they might appear. If the Navy clearly signals that it values innovation, firms will work hard to develop the most innovative ships possible. As the teaming arrangements for the LCS program demonstrate, the firms can be expected to search the commercial world for new concepts, technologies, and materials to satisfy their customer. They will also happily use their in-house resources to push technological boundaries. Both the General Dynamics- and Lockheed Martin-led teams feature smaller shipyards with experience in modern shipbuilding designs, techniques, and materials. They will innovate with an eye toward the approaches taken by their competitors, who also seek to please the customer with their own strategies.

NCW AND SHIPBUILDING: NEW PERFORMANCE METRICS?

The most contentious part of the Navy's debate about network-centric warfare has concerned its implications for the types of ships that Congress should buy, the Navy should plan for, and the shipbuilding industry should produce. At their most extreme, transformation advocates argue that traditional major combatants—from big-deck, nuclear-powered aircraft carriers to extremely capable, multirole Arleigh Burke–class destroyers—will not have a place in the future Navy. This extreme position must be tempered by the reality that the Navy will not immediately replace all legacy ships with new ones; even a high rate of peacetime procurement would buy only a few ships per yard per year.[20] Serious current proposals plan first to demonstrate the characteristics of a network-centric force using a relatively small portion of the total fleet. Some transformation proposals call for a much larger fleet, the bulk of which would be LCS or even smaller designs derived from LCS.[21] But realistic ship construction plans suggest a smaller fleet, and the Navy now acknowledges that it will not meet its one-time headline goal of 375 ships by 2023.[22] Shipbuilding plans announced shortly before then-Chief of Naval Operations Vern Clark stepped down in the summer of 2005 projected a fleet of between 260 and 325.[23]

Many recent arguments concern the requirements that will define the new ship designs—the performance metrics by which the LCS will be evaluated. Specifically, what sort of test bed will the LCS be? Given the mix of sustaining and disruptive innovations planned for the LCS, it is no surprise that traditional and nontraditional Navy suppliers are involved in joint ventures in the LCS program. The requirements that call for enhancements of traditional performance metrics (sustaining innovation) put traditional shipyards in a good position to contribute to LCS. But other design requirements use new performance metrics (call for disruptive innovation), introducing a role for new suppliers.

As even a cursory review of its current fleet reveals, the U.S. Navy has long preferred naval platforms that are large, multimission, complex, and consequently expensive. Military leaders naturally want to deter potential adversaries (or fight actual enemies) with the most capable ships possible. At the same time, political incentives have pushed the Navy toward smaller numbers of larger, more capable, and even more expensive ships rather than larger numbers of smaller, less-capable, and less expensive ones: so-called "gold plating" is a natural response to political uncertainty.[24] When faced with high cost estimates for new platforms—estimates reflecting real technological uncertainty that might undermine political support for acquisition programs—advocates naturally promise that their favored innovations can help with additional missions. The idea is to broaden the political coalition that supports the weapon system, yielding a kind of mission or capabilities "creep" that in turn produces complex, high-performance, multirole platforms.[25]

The Big Six shipyards have repeatedly demonstrated their ability to build those high-end ships. The yards have developed particular core competencies to perform the complex integration of subsystems within relatively large hulls. For example, the hulls of the Arleigh Burke destroyers are roughly the size of those of traditional cruisers. Individual ships of that class are intended to fight antisubmarine and antiair warfare battles at the same time that they prepare for (and perhaps execute) land attack/ strike missions. The Arleigh Burke design thus bristles with antennas, squeezes an enormous amount of equipment into a confined space, and relies on weapon systems (like vertical launch tubes) that can handle many types of missiles. The designs of aircraft carriers, amphibious ships, attack submarines, and even combat-support ships reflect the same core competencies in naval architecture and complex craftsmanship that make the Arleigh Burke–class ships tremendously capable.

Left to their own devices, the shipbuilders would like to capitalize on those established core competencies. They are more likely to embrace sustaining than disruptive innovation. General Dynamics and Northrop Grumman have on occasion encouraged the Navy to invest in incremental changes to existing designs rather than starting "clean sheet" redesigns. Electric Boat's proposals for sa next-generation attack submarine were clearly modifications of the current *Virginia* (SSN 774) class. Newport News Shipbuilding did not resist the U.S. Navy's decision to abandon the clean-sheet approach to its new aircraft carrier programs.[26] Evolutionary improvements in the performance of familiar products, regardless of the size of the necessary resource investment, reinforce barriers to entry and allow established firms to entrench their technological advantages.

But advocates of network-centric warfare want to acquire future platforms that, they argue, are substantially different from the legacy force. The following paragraphs elaborate some of the performance metrics that will be used to evaluate the LCS. The question is to what extent the transformational ships, which NCW advocates intend to be used substantially differently by warfighters, will also be different from the perspective of the performance metrics that matter to the shipyards.

Some of the performance metrics for evaluating LCS are actually quite traditional—meaning that the designs will require sustaining rather than disruptive innovations. Other transformation objectives, however, establish new performance metrics, and some of the resulting ships will certainly perform less well than legacy ships in terms of traditional performance standards. As a result, the network-centric Navy may require disruptive innovation in the shipbuilding sector and thus the establishment of some new industrial arrangements.

SPEED

Transformation advocates invariably emphasize speed.[27] Increased speed is supposed to be achieved through, among other things, the development of new propulsion systems and the introduction of new hull forms.[28] Speed, of course, has been at a premium throughout much of naval history, helping warships make passages more rapidly, outrun more powerful pursuers, get within engagement range of evasive targets, and outmaneuver adversaries. Moreover, speed has different meanings in tactical, operational, and strategic contexts.

In recent decades, however, with the advent of missiles and the increased power of naval aviation, speed has become less important than it was when ships exchanged gun salvos. But NCW may reverse that trend. Increased speed may help warships to swarm, and it may allow intra-theater transports to reach the battlespace more quickly from over the horizon. Moreover, NCW proponents may be willing to accept a different design outcome in the traditional matrix of tradeoffs between speed and payload. In network-centric operations, reduced weapon payloads may be acceptable, because, for example, strike weapons are now more lethal and more accurate. Alternatively, if ground forces are less heavily equipped because their lethality arises from their connections to air, sea, and space-based assets, intra-theater transports might reasonably sacrifice lift capacity for speed. Note, however, that in neither of these examples is the metric of speed different from that which has been used in previous periods; rather it is the use to which speed is put that is changed by network-centric warfare.

Investment decision-makers at traditional military-oriented shipyards will understand how to evaluate technological proposals that promise to yield faster ships. They understand from long experience the inherent tradeoffs associated with decisions about surge speeds, sustained speeds, payloads, hull designs, and fuel capacity, among other factors. Customer demand for more speed thus calls for sustaining rather than disruptive innovation.

STEALTH

Transformation advocates often discuss the availability of new technologies that promise to reduce the sensor signature of American platforms, including the use of composites to decrease shipboard emissions.[29] Information dominance requires improved sensors that will reveal enemy positions, while concealing friendly forces from enemy sensors. With vessels as large, slow, and bound to two-dimensional travel as warships, stealth is a relative term, no matter how small the ship in question. Adjustments in hull design, superstructure architecture, surface materials and coatings, and emissions from engines and electronic equipment, however, can reduce chances for long-range detection and targeting of new ships like the LCS.[30]

Again, however, stealth is a well-established performance metric for existing naval shipyards. Since the introduction of long-range antiship missiles, low signatures have been crucial for preventing enemy target acquisition and increasing the difficulty of terminal guidance for enemy weapons. Stealth, improved electronic countermeasures, ship self-defense systems, and combat air patrols over the battle group worked together to defend ships during the Cold War. Submariners have long emphasized their advantage as "the silent service." In sum, the difference in the emphasis on stealth by today's fleet and by the next generation of warships is largely a matter of degree. Improved stealth will be the result of sustaining rather than disruptive innovation.

BATTLE-GROUP COOPERATION

In network-centric operations, ships will be deployed in relatively large numbers. "Swarming" and "self-synchronization," based on shared access to data from sensors, will make operational coordination an emergent property of decentralized decision-making by individual ship commanders. The LCS is explicitly intended to operate this way.[31] As we shall see in chapters 5 and 6, on communications and systems integration respectively, one of the major reasons why improvements in these sectors is crucial for the successful implementation of network-centric warfare is the ability to integrate nodes like the LCS into a fully netted force.

Buying ships with the ability to operate with other ships in the battle group—especially in relatively close proximity—has been an important acquisition criterion for many years. Complex fleet maneuvers were vital tactics for sailing ships-of-the-line; destroyers and dreadnaughts cooperated in World War I-era fleet tactics; and battleships turned out to contribute crucial air defense to World War II naval task forces led by aircraft carriers.[32] In recent years, the development of the Cooperative Engagement Capability (CEC) has led to a major investment in high-speed, inter-ship networking and data processing equipment to improve awareness of "tracks" along which enemy aircraft and missiles are flying and to improve cuing of the battle group's responding fires. The idea that ships should fight together to maximize their effectiveness is well established.

Requirements for basic communications interoperability have forced platform designers and operators to cooperate with external organizations—designers of other platforms that will serve in the same battle groups. Unfortunately, organizational boundaries have been a problem; interoperability requirements are often among the first to be sacrificed during the development process, and operators are forever asking fleet-support engineers and technicians for "quick fixes" before platforms go to sea together.[33] If the organizational problems can be solved, calls for a common operational picture will be simply continuations of long-term demands for reducing the fog of war and improving interoperability. New and improved methods of sharing data may reduce the dependence on active command and control (a development that could completely reshape the Navy's operations and command structure), but new equipment to make that change possible will advance along a well-known path—it will be a sustaining innovation. However, the increased emphasis that battle-group cooperation receives in connection with transformation will require adjustment on the part of shipbuilders and firms providing shipboard subsystems.

AFFORDABILITY

Given continued budgetary constraints, the requirement for larger numbers of ships dictates that new platforms be less expensive than legacy designs. Even with the defense budget increases of the early twenty-first century, the naval shipbuilding account is unlikely to grow enough in the coming years to buy dozens of ships at current prices; even relatively modest warships currently cost more than half a billion dollars each. In the defense budget debates in both 2004 and 2005, Congressional appropriators trimmed plans to procure ships.[34] While the official Navy position is that the cut from nine warships procured in 2005 to four in 2006 is a natural part of the transition to next-generation vessels,[35] knowledgeable analysts have long questioned whether the Navy can sustain even its current fleet size.[36] Either way, the Department of the Navy and its critics agree that more affordable ships, including the LCS, will improve the prospects for keeping up numbers.[37]

Yet acquisition-reform advocates have routinely tried—and failed—to make cost an important performance metric for the DoD acquisition community and the defense industry. In resolving the tensions between costs and capabilities, price considerations have rarely won the day.[38]

Buyers naturally prefer lower prices for any given capability. That was true even during the Cold War, when the pressing threat from the Soviet Union drove military requirements. Nonetheless, the acquisition community has weighted combat performance as more important than low cost in tradeoff studies—generally for understandable reasons.[39] In the post–Cold War environment, despite the introduction of "cost as an independent variable" in acquisition regulations, the buyer continues to weight non-price performance concerns highly in acquisition decision-making; "pork barrel" politics are important in the low-threat environment. Network-centric warfare may add military pressure to budget pressure for making affordability an important performance metric, but political resistance will continue.[40] Traditional shipyards may have some incentive to adapt their designs to the goal of cost reduction, but the political safety valve will limit the likelihood that affordability will force major change in the industrial landscape.[41]

Low cost has not been a traditional performance metric for the Big Six shipyards, so if network-centric warfare advocates truly have their way, affordability may require disruptive innovations from the shipbuilding sector. Based on past sales of frigates and corvettes to foreign navies, some non–Big Six shipbuilders claimed prior to the initiation of the LCS program that they would be able to build STREETFIGHTER-like ships for around $250 million a copy.[42] If demand for swarms of ships makes affordability truly crucial for the acquisition community, then these nontraditional suppliers may have an opportunity to break into the U.S. Navy market. In fact, the General Dynamics-led LCS team will build its versions of the Littoral Combat Ship at Austal USA's Alabama shipyard rather than at Bath Ironworks in Maine, and the Lockheed Martin–led team does not include any of the Big Six yards at all. On the other hand, the Bath yard does not have a clear follow-on project lined up after it completes its current set of four Arleigh Burke destroyers, and the pressures to expand the LCS' list of requirements may drive up the cost and downplay the affordability performance metric enough to mitigate this potential demand for disruptive innovation in the shipbuilding sector.[43]

Early reports suggest that the Littoral Combat Ship may have difficulty meeting affordability criteria. Although Assistant Secretary of the Navy John Young has said that he hopes that competition will keep the long-term cost of each LCS ship below $250 million, Congress is spending $214 million on prototype LCS construction for the hull alone, not counting the mission modules that will make the ship a useful combatant.[44] Not too long ago, the Navy's surface warfare directorate estimated that the first LCS would cost approximately $542 million.[45] Although this figure is lower than similar estimates for the cost of the Navy's larger next-generation ships, it still seems too large to allow the procurement of sufficient numbers of LCS for swarming, and the Navy will be hard pressed to satisfy its peacetime forward-presence requirement with small ships at that price.

SINGLE-PURPOSE SHIPS

Network-centric warfare advocates call for single-purpose ships, in part to eliminate the problem of "tactical instability." The loss of one large, multimission platform in a battle group or amphibious ready group would severely cripple the fleet's capabilities and would be so expensive in lives and resources as to make it difficult for American commanders to properly employ the fleet during crises. The high cost to U.S. forces of losing a ship gives potential adversaries a weakness to exploit and a technological aim-point: America's adversaries seek cheap weapons capable of knocking out a major American combatant. NCW advocates stress that decentralization of capabilities would solve this problem: a particular node might be lost, but the overall network will remain highly capable.

Transformation calls for ships optimized for a single mission (such as antisubmarine warfare). Losses of one or more single-mission ships, while costly and tragic, would not weaken the fleet's ability to perform its other assigned tasks. Furthermore, at least in theory, a single-mission ship might perform a particular task better than a multipurpose ship that must compromise among the performance metrics associated with different missions.

Whether buying single-purpose ships would require disruptive innovation from the shipbuilding sector depends on how small a single-purpose ship design the Navy actually wants. "Tight packing" of subsystems is a performance metric associated with multipurpose ships, but it may be less important to the network-centric Navy. Over the past several decades, the Big Six have learned to handle the complicated engineering and manufacturing necessary to fit the many complex subsystems required for multirole ships into tight spaces; as the Arleigh Burkes show, even a large hull can be space constrained if you wedge enough equipment into it. By contrast, single-purpose ships should generally require less space for their mission systems, because they require less functionality. Even if designers increase the capability of the single-purpose ship by expanding the space allocated to its mission systems (which might benefit, for example, from adding cooling capacity or additional signal processors), the Navy should be able to get a single-purpose ship that is significantly smaller than its current multi-role platforms. That prospect would allow the Navy to gain the tactical-stability benefit of its single-purpose ship while also simplifying the naval-architecture task—and it might introduce demand for disruptive innovation in the shipbuilding sector.

Successful proposals for network-centric ships might perform less well on the "tight packing" performance metric: the planned prototypes for the LCS are not especially small, at least compared to LCS' STREETFIGHTER inspiration and to other classic naval vessels such as corvettes, frigates, and patrol craft. As a result, it is no surprise that nontraditional suppliers have been assigned major roles in development and production of the LCS prototypes: even though the nontraditional yards have not invested in complex naval architecture as a core competency, they can handle the demands of the LCS. If the Navy remains relatively liberal with size as it defines future requirements, the nontraditional suppliers may have a long-term advantage in design competitions for relatively large single-purpose ships.

On the other hand, Navy doctrine writers may decide that single-purpose ships should be much smaller than legacy ships—and that is certainly their goal, because smaller ships tend to be stealthier, faster, and cheaper. Striving for smallness would also be consistent with the new-economy theme of miniaturization. Consequently, the ratio of mission-system size and complexity to hull size may not change at all—and that ratio might even increase, demanding still greater contortions from shipbuilders as they design the guts of future ships. This version of transformation could reinforce the value of traditional shipyards' skills, making the shift to single-purpose ships call for sustaining rather than disruptive innovation.

On a broader scale, though, the idea of single-purpose ships could still introduce a different demand for disruptive innovation. The ideal ship in a networked Navy need not have many on-board capabilities, because it can distribute requests for, say, air defense to other nodes in the network. The flip side of this premise is that an individual ship will be less capable than a non-NCW platform if it must engage the enemy without access to the network, whether because of battle damage, enemy jamming, equipment failure, or unexpected dispersal of friendly units. But NCW dreams of simple ships with less organic self-defense capability, fewer sailors, and less capacity to manage battle damage have given way to the reality that the Navy cannot send ships into battle with limited survivability. If shipbuilders, both the yards themselves and integrators charged with populating hulls with various ship systems, need to reorient to make network-only ships, the key performance metrics will shift dramatically toward making sure that ships are never cut off from their battle groups.[46] In this scenario, the network-centric ships will both require a new performance metric (unbreakable connectivity) and perform worse on a traditional metric (organic self-defense capability)—meeting the classic definition of disruptive innovation that would open the way for turmoil in the industrial landscape.

Even so, future ships may be designed with the full panoply of capabilities to fight independently, overlaid with network-based capabilities. This less extreme version of NCW seems to be taking shape in the LCS program, and it is likely to be selected for future designs on both military-operational grounds (commanders prefer maximally capable ships under all possible fighting conditions) and political grounds (politicians are unlikely to vote for ship designs that offer anything less than maximum protection for American sailors). Thus, the extent of disruptive innovation associated with network-centric warfare and its emphasis on single-purpose ships will likely be limited.

MODULARITY

Modularity has had several meanings in the shipbuilding sector over the years. In the past, it was applied to construction—ships that were built section-by-section and then "snapped together."[47] In another meaning, single-purpose ships built for strike, antiair warfare (AAW), antisubmarine operations (ASW), and reconnaissance, for example, would share a basic design with many common parts, thereby achieving economies of scale in production.[48] As part of military transformation, these definitions would imply that modularity should be seen as a component of the new emphasis on affordability, providing that issues such as overhead costs of supporting modularity can be worked out. While this form of modularity would surely yield scale economies and help relieve the shipbuilding sector of some of the burdens of low-rate craft production, it would also add tremendous complexity and cost in the ship-design stage. The resulting ships would gain whatever benefits for tactical stability the single-purpose performance metric will provide, but they would also require exactly the kind of demanding naval architecture and construction skills that the Big Six shipyards and the leading naval-design and professional-service consultancies have nurtured (for example, Gibbs & Cox, a member of Lockheed Martin's team on the LCS, or SYNTEK, which played a key role in the Arsenal Ship program before it was cancelled). From an industrial-landscape perspective, this form of modularity could actually reduce the disruptiveness of the innovations required by transformation.

For the most part, transformation visionaries are enamored with a more ambitious version of modularity. Ideally, new ships developed for network-centric warfare could be optimized for missions in one environment and then rapidly reconfigured for other missions in other environments. NCW proponents argue that modern information technology should allow the Navy to develop modular mission systems that can "plug and play"—to install different payloads, depending on specific mission requirements and battle-group composition, without extensive retrofitting in a depot or shipyard. The LCS requirement calls for "swappable mission modules." To date the LCS program has focused on three specific modules: "one type of mission module will contain improved detection, surveillance and defensive equipment for antisubmarine warfare. Another will include systems for defeating surface threats, such as small boats. A third type of module will contain equipment to accelerate mine warfare missions."[49] Each of these options provides capabilities required for littoral combat, but in theory at least there is no reason why the Navy could not develop other types of mission modules optimized for antiair operations, projecting power ashore, or specialized intelligence, surveillance, and reconnaissance missions.

While few continue to believe that this modularity will involve simple changes that could be accomplished while the ship is underway, in principle it does not seem impossible for the established defense industry to provide modular ships. The Navy already fires a variety of missiles from the Vertical Launch System on its destroyers, cruisers, and submarines, and each ship goes to sea with a different configuration of munitions, depending on its expected mission profile.[50] Changing sensor suites in addition to the weapons payload is an order of magnitude more complicated, but the idea to pack modular systems into a ship design is not all new. As a result, this expanded modularity as part of network-centric warfare might be best classified as a particularly difficult, sustaining innovation.

REDUCED MANNING

Advocates of naval transformation frequently stress the need to build ships that smaller crews can operate and fight—to reduce costs, ease problems with recruitment, and put fewer lives at risk during combat. Furthermore, over the life of a ship, personnel costs loom large compared to those of design and production. As salaries have risen in an attempt to meet recruitment and retention challenges, the failure to maximize the productivity of human capital aboard ships has become a glaring target of criticism. Finally, one of the defining characteristics of NCW nodes/platforms is that they provide greater tactical survivability and risk fewer lives. "Optimal" manning in the Navy jargon is a key characteristic of the LCS; the Navy target for the LCS crew complement ranges from fifteen to fifty crew members with the ability to carry another fifteen to sixty personnel to man the mission modules.[51]

In the shipbuilding sector, reduced manning was not a priority in the past; if anything, ship designers were pressured in the opposite direction. Warships were designed and produced to accommodate a built-in surplus of personnel—to operate weapons that in peacetime operations are seldom used and to provide extra damage-control capability. The developmental Advanced Gun System for the next-generation destroyer, the DD(X), is the first naval gun to take sailors out of the magazine; greater efforts to automate both mission and ship systems can be expected in the future.[52] Crew allocations are also changing now, as certain functions are moved off-ship by advances in telecommunications and computing. Transformation may extend these changes into future overall ship designs—possibly introducing a new performance metric and therefore a demand for disruptive innovation.

Commercial vessels have long operated at lower manning levels than naval ships.[53] It may be that firms with more experience building commercial ships, even smaller and much less complex vessels than warships, have core competencies in areas like automated damage control and ship handling. These skills may prove advantageous in design competitions for future NCW-friendly ships, helping new entrants establish positions in the American naval market.

A MIXTURE OF TECHNOLOGICAL INNOVATION

The list of performance metrics for ships touted by advocates of network-centric warfare includes a mixture of established and new standards for evaluating designs. Speed, stealth, modularity, and perhaps battle-group cooperation and the single-purpose platform all suggest an important role for sustaining innovations in naval transformation. On the other hand, emphasis on affordability, reduced manning, and more ambitious conceptions of single-purpose ships will pull demand toward disruptive innovations that may encourage some restructuring of the shipbuilding sector. With this blend of types of technological innovation embodied in the LCS designs, it is not surprising to find joint ventures in which Big Six shipyards and nontraditional suppliers work together to produce the new ships.

CUSTOMER–SUPPLIER RELATIONSHIPS

To the extent that transformation requires some disruptive innovation, the close customer–supplier relationship between the Navy and the Big Six shipyards may delay, if not undermine, the process. The Big Six may be reluctant to change standard operating procedures, to invest in new production technologies, and to develop teaming relations with potential competitors and nonmaritime defense firms. Conversely, established relationships may help promote sustaining aspects of transformation and may allow the Big Six to serve as platform integrators, brokering connections among new entrants unfamiliar with military operations and requirements, suppliers of military mission systems, and the military customer. The established firms' lobbying power may also prove vital to convincing Congress to fully fund transformation.

The close relationship between the Navy and its traditional private shipyards has developed over a long history. Until relatively recently, shipbuilders of necessity worked closely with the Navy, if for no other reason than that the Navy reserved design and engineering functions to such organizations as the Naval Sea Systems Command (NAVSEA). Further, the Navy maintained its own yards to provide the bulk of the maintenance and upgrades required by the fleet. In day-to-day terms, naval officers supervised the production of ships and submarines and then worked hand in glove with private yards throughout their shakedown cruises.

Over the course of the past decade or more, the Navy has ceded a great deal of responsibility for ship design to private firms. The Navy's acquisition workforce has been cut back in the name of efficiency, and those cuts fell disproportionately on the Navy's technical staff. The government cannot shed many contract-writing and program-management positions that respond directly to statutory requirements, and to some extent demand for government employees who enforce acquisition rules has only increased as outsourcing has become more prevalent in defense acquisition. As program offices have often been asked to handle more work with fewer workers, technical staff members have frequently been the easiest to let go in the waves of downsizing.[54] These cuts in specialized design expertise have only been possible because of the close relationship between the Navy and the Big Six shipyards and specialty technical advisers that have picked up the work: the Navy is generally confident that those firms well understand its core interests.

Some NCW advocates fear this close relationship, pointing out that many technological advances are brewing in shipyards outside the Big Six. As a result, the advocates hope the Navy will break its ties with established suppliers so that it can gain access to the new technologies. Existing commercial shipyards, especially in other countries, are now pushing the boundaries with new hull designs, production processes, and propulsion systems that might fulfill future requirements. The Visby, La Fayette, Jervis Bay, WestPac Express, Triton, Skjold, and other innovative designs come from Swedish, French, Australian, British, Norwegian, and other overseas shipyards. Those shipyards, despite their various licensing and experimentation agreements with the U.S. Navy (and the other services), do not have ties as close as those enjoyed by Northrop Grumman and General Dynamics.

Yet, even for the more disruptive platform innovations, the Navy is unlikely to entirely abandon established defense firms in the pursuit of transformation, as seen in its choices of the LCS teams. Each established defense firm, in addition to its technical skills, has developed a core competency in working with its military customers. Firms outside the defense sector, while able to offer sophisticated technical solutions that serve nontraditional performance metrics, are unfamiliar with the language in which the military describes its requirements and do not necessarily understand the operational environment in which military products will be used.

Commercial and foreign shipyards thus may lack the real advantages that a close customer relationship would bring to the transformation process. After working with the military customer for many years, the Big Six shipyards generally understand naval operations. The Big Six also follow the Navy's requirements-generation process, so they are able to respond with alacrity and focus to new requests for design proposals.[55] Yards outside the traditional industrial base have other customers, whose demands will limit their ability to commit all of their investment resources to the desires of the Navy. The question for the future industrial landscape in the shipbuilding sector is whether transformation proponents can engineer suitable teaming arrangements to capitalize on the platform-integration skills and customer-relationship advantages of the Big Six shipyards and also on the sources of innovation (especially disruptive innovation) outside the established industrial base.

The Big Six also understand the impact of the customer's preferences on subcontractor relationships, and they maintain large databases of suitable subcontractors. In some ways, those subcontractor relationships may be a drag on the implementation of disruptive innovations at the subsystem level, but many of the new plumbing or wiring innovations that one could imagine for ships are actually sustaining innovations. They ease space or cooling constraints, or they lower manufacturing costs.

New-entrant shipbuilders, on the other hand, might find it difficult to manage subcontractor relationships in the way that the Navy requires (with minimum efficiency losses in the face of complex acquisition regulations). They also might find it difficult to scan the overwhelming flood of technological innovations that could find places on a major new ship design for the Navy—a much more complex process than the relatively simple platform-integration tasks that are required for commercial or foreign naval vessels.

Finally, outsiders also lack the standard operating procedures that have been developed by defense firms to manage the unique oversight requirements of selling to a government customer. For the military buyer, efficiency (minimizing transaction costs) is an important goal in the contracting process, but the government also has other crucial goals that no acquisition-reform proposal can wish away—military effectiveness, accountability for the public trust, and social policies, for instance. Efficiency is not as important as it would be for a customer in private industry, and defense firms have adapted accordingly.[56] The transformation process needs to work in harmony with the American political process, or it will risk being derailed. The established Navy shipbuilding sector has demonstrated its ability to work within that process.

THE POLITICS OF BUYING SMALL SHIPS

The final step in implementing the NCW vision of buying small ships is to maintain the political coalition that has funded the LCS program. The short-term effects of trying to buy from nontraditional suppliers could undercut political support for transformation. But the LCS program has found roles for important political constituencies, and those groups have mobilized to protect the transformation project.

The major shipbuilders and their suppliers are organized into hefty lobbying groups like the American Shipbuilding Association (ASA). They work closely with members of Congress and Navy officials. Their approach is not subtle.[57] Building capital ships means money and jobs—many jobs and a great deal of money concentrated heavily in a limited number of coastal states (and indeed a limited number of specific communities). The ASA has a long list of powerful Congressional allies who are kept well informed about what the industry means for their constituents. Essentially the Association argues that more ships equal more military power, which in turn serves American geopolitical interests. Little if any mention is made of the greater aggregate firepower of today's ships compared to their more numerous predecessors. The ASA also does not question whether the network-centric approach to future military platforms developed by Vice Admiral Cebrowski and other transformation advocates is actually suitable to the current and future international environment. Instead, their lobbyists and public-affairs experts tout the capabilities of the new ships—and the "good jobs" that the projects bring to the United States.[58]

Indeed, the Navy and the ASA have occasionally worked at cross-purposes.[59] Although senior naval officers generally favor building and maintaining a larger fleet, they have other important goals as well. During wartime they must focus on operational readiness, for example, and even in peacetime they must balance the needs of the various naval communities—surface warfare, submarines, and aviation.[60] ASA is interested solely in building more ships, especially of the types produced by its members. When the Navy's commitment to the procurement account appears to waiver or the Navy hints that some nontraditional shipbuilding strategies might be appropriate, tensions arise with the shipbuilding lobby and its Congressional supporters.

These tensions were apparent in Congressional uncertainty about how rapidly to fund construction of the LCS prototypes as opposed, perhaps, to procurement of additional ships in established classes.[61] The current and planned large, multipurpose ships (and their predecessors) have served the nation very well for more than one hundred years. They already work together in battle groups through existing communications, and the modernization of these systems does not necessarily require new smaller, faster, and lighter "nodes." Strategic, operational, and tactical innovations, such as preparing for littoral warfare and projecting power farther ashore using naval ordnance, remain controversial. The interest in littoral warfare begs the question, why?[62] And the quest for Navy-launched deep strikes on land targets runs squarely up against long-standing interservice rivalries over roles and missions.[63] Individual shipbuilding firms and their lobbying arms make strong arguments that build on legislators' self-interest, and, especially if pressed, they sometimes raise serious questions about the need for network-centric transformation.

In the summer of 2004, the interaction of Congressional politics, Navy force structure planning, and contractor lobbying determined the LCS program's fate. House authorizers tried to delete funding for the procurement of LCS from the defense budget. Specifically, Rep. Roscoe Bartlett (R-MD), the head of the House Armed Services projection forces subcommittee, argued that the LCS concept was "immature," and he convinced the full House to make the cut in the defense authorization bill—offering to fund two additional Arleigh Burke destroyers to allay the Navy's concerns about its industrial base and force structure.[64]

The threatened cut coincided with the Navy's planned announcement of the selection of two teams to build the Flight 0 LCS from a menu of three design proposals. Lockheed Martin, in cooperation with its proposal teammates, launched a lobbying and media campaign that simultaneously hoped to tilt the Navy competition in its favor and to rally Congressional support for the overall LCS program.[65] The Navy simultaneously argued that they could not fully make the case for the program's maturity until the two finalist contractors (Lockheed Martin and General Dynamics) had been selected, and service–contractor cooperation kicked into high gear to rescue the program in Congress.[66] By choosing two LCS teams to actually build Flight 0 ships, the Navy broadened its supporting coalition. By making Lockheed Martin, not a traditional shipbuilder, one of the team leaders, the Navy added still another reservoir of political support. And finally, by working with joint ventures that promised to produce the ships in new shipyards (Marinette Marine, Bollinger, and Austal USA), the Navy broadened political support for the shipbuilding industrial base still further—as long as the Big Six also received contracts somewhere in the FY2005 defense budget (which they did) and could even hope someday to produce littoral combat ships themselves (especially at Bath Iron Works).

Then-Navy Secretary Gordon England clearly understood the implications of adding three new shipyards to the Navy's stable of suppliers: it would create three new political supporters of Navy programs, but also three new mouths to feed with future acquisition contracts.[67] Ultimately, the Congressional authorization conference committee report "note[d] the concerns" that Representative Bartlett had expressed and warned that the LCS acquisition plan should not undermine any players in the industrial base. The final spending authorization bill actually ended up fully funding construction of two ships at a higher level than had been proposed by the Navy or either house of Congress in the authorization bills.[68]

These political dynamics show that unnecessarily alienating the Big Six, their suppliers, and the shipbuilding industry association could weaken the political support that the Navy needs for its investment plans for ships small or large. Internecine fighting may also help expose some of the strategic and doctrinal flaws in NCW concepts. In the broad context of transformation and doctrinal change—in line with scholars like Owen Coté, who emphasize the importance of intra- and interservice rivalries as the source of innovative and effective military doctrine—this rivalry may be very healthy for U.S. national security. But for the service subject to such criticism and for its private-sector suppliers, such dissention and debate may be counterproductive. It is no surprise, then, that supporters of LCS have built a political coalition—through joint ventures with established shipyards and major prime contractors—to keep the LCS program on track.

SMALL SHIPS IN A NETWORK-CENTRIC FUTURE

If the Navy chooses to acquire more network-centric ships in the future, shipyards other than the Big Six might be enticed to enter or reenter the business of building Navy ships, thereby transforming the landscape of the shipbuilding sector. The first LCS are being built at yards other than the Big Six's facilities. It is no secret that the American shipbuilding industry lags behind major international competitors in a number of areas, including small-ship design and manufacturing technology. Of course, the systems integration aspect of shipbuilding would remain an advantage of the traditional producers, but smaller yards such as Austal and Bollinger can overcome that advantage by teaming with systems integrators or Big Six yards. Indeed, like Austal, Bollinger, and Marinette Marine in the LCS teams, another smaller shipyard, Halter Marine,[69] has teamed with well-known defense-industry prime contractors in its work for foreign navies.[70]

The Big Six could also face challenges in the Navy's network-centric future from large defense contractors that specialize in systems integration rather than shipbuilding, but this challenge is considerably less likely to revolutionize the defense industrial landscape than is the prospect of joint ventures with commercial or foreign shipyards. Many people see an intuitive connection between network-centric warfare's shift in emphasis from platforms to networks and a shift in emphasis from hulls to internal electronics in shipbuilding.[71] Consequently, traditional prime contractors in the aerospace and electronics sectors of the defense industry hope to take the lead role in integrating naval platforms in the future. Raytheon has struggled in its role as prime contractor on the LPD-17 amphibious ship program, but it hopes that it has now "learned the ropes" so that it will perform better on future transformational ship-building projects.[72] Raytheon lost the competition for a contract to build an LCS prototype because its team "did not measure up in management and design skills," but Lockheed Martin won that contract without recent shipbuilding experience or a Big Six partner.[73] The open question is whether problems on these contracts so far are natural "teething troubles" or are more fundamental, indicating that systems integration contractors from the aerospace business may not truly understand the complex world of shipbuilding.

In any case, trying to force the Navy acquisition community to rely on nontraditional suppliers of ships in the interest of military transformation is undesirable, because it throws away the benefit of a core competency of the established prime shipbuilders. They actually specialize in the complex integration of electronics into naval platforms—dealing with space, power supply, cooling, antenna placement, and other issues that must be balanced with the structural demands of ship design. Moreover, the leading naval shipyards have established procedures for subcontracting for naval electronics systems—sometimes even working with units of the same aerospace primes that are trying to move into the systems integration role for shipbuilding. The established shipyards' ability to solicit bids from suppliers of subsystems and to manage subcontracts that meet defense department acquisition requirements is a key advantage compared to potential commercial and foreign ship suppliers.

In the end, the Navy is on track to acquire the transformative ships it says it needs. The final products may be less radical in design and production than the visionaries once hoped for, but small ships are going to join the fleet—and perhaps a lot of them will be built in the years to come. However, nontraditional suppliers almost certainly will not take the lead role in the acquisition programs. Instead the Big Six yards and well-known defense-industry prime contractors will work with teams of smaller shipbuilders and other nontraditional suppliers. The early contracts for the LCS certainly follow this model.

CHAPTER FOUR

UNMANNED AERIAL VEHICLES

Unmanned vehicles are ubiquitous in both visions of the transformed military and the most recent armed conflicts.[1] Unmanned aerial vehicles (UAVs) are the most successful type thus far, widely praised in journalists' accounts of America's recent wars. In transformation plans, they bring a number of critical capabilities to the fight. They can be employed as intelligence, surveillance, and reconnaissance assets to gather data by carrying a wide variety of different sensor payloads. They can be used to launch precision strikes, especially against targets in very dangerous environments. And they can serve as communications relays, helping friendly radios to connect over the horizon. Many, though not all, of the tasks envisioned for UAVs in the future are currently performed by manned aircraft or satellites. Transformation advocates suggest that UAVs will cost less than those alternatives and at the same time will perform better for many missions. UAVs may have more impressive physical characteristics (size, stealth, loiter time, etc.), and tactical and operational commanders can tailor their mission profiles (launch timing, payload, flight path, etc.) to their specific needs. As NCW has become the common doctrine underlying military transformation, each of the services is preparing to acquire a large number of unmanned platforms that will be assigned an increasing number of roles, missions, and functions.[2]

American UAVs, including most prominently General Atomics' Predator and Northrop Grumman's Global Hawk, have already fought in recent conflicts from the Balkans to Afghanistan to Iraq. Their utility has increased from one conflict to the next, as the UAVs' technical capabilities have been enhanced and commanders have learned how to use them. Ten different types of UAVs flew during Operation Iraqi Freedom, compared to the single UAV system fielded for reconnaissance during the 1991 Persian Gulf War.[3] After-action reports and early assessments of the recent campaigns confirm UAVs' versatility.[4] Global Hawks, for example, were praised for enabling time-critical strikes in Iraq against surface-to-air missile (SAM) launchers, their support vehicles, and a large number of enemy tanks.[5]

With the improved performance, the market for existing UAV manufactures and other firms hoping to sell unmanned systems has grown by leaps and bounds. Visionaries have proclaimed that the F-35 tactical fighter aircraft, in versions currently under development for the Air Force, Navy, and Marine Corps, will be the last manned aircraft bought by the United States military.[6] Even if turns out that other manned aircraft programs follow the F-35, transformation advocates' eagerness to replace manned systems and the hype surrounding UAVs show the upside potential for growth of this segment of the defense market.

MILITARY TRANSFORMATION AND UAVs

Network-centric warfare doctrine plans to employ UAVs in many roles: to support the network as long-endurance communication relays; to support a common operational picture by carrying small, inexpensive, fast-moving, hard-to-detect sensors; and to launch precision strikes against targets that are too difficult or dangerous for manned platforms to engage. Today, the U.S. military operates three types of UAVs—small, tactical, and medium-endurance—primarily to carry sensors.[7] Technologists call for descendants of all three of these types plus "micro" air vehicles that may be as small as a sparrow or even an insect[8] and long-endurance UAVs that might remain at high altitude "over a given spot for a day or more."[9] To accomplish the full range of network-centric tasks, these future UAVs will rely on technological advances both in the mission systems carried by the UAVs and in the autonomous or remote-controlled operation of the UAVs themselves.

Perhaps the greatest contribution envisioned for UAVs is to real-time situational awareness. The dominant battlespace knowledge promised by *Joint Vision 2020* is supposed to be achieved in substantial part using UAVs equipped with a range of specialized sensors (for example, thermal and electro-optical cameras).[10] Unlike space-based assets that pass infrequently over the battlespace and manned aircraft that have a limited ability to loiter, some UAVs will be able to linger over areas of interest for long periods of time. Moreover, assuming that they are affordable enough, different kinds of UAVs will be available to all levels of command responsibility. Each commander will be able to direct a reconnaissance asset to focus closely on targets that he views as critical to his particular mission objectives: tasking will be controlled by those closest to the action, improving the intelligence value of the data stream. If it becomes possible to feed information through the network from all UAVs in the theater to all potential consumers—or, rather, when that becomes possible, according to transformation advocates—the United States military will be much closer to creating a common operational picture and the dominant battlespace knowledge that could drastically improve military effectiveness.

The most optimistic proponents of both UAVs and network-centric warfare also foresee a day when UAVs will operate in swarms.[11] Commanders will describe their intent and the rules of engagement, and nodes will then function free from centralized control, although they will communicate and react to each other. The result will be self-organizing, effectively autonomous behavior—adaptable and resilient in the face of obstacles. Even if attrition were very high on the fluid battlefield of the future, it would be unlikely to prevent a swarm of UAVs from carrying out its assigned mission, because the swarm would adapt to obstacles and the loss of individual units.[12] Similarly, self-organizing mini-UAVs, serving as sensors, would be difficult for an enemy to find and destroy; they could work with forward air controllers or even serve directly in hunter-killer packs to suppress enemy air defenses or accomplish other difficult tasks.[13] Test flights of UAVs have included up to four vehicles interacting with each other, and two UAVs have cooperated in a test to decide autonomously which one had a better shot at a partially obstructed target.[14]

If the theorists are correct, swarms will be formidable weapons for the American military. Yet as a National Academy of Sciences report noted in 2000,

The ONR [Office of Naval Research] vision pictured swarms of cooperating and totally autonomous UAVs that distribute and share information and assignments and that self-adjust for operational changes, losses, sensor blinding, electronic jamming, and software crashes, all the while still accomplishing their assigned mission without human intervention or active involvement. None of this is remotely possible today.[15]

Since this report was issued, scientists and engineers have invented few breakthrough UAV technologies. Before UAVs reach the point where they can operate without continuous guidance from human operators, a great deal of money will have to be spent on basic science and technology research. Later, the fruits of that investment will have to be applied to specific UAV development and procurement projects.[16]

Sensor-carrying UAVs and unmanned combat aerial vehicles (UCAVs) also have additional important roles in network-centric warfare. They will be able to undertake the most dangerous and difficult missions such as the suppression of enemy air defenses to help assure access for follow-on American forces. Flying to the battlespace from ships at sea or distant land bases in friendly countries, they will locate and track critical targets and provide the precise data necessary to launch long-range weapons from safe areas. UCAVs may even be able to launch the access-enabling attacks themselves rather than calling for fires through the network.

UAVs may increase not only the effectiveness but also the pace of access-enabling operations. For example, theater commanders generally have had to wait for combat search and rescue equipment to arrive before initiating manned aircraft operations at the start of a campaign.[17] UAVs do not need combat search-and-rescue, so they can launch sooner. And network-centric warfare theorists believe that very fast attacks that begin before the adversary is psychologically prepared for battle can achieve disproportionate effects on the enemy's political calculus. Directly influencing the enemy's high-level decision-making, called "effects-based operations," is one of the key goals of network-centric warfare.[18]

Depending on the mission packages they carry, UAVs may also contribute to improved connectivity within and among units from the various services. The most autonomous of the UAVs used in Afghanistan and Iraq, the Global Hawk, is a notorious consumer of bandwidth—partly to transmit flight-control instructions but mostly to send sensor data back to the ground station.[19] Future systems will depend on either having more bandwidth available or improving the processing and analysis power on board the UAV itself so that less raw data needs to be beamed elsewhere. But in the vision of network-centric warfare, high-altitude UAVs like the Global Hawk become a solution rather than a contributor to the bandwidth problem by carrying extra antennas rather than extra sensors. UAVs used as communications relays can act as "poor man's satellites," reducing the need to transmit via geosynchronous communications satellites and allowing units to connect to each other over the horizon without depending on the greater power and transmission time needed to reach high-earth orbit.[20]

To date, incremental progress has been made in improving the current generation of UAVs. DARPA, the services, and several versions of a joint program office created for UAVs have funded many research projects and plan to fund many more in the years to come. In 2002 DoD's UAV Planning Task Force identified forty-eight performance goals in its *UAV Roadmap, 2002–2027*.[21] But the technical limits of UAVs remain uncertain, and predictions about the pace and trajectory of UAV development remain haphazard compared to the well-understood process of acquiring new manned systems.

THE GROWING UAV SECTOR

UAVs have been used by the U.S. military at least since the Lightning Bug was deployed in Vietnam; as a RAND report noted, "[i]t has been technically possible to build generic UAV platforms for several decades, and many have been built and used as aerial targets and reconnaissance drones."[22] But over the years, the large number of UAV projects announced has mostly yielded a large number of project cancellations rather than deployed systems.[23] Some projects like the Hunter were canceled before they even reached the initial production phase; even relatively successful UAVs like the Pioneer were deployed in small numbers and suffered from performance limitations. Analysts stress institutional and cultural resistance to UAVs as well as an absence of clear demand because of competition from a diverse array of platforms that can perform similar missions.[24]

In the United States, the UAV sector includes the few firms currently designing and building unmanned aerial vehicles for the U.S. military and other government buyers such as the Department of Homeland Security. Northrop Grumman Integrated Systems (owner of Ryan Aeronautical),

General Atomics Aeronautical Systems, and AAI enjoy the advantage of having built deployed UAVs.[25] Boeing and AeroVironment have also built prototypes recently for DoD, NASA, the U.S. Army, and the U.S. Marine Corps.[26]

A more complete survey should include potential suppliers because, in many respects, the UAV sector has emerged only recently, and the number of firms that ultimately will enter the market remains uncertain.[27] Many firms claim to have the technical expertise and production capabilities to build UAVs, and in some cases they have even built flyable prototypes. Given the projected dramatic expansion of demand—both in terms of number of vehicles and the diversity of vehicle types—it is plausible that other firms could join the sector without undercutting the existing suppliers. Three other types of firms may eventually enter the UAV market: (1) traditional defense firms that have built UAVs in the not-so-distant past; (2) startup firms that may offer innovative solutions to long-standing technological challenges; and (3) foreign UAV manufacturers that already make products for foreign militaries.

Aircraft prime contractors are clearly capable of designing and building UAVs, even if they have not designed or built such systems in recent years. For example, General Dynamics proposed a modified Gulfstream G550 (a commercial business jet) as an unmanned replacement for the Navy's manned EP-3 electronic intelligence-gathering aircraft.[28] Once Boeing lost out to Lockheed Martin in the JSF competition, it quickly turned its attention to UAVs.[29] Boeing officials were quoted saying that "[u]manned systems are the future of aerospace," and "[o]ur goal is to develop a large business out of unmanned systems."[30] Although the larger primes initially did not have much experience producing UAVs, they have quickly entered the market.

Particular attention should also be paid to the prospects for startups: in theory at least, aggressive nontraditional suppliers could offer better solutions to outstanding technical challenges. The current stage of industry development emphasizes technological entrepreneurship, and UAV concepts generally do not require large fixed investments to take through the system-development phase.

Meanwhile, foreign suppliers have had some success penetrating the U.S. market: in mid-2004, the Department of Homeland Security leased two Israeli-made Hermes 450 UAVs for testing, and a joint venture of AAI and Israel Aircraft Industries makes the Army's Shadow 200.[31] Moreover, the range of potential international suppliers is expanding:

TABLE 4.1 U.S. UAV MANUFACTURERS

AAI Corporation
Advanced Ceramics
Aereon Corp.
AeroVironment
Alliant Defense Electronics Systems Co.
ARA
Aurora Flight Sciences
BAE Systems, North America
BAI Aerosystems, Inc.
Bell Textron
Boeing
Center for Interdisciplinary Remotely Piloted Studies
Dara Aviation
Dragonfly Pictures, Inc.
DRS Unmanned Technologies
Frontier Systems, Inc.
Genera Atomics
General Atomics Aeronautical Systems, Inc.
Honeywell
Imaging Microsensors, Inc.
Kaman Aerospace Corporation
Lockheed Martin Corporation
MMIST, Inc.
Northrop Grumman Corporation
Nurad Technologies, Inc.
Piasecki Aircraft
Pioneer UAV, Inc.
Raytheon Company
R&D Aeronautical Engineering Co., Inc.
Scaled Composites, LLC
Scheivel Technology, LLC
Secra Group, Inc.
Systems & Electronics, Inc.
Teledyne Brown Engineering
Titan Corporation
Trek Aerospace, Inc.

Sources: Peter Partridge, ed., *Jane's International Defence Directory 2005* (Surrey, UK: Janes Information Group, 2005), p. 752-754; Office of the Secretary of Defense, *Unmanned Aircraft Systems Roadmap 2005-2030*; Authors.

in 2001, nineteen companies in France, Germany, and the United Kingdom alone were actively engaged in the UAV market; in 2005, forty-
three countries are home to UAV manufacturers, ranging from Botswana
to the United Kingdom.[32] These firms are naturally interested in entering the U.S. market, because the United States is expected to account
for 90 percent of the spending for UAV technologies and 70 percent of
official procurement worldwide in the coming decades.[33]

By defense-industry standards, the industrial landscape of UAV manufacturers is thickly populated, when potential producers are counted (see
table 4.1). On the other hand, the established suppliers who currently sell
Global Hawk, Predator, and Shadow to the military would prefer to do any
additional UAV work themselves rather than making room in the sector
for more firms.

UAV PERFORMANCE METRICS

The designated tasks of UAVs developed in the past bear only a passing
resemblance to the roles and missions envisioned for UAVs in network-
centric warfare. The gap in conceptual and technological terms between
UAVs operating in 2005 and those proposed for 2025 may be as large
as the gap between the first unmanned drones used as disposable targets
and early UAVs.

Earlier UAVs were generally single-purpose vehicles—mostly scouts
for military units lacking direct or sufficient access to operational and
strategic ISR systems that in any case were ill suited to providing timely,
detailed information to small units. UAV manufactures concentrated
on producing systems with modest capabilities and foresaw relatively
little program growth. The widespread expectation that UAVs would be
cheap constrained investment in advanced capabilities and mission payloads—and often led to disappointment in the systems' performance and
ultimately to projects' cancellation.[34] In terms of program size, UAVs
paled in comparison to manned systems. The need for large numbers of
unmanned systems was not widely recognized, except during wartime
when operational considerations overruled theory and doctrine.[35] As
a consequence, large defense contractors left UAV manufacturing to
small firms or divisions of their own firms that were outside the corporate mainstream.

With the growing acceptance of military transformation and the operational successes of existing UAVs in the 1990s and early 2000s, however, UAVs have emerged from the defense industrial backwater. UAVs will no longer be relegated to the limited role of tactical surveillance; instead they will come in all shapes and sizes, stuffed with all manner of mission payloads. The Department of Defense has begun to identify UAV performance metrics for the coming wave of acquisition investment.[36] The forty-nine metrics listed in DoD's UAV roadmap are quite detailed and do not establish comprehensive program goals that could help determine what sort of firms are best suited to producing UAVs for military transformation.[37] Which firms will prosper—and the potential for attracting political support from powerful defense-industry lobbyists for this part of network-centric warfare—will depend on whether the broad performance metrics for the new UAVs will demand sustaining or disruptive technological innovation.

Both alternatives are reasonable possibilities. According to one school of thought, UAVs have been built for years; they resemble other, already successful products from autopilots on commercial aircraft to various forms of cruise missiles and unmanned target drones. Once the military determines what roles UAVs will play in future conflicts, existing suppliers will be able to build them in large numbers, because the performance metrics will be the same as for the similar systems. In this view, the technological challenges can be solved with sustaining innovation.

A second school believes that UAVs are unique and that future UAVs will be quite different from the false starts of the past. Major changes in what the customer is looking for would require disruptive innovation and, likely, a new set of suppliers. At present, the industry faces genuine uncertainty about the characteristics of UAV demand. We have identified a set of four performance metrics for UAVs in network-centric warfare, based on our interviews and interpretations of the technical and operational issues at stake.

FORCE PROTECTION

Eliminating risk to pilots is both the most obvious and probably the most important feature of UAVs discussed by NCW advocates: using UAVs connected to the network, the military will be able to carry out missions that would simply be too risky or physically taxing using manned systems.[38] UAVs compete with systems that put their operators at risk (except for space-based assets). Navy and Air Force aircraft that perform close air support or deep strikes may be shot down, risking the death or capture of the flight crews. By contrast, if a Predator equipped with Hell-fire missiles is shot down, only equipment is lost. This same logic applies to non-strike missions—notably, reconnaissance aircraft intentionally fly close to the enemy, and their mission performance depends on close proximity to the battlespace. The risk to reconnaissance pilots stimu-lates demand for tactical UAVs: replacing today's Joint Surveillance and Target Attack Radar System (JSTARS) with tomorrow's sophisticated UAVs, for example, would mitigate the risk.[39]

Trying to protect pilots is nothing new for the aircraft industry: stealthiness, speed, and maneuverability are familiar metrics, and some airplanes like the A-10 have been praised for their ability to keep flying when damaged. The point is that military missions are inherently danger-ous, and often the best force protection would be to remain out of harm's way entirely—that is, to stay far outside your adversary's reach, ideally at home. In effect, that is exactly what the military has been doing for some of the tasks that transformation advocates plan to assign to UAVs. If UAVs and the network work well enough, though, the military will be able to accomplish those additional tasks, because of the significant increase in force protection that the UAVs would offer.

Even though all UAVs leave their pilots at the ground station, reduc-ing soldiers' direct exposure to enemy fire, not all UAVs should be mea-sured as equally capable with respect to force protection. The real ques-tion is whether UAVs will be able to achieve sufficient levels of mission performance while keeping airmen away from the enemy: a UAV's value depends on the likelihood that it will complete a particular mission com-pared to its UAV peers or to a competing, manned system.

Force protection and mission performance both require situational awareness—understanding the environment in which the vehicle is operating. For manned aircraft, the pilot acts as both a sensor looking out the canopy and a processor/analyzer of information provided by instruments and subsystems onboard the aircraft. As the primary deci-sion-maker, the pilot can make rapid choices to reorient sensors, change targets, respond to failures that affect his or her aircraft's flightworthi-ness, and take advantage of opportunities presented during flight. The operator of a UAV, sitting in a ground control station, ideally will be able to make the same choices—as long as the data link works well enough and is designed to transmit the right information to the operator, and as long as the operator has enough "feel" for flying the UAV. But at present, "UAVs simply do not have the capacity to absorb, process and relay the same amount of data as a pilot in the cockpit, who can maintain 360-degree situational awareness with his or her radar, wingman and eyesight."[40] Without the pilot in the cockpit, the vehicle loses a critical sensor, analytic processor, and decision-maker. As a result, UAVs are likely to perform less well than manned aircraft. The question is whether they can perform well enough to meet the high expectations of transformation advocates.

Other aspects of UAV design may offer opportunities to enhance performance. Just as for manned aircraft, force protection for UAVs requires avoiding enemy tracking and targeting systems.[41] Ideally, UAV designs that do not need to make room for a pilot and that do not need to take account of the pilot's fragile physiology will be stealthier and more maneuverable, and thus UAVs may achieve more operational success than their manned counterparts. On the other hand, UAVs inherently need more communications antennas built into their designs, which limits their stealthiness.[42] Moreover, if a remote UAV pilot turns too quickly or tries to execute the sort of complex maneuver that a creative pilot might try in a manned aircraft, he is liable to break the communications link from the ground station to the UAV. A temporary interruption of the data link might simply reduce the operator's situational awareness or the UAV's value as a sensor; more likely, it will make the UAV, suddenly operating autonomously, a sitting duck for enemy fire, or in the worst case, it could lead directly to a crash. The net effect of these positive and negative impacts on mission effectiveness of removing the pilot from the platform will be the major factor determining the extent to which UAVs meet the expectations of transformation proponents.

Force protection, which appears at first glance to be a simple performance metric, is actually fairly complex. It has always been a consideration in the tradeoff matrix used by designers of military equipment, and in that sense UAVs represent a sustaining innovation: defense industry leaders can comfortably assess the value of taking the pilot out of the platform compared to the value of improvements on other measures like stealth and armor protection. The established defense industry should have no conceptual problem accepting and investing in the force-protection aspect of UAV technologies.

However, the breadth of the category—force protection defined relative to some measure of mission effectiveness—suggests the limits of the approach of separating technological innovations into sustaining and disruptive categories. Force protection is really an aggregation of several familiar performance metrics that are traditionally traded off against each other: for instance, an airplane might gain some resilience to enemy hits by giving up some maneuverability. UAVs introduce additional complications to the tradeoffs among the well-known performance metrics and a new extreme on the potential value of pilot protection that has not been available on any system in the trade space in the past. If future UAVs eventually are expected to fly missions that have been ignored by the military in the past as too dangerous to attempt, then UAV manufacturers will have to learn a new set of operational requirements in order to make reasonable choices about optimizing UAV design. A new concept or two probably lurks somewhere in this process, which would typically introduce an element of disruptive innovation, even if UAVs' direct effect is measured entirely by familiar performance metrics. On balance, though, UAVs' ability to increase force protection is mostly an improvement on a familiar technological trajectory—a sustaining innovation.

AFFORDABILITY

Affordability is purported to be a key advantage of unmanned systems relative to their manned counterparts. Like force protection, UAV affordability needs to be assessed relative to the systems' ability to perform certain tasks: DoD's *UAV Roadmap* says, "It is not necessary that a single UAV replicate its manned counterpart's performance; what matters is whether the UAV can functionally achieve the same mission objectives more cost effectively."[43] But that statement makes clear that the expectation that UAVs will be relatively inexpensive is central to the case for buying more systems. Especially if NCW requires populating the future battlespace with many UAVs performing a diverse array of missions, cost will be a major issue.[44]

Advocates expect that UAVs will reduce acquisition costs in several ways. They hope that UAVs can be smaller and simpler because they do not need to carry pilots with them. Designers generally expect that UAVs will be less expensive to manufacture and will experience fewer maintenance problems and operational failures because they will consist of fewer components than manned systems. They also hope that UAVs will require less labor-intensive maintenance and training. Finally, UAV advocates also hope to reduce the number of expensive pilots that are needed in the force structure.

Expectations of greatly lower costs may not be fulfilled. First, even if UAVs are relatively inexpensive to design and build, they will not be as affordable as predicted if they frequently fail. Available data suggest, "UAVs currently suffer mishaps at 10 to 100 times the rate incurred by their manned counterparts."[45] A system that crashes in bad weather or from a single point failure in a subsystem—problems suffered by the current generation of UAVs—will not be reliable operationally. Nor will the total cost of buying several unmanned systems be less than the cost of buying a single, more reliable manned system. A shorthand way of thinking through the reliability issue is to measure UAV systems' mean time between failures: how long the UAV can remain in the air without experiencing either a catastrophic equipment failure or an operator error from which recovery is not possible. Current research and development projects emphasize the goal of giving UAVs the ability to "degrade gracefully" in the event of a system failure.[46] Unless these projects succeed, UAVs will struggle on the affordability performance metric.

Second, UAVs do not reduce personnel requirements as directly as the caricatures provided in news reports often suggest. While UAVs have no flight crews, they still require remote operators; for most current systems, ground control stations can control only a very few UAVs at any given time, and each UAV essentially needs its own pilot or pilots.[47] Moreover, the U.S. Air Force insists that only licensed aviators fly UAVs, despite claims by some proponents that "operating these aircraft . . . is like playing a video game."[48] With the high operating tempo demanded by Iraq, Afghanistan, and the global war on terror, trained aviators for manned systems are in short supply, and UAVs often must compete for pilots.[49] At best, future systems may improve aircraft autonomy, avionics, and data links, which would then reduce the pilot manpower required for the overall network.

UAVs also require maintenance and support crews, and although mobile ground stations surely require less than even a rudimentary air base, supplying the UAV with fuel, spare parts, mission packages, and other logistical support will not be a trivial task. UAVs themselves have also traditionally been relatively fragile, meaning that they need a lot of maintenance effort—often technically complex maintenance that cannot readily be accomplished in the field by the enlisted personnel usually given that task.[50] The best case for UAVs is that they may at least reduce the time and money needed for training: UAV system developers can readily incorporate simulator functions into flight control stations. In total, the UAVs' ability to shine on this contribution to affordability remains a question for the future.

Finally, leaving aside these operational issues, UAVs' supposedly simpler system design and manufacturing may not turn out to reduce costs. The acquisition process for UAVs is vulnerable to the same "gold plating" pressures that plague other programs. Individual vehicles are already being asked to perform more and more tasks, increasing development cost, requiring larger unmanned platforms to accommodate all the mission payloads, and reducing the ability of designers to optimize performance for specific missions.[51] System costs have surged. The Global Hawk, for example, began as an Advanced Concept Technology Demonstrator program with a budget goal of $10 million per copy, yet a recent estimate put the out-year cost at roughly $75 million per system.[52] Northrop Grumman and Boeing are currently building prototypes of the Joint Unmanned Combat Air System (J-UCAS), which will be a "drone only slightly smaller than an F-16 fighter to drop guided bombs to suppress enemy defenses deep in enemy territory."[53] Of course, the large size and high cost of the J-UCAS may simply result from the difficulty of its assigned mission, and the costs may be worth paying. It is very difficult to identify gold plating *ex ante*. But even if UAVs are expensive only because they are technologically challenging to design and build and because they are tasked with heroic missions, an expensive UAV will still be assessed as a poor performer on the affordability metric.

Affordability is a familiar goal of defense acquisition programs, although it is frequently a goal that receives disproportionately low weight in the overall acquisition decision process. For UAV manufacturers and transformation advocates attempting to attract new users to new missions, though, price is a selling point, and affordability as a performance metric may have even more appeal to Congressional appropriators than usual for other military systems. Improving on an established performance metric is the definition of a sustaining innovation; however, increasing the relative weight attached to one performance metric versus the others might introduce some characteristics of disruptive innovation.

If UAVs perform well enough and stay within budget constraints, some service communities may even prefer them to systems that perform better but remain prohibitively expensive. That circumstance is quite close to the caricature story of a disruptive innovation—an innovation that is accepted by a user that did not buy the preexisting products because they were too expensive and provided more capability than the new user needs.[54] Such innovations only disrupt the established supplier base if the performance of the new product improves rapidly on the performance metrics on which it initially did worse than the established products. That trajectory of improvement will determine whether UAVs replace or supplement current manned and space-based systems. It will likewise help determine whether UAVs will be vulnerable to powerful political opponents that will make it difficult to implement transformation and will therefore limit military innovation.

BATTLESPACE INTEGRATION

According to the doctrinal vision of network-centric warfare, each friendly platform in the battlespace will serve as a node in the network—as a potential communications relay, as a sensor, and possibly as a shooter—and UAVs will make a significant contribution only to the extent that they are tightly linked to other nodes. New systems will be optimized for NCW, meaning that they will be simpler and will rely more on the network for functionality. UAVs not only must have sufficient communications capabilities to interact with other nodes, but they also need to be designed to physically fly safely in the same airspace as manned systems and other UAVs.[55] Air Force Chief of Staff General John Jumper highlighted this problem with approximately 750 UAVs of various types operating in the skies over Iraq: as of May, 2005, he said, "we've already had two mid-air collisions between UAVs and other airplanes." Jumper also noted that UAVs are "jamming each other in the radio frequency."[56]

"Playing well with others" is a difficult technical problem. As one industry expert argued, "DAPRA has been focusing on collision avoidance because it is a DARPA-hard problem."[57] DARPA's Organic Air Vehicle (OAV) will have a collision avoidance subsystem integrated into its flight control system to allow it to operate in the same airspace as other UAVs, manned aircraft, and obstacles such as telephone lines and rough terrain.[58] Industry leaders such as Boeing are working on other advances including operating UAVs in formation; two X-45s flew in "loose" formation for the first time in the summer of 2004.[59] Ultimately, the goal is solving the "sense and avoid problem for achieving manned-like aircraft capability among multiple autonomous aircraft, enabling us to detect and avoid both cooperative and non-cooperative aircraft in the same space."[60]

The physical problem of battlespace integration for UAVs is not limited to airspace management. If significant numbers of UAVs are launched and recovered from an aircraft carrier or another ship, the Navy will face a special problem in managing operations, especially if enough UAVs are involved to work in swarms, as called for in NCW doctrine. Current manned aircraft recoveries by aircraft carriers still rely on the visual acuity of pilots. Pilots control their own landings, and they need to see the carrier and other aircraft waiting to land. UAVs currently do not have nearly adequate sensor capabilities, because most of their sensor systems are oriented toward mission performance (e.g., surveillance or weapons targeting). They have not been designed to observe their airspace or to process the resulting information.

To implement network-centric warfare and to work with other nodes in the battlespace, UAVs will need substantially improved situational awareness. The components to provide that improvement, even if based on tremendous, yet-to-be-invented technologies, will increase the UAVs' complexity and cost and will take up payload space and weight that could otherwise be assigned to mission systems. But UAVs do have one natural advantage that could be critical in their quest to achieve their technical goals: UAV ground stations can expand even while the UAV itself stays small, stealthy, and mission-oriented. While it is difficult to accommodate extra personnel in a manned aircraft, a ground station can fit several people, each of whom might control a different aspect of the UAV—e.g., a pilot and a flight engineer dedicated to monitoring sensors. And at the same time, the ground station can carry a larger, more powerful computer with enough processing power to solve data management problems that would overwhelm a manned aircraft flight crew. But as usual, the ability of the UAV to capitalize on the flexibility of its ground station will depend on the quality of its data link and on improvements in other basic equipment like displays and all-aspect sensors that would facilitate situational awareness. Expanding ground stations may also add to the cost of UAV systems.

The military's battlespace integration problem did not arise for the first time with the recent interest in UAVs and NCW. One of the issues in the long-standing debate between advocates of single-seat and two-seat tactical aircraft has been whether the second flight crew member makes enough of a contribution to situational awareness and real-time battle management to justify the additional aircraft size, cost, and risk to American personnel.[61] Debates about the ideal formations and tactics, techniques, and procedures for air-to-air engagements in essence are debates about the best form of battlespace integration. Similarly, American ground-attack sorties are complex ballets involving combat air patrol flights, electronic warfare aircraft, support aircraft such as tankers, and of course the actual bomb-droppers.[62] Aircraft proposals have long been evaluated in terms of their ability to fit into the Air Force's overall system—and more recently their ability to fit into the joint force. Despite routine complaints about the failure of system designers to adequately implement communications interoperability standards, American forces, especially intra-service organizations, have done a remarkably good job of managing battlespace integration of existing platforms.[63]

The bar is set quite high for the expected performance of future UAVs, especially if NCW requires them to depend on battlespace integration to an even greater degree than the legacy systems have. But the idea of battlespace integration is not new. The call for rapid improvement in UAV capabilities on this metric is a call for sustaining innovation.

END-USER CONTROL

In complex terrain, facing clever adversaries, local forces generally know much more than higher echelon commanders about the information that they need to complete their missions. Soldiers on the scene also can be much more precise about the location and priority of various targets for indirect fire from artillery, missiles, or air support, as shown by the success that Special Forces teams enjoyed directing strikes in Afghanistan. Advocates of network-centric warfare hope to capitalize on those local advantages by distributing capabilities to small-unit commanders, whose ties to the network will give them a better conception of their role in the evolving battle and of the theater-wide resources available to back them up. Giving command and control of UAVs to all levels of the American military under NCW will help tailor intelligence, surveillance, reconnaissance, and strike to the requirements of the rapidly evolving battlespace.

The practical issue of local control tracks with the concern of many transformation advocates for decentralized decision-making and self-synchronization. Providing warfighters understand their commander's intent (as they are supposed to under the precepts of network-centric warfare), they will be better able to fulfill that intent if they have the operational freedom and the information about their specific local environment that they need to act. Control over a UAV's sensors will allow for better and more timely decision-making by those most directly involved operationally and tactically.

In the past, deployed Army and Marine units have sometimes found it time-consuming to request support from Air Force and Navy assets—or even from assets controlled by higher echelons of their own services. Their requests have also sometimes been refused at critical moments, although cooperation and responsiveness in joint operations have improved markedly over the past twenty years.[64] After-action reports from Operation Iraqi Freedom stressed that joint fires are now much more reliable than they were in the past: the Army insists that it now trusts the Air Force to provide close air support.[65] But NCW advocates consider this relative success to be only a way station on the road to fully integrated, networked forces.

One of the problems in transferring control of sensors and responsibility for target designation to forward forces has been that they often outrun their ability to communicate effectively with higher-echelon commanders.[66] UAVs may provide the critical "last mile" of connectivity between tactical nodes and the Global Information Grid.[67] UAV communication relays could enable better data interchange, more effective calls for indirect fire, and efficient requests that high-level intelligence assets be committed to tasks critical to warfighting.

But reducing communications delays and giving joint commanders the appropriate incentives to respond to requests will not be sufficient to achieve information dominance, precision strikes, and the full benefits of network-centric warfare. Even when requests can pass rapidly up the chain of command in a form that enables immediate decision-making, the higher-echelon assets may already be occupied with other missions. At best, the local commander can only "bid" for attention, and the higher-echelon commander might still allocate the assets to a higher-priority mission. On the other hand, a commander of a distributed UAV would not have to compete with the rest of the military. UAVs directly attached to local commanders will, by definition, be more responsive to local needs.

Resolving the issue of end-user control is not necessarily straightforward. Simply because a UAV is a Marine asset does not necessarily mean that Marines engaged with an adversary or undertaking tactical operations will have direct control over it. UAV ground control stations, in all like-lihood, will be located as far from the battlespace as possible in order to maximize force protection. The interface that links ground forces to UAV operators may depend on forward air controllers, replicating the institu-tions that link them to manned aircraft. Assigning ground troops to fly UAVs seems to introduce problems, because their organizational culture does not include a "feel for flying"; allocating UAVs to relatively forward-deployed specialist airmen reintroduces layers of command and control like those that currently separate in-theater commanders from the use of, for example, space assets.[68] Optimizing operational control of UAVs requires that numerous technical and organizational issues be resolved.

The military services have sought for years to increase their respon-siveness to the needs of soldiers at the forward edge of the battle area, but they generally have emphasized communications improvements and higher-echelon battle-management techniques and training rather than true decentralization of control.[69] Even the Navy, which is most famous for delegating responsibility to captains "over the horizon," has mixed feelings about end-user control.[70] To the extent that NCW's com-mitment to decentralization and self-synchronization is implemented through the acquisition process, this performance metric will take on a substantially new role and importance—introducing demand for disrup-tive innovation. Potential UAV suppliers that want to offer products to increase end-user control face technical decisions, including where to locate processing and analysis capability (i.e., on the UAV itself, at the ground control station, or elsewhere in the network) and how to deliver data in a useful form. But their more important task will be to learn to analyze projects using this new performance metric and to harmonize their investment plans with their customers' transformational intent. The emphasis on end-user control is likely to offer more of an advantage to new suppliers than any other UAV performance metric.

THE IMPLICATION OF EMERGING PERFORMANCE METRICS FOR UAVS

Which performance metric, or group of performance metrics, will set the standards for UAV designers and builders will be revealed gradually over the next several years as the results of testing, experimentation, and operational experience become available. In some respects, the high operational tempo of the U.S. military during the campaigns in Afghanistan and Iraq may accelerate the process of sorting through appropriate measures of UAV effectiveness. The services today have a much greater database of lessons learned and much more tacit knowledge of actual UAV operations than before 9–11 provoked the War on Terror.[71]

Although most emerging UAV metrics appear to require sustaining innovations, the development of transformational UAVs also demands more elements of disruptive innovation than other areas of NCW investment. The dominant role of familiar performance metrics suggests that established suppliers can satisfy the demand, but it is possible that new firms will prove more adept at providing the military with products maximizing particular disruptive performance metrics. For instance, a new firm could develop UAVs capable of reliable autonomous operations. Greater autonomy could prove disruptive, because most UAV manufacturers have not, to date, made this their primary focus or invested heavily in the technologies that would allow for it. Yet successfully resolving the autonomy challenge might be attractive to consumers; it would, for example, help reduce the manpower required to operate UAV ground control stations.

Until questions about specific disruptive and sustaining performance metrics are resolved through research and experimentation, firms with proven track records will remain in the driver's seat. Late entrants and startups will seek to break into the marketplace based on new technologies and skills adapted from the design and production of other weapons systems. In this still-evolving sector, it is not yet clear whether customer requirements will be met predominantly by sustaining or disruptive innovation.

Customer–Supplier Relationships

Performance metrics alone will not determine which types of firms will thrive by supplying UAVs for transformation. Existing and emerging customer relationships will also shape the future industrial landscape and the availability of political support for innovative UAV acquisition. Because the services have not yet purchased many UAVs, neither acquisition organizations nor their technical advisers have formed close relationships with particular contractors in this sector. Instead, several firms have modest track records,[72] and a larger group of companies can claim either direct experience with, or demonstrable technical potential for responding to, requests for proposals. These limited ties must translate into a comfortable working relationship if suppliers are to be able to make the products that the military really wants and if the military is to rely on the suppliers to help build Congressional support for military innovation.

The relationship-building experience of the contractors that are currently selling UAVs to the U.S. military shows the nascent state of the sector. General Atomics explicitly hopes to profit from its track record: the Predator and its follow-on, the Predator B, have already flown combat missions with some success. Based on that operational experience, the company is now adapting its line of UAVs to carry larger payload, fly at higher altitudes, and operate using man-portable ground stations.[73] In the past, General Atomics executives have complained sharply that some potential customers, such as the U.S. Navy, have not appreciated the capabilities of their products and have continued to develop doctrine and establish requirements through paper studies rather than experiments with actual vehicles procured from the production line.[74] In the Army's extended-range multi-purpose UAV competition, General Atomics has opted to team with AAI, because AAI has established a relationship with the Army by selling it the Shadow UAV.[75] As much as General Atomics would like to have a close, trusted relationship with the military, the firm has not yet achieved its wish.

Having acquired the established UAV manufacturer Ryan Aeronautical and subsequently developed the Global Hawk, Northrop Grumman appears to have bought itself credibility within the UAV community. However, Global Hawk has not yet demonstrated peak performance for extended periods, and chronic equipment failures suggest that Northrop Grumman will have to work hard to maintain the position that it has attained.[76] Although the program was subsequently revived as part of the Army's Future Combat Systems, the Navy terminated the Fire Scout, Ryan Aeronautical's prototype vertical-takeoff UAV, at the flight test stage, even though the contractor felt that the vehicle was meeting performance expectations.[77] Northrop Grumman's strongest advantage in the UAV business may not even come specifically from its Ryan Aeronautical group: the parent company has invested more than some of its competitors in understanding the military's vision of network-centric warfare—or at least Northrop Grumman has spent more resources developing its public image as "an RMA company."

Boeing, too, has gone to great lengths to demonstrate network-centric expertise. It claims to have spent more than $500 million to produce extensive independent analyses of NCW, supplement the military's strategic planning documents, and build the Boeing Integration Center to explore the implications of information-sharing through communications networks.[78] The Army in particular has used the simulation capabilities of the Integration Center to test concepts for its Future Combat Systems, surely a sign of a close customer–supplier tie—but a tie at the corporate level rather than specifically within the UAV community.[79] Boeing's future as a producer of UAVs hinges on the success of its prototype UCAV, the X-45.[80] If the X-45 turns out to be a technical success, it will help Boeing to shape emerging UAV performance metrics. But even if the X-45 itself does not perform well, the program could provide Boeing with inside information and a comfortable relationship with evolving military requirements.[81]

Any problems that existing UAV producers face in their relations with the military pale in comparison with the difficulties facing startup firms and other small companies. Officials from mainstream UAV manufacturers and the military's acquisition organizations joke about the stereotypical wild-eyed tinkerers who work in their garages to produce "big model airplanes," which they hope can serve as militarily useful UAVs.[82] It would be tempting to dismiss their scorn as uninformed or self-interested, but some small UAV ventures seem to invite such criticisms. Some UAV startups do work out of "garages," employ engineers with little understanding of military requirements, and use business models often hinging on joint ventures with, or acquisition by, firms that have established relationships with the military customer. Technically skilled new entrants are not familiar with military culture, warfighters' professional expertise, and the platform-level systems integration capabilities that producers of manned aircraft have developed since the 1930s. In short, there are long odds against serious challenges by new entrants for leadership of the UAV industry.

The Politics of Future UAV Acquisition

Especially in reaction to reports from Afghanistan and Iraq, UAVs have become popular with politicians. The successful attack on a high-value al-Qaeda target in Yemen by an armed Predator in 2002 was great advertising for the UAV community.[83] But the demand for weapons and systems that work now and the need to replenish supplies of systems, including UAVs, lost during operational deployments may diminish the funds and importance of UAV research and development efforts. In the rush to field successful systems, the services and manufacturers may slow long-term UAV progress down.

The future of this sector depends on the strength of the military services' commitment to UAVs as part of NCW-style transformation. Until recently, the services hesitated to commit strongly to UAV acquisition, and their resistance played out in the planning, programming, and budgeting process.[84] Of the services, the Navy has lagged the most; the Army by contrast plans to have 6,000 UAVs within a decade, including 5,000 micro- and mini-systems.[85]

The trickle of support to UAV firms before transformation really infused the Pentagon ethos came from interested congressional leaders. Senator John Warner (R-VA) ensured some resources for UAV development.[86] In 2003, as DoD's interest in UAVs grew, Representative Curt Weldon (R-PA) argued that one-third of American deep strike assets should be UAVs.[87] Other Congressional leaders, including Rep. Jerry Lewis (R-CA), Rep. C.W. Young (R-FL), and Senator Ted Stevens (R-AK), have "added money for Predators in the defense appropriations bill, ensuring the programs survival when Air Force support was tepid."[88] This Congressional interest provides a core of potential support for military innovation that transformation advocates and UAV suppliers can exploit. R&D funds are now flowing to help resolve remaining technical hurdles, and planning documents such as the *UAV Transformation Roadmap* envision purchases of UAVs in sufficient numbers to generate interest among major defense firms.

The UAV sector does not yet have a powerful lobbying vehicle comparable to the shipbuilding sector.[89] There is no real equivalent to the American Shipbuilding Association to jealously guard the interests of domestic firms versus international manufacturers and provide information and analysis about the impact of UAV procurement decisions on the industry as whole. The potential remains, however, that such a peak association will emerge as the financial stakes for selling UAVs rise. Already, Arlington, Virginia, hosts an international association, the Association for Unmanned Vehicle Systems International (AUVSI) with a membership drawn largely from North America. A more cosmopolitan organization, the Unmanned Vehicle Systems International (UVS International), is based in Paris and boasts 209 corporate, military, and institutional members from at least 32 countries.[90] As relatively new organizations, their lobbying power remains modest relative to the efforts for other military platforms, including ships, manned aircraft, and ground vehicles.

The sole UAV association based in the United States and consisting solely of U.S.-based members is UNITE (UAV National Industry Team).[91] Formed by six producers of military UAVs (AeroVironment, Aurora, Boeing, General Atomics, Lockheed Martin, and Northrop Grumman), the association has collaborated with NASA, DoD, and the FAA to give high-altitude, long-endurance UAVs routine access to civilian airspace in the United States. The stated rationales for this effort were to remove FAA obstacles to flying UAVs for civilian uses and to ease the burden on the military for transporting UAVs between bases and conducting scientific research. Clearly, however, removing obstacles to flying in civilian airspace would help all the manufacturers of military UAVs to broaden their market and potentially reduce unit costs of UAVs through economies of scale. UNITE's explicit goal is to build a "partnership" with the government, bringing UAV makers into the political and regulatory process.[92] Building over time from the nascent organizations' limited goals, UAV-makers' representation in the political process is likely to grow—and needs to grow in order to maintain support for this aspect of the military transformation initiative.

Individual UAV firms, too, are increasing their ability to influence defense budget priorities, often using partnerships among established defense contractors, startup UAV specialists, and in-house experts in military operations. Already major defense contractors have begun the process of acquiring smaller firms with cutting-edge technologies. For example, Boeing bought Insitu, a small UAV manufacturer in Oregon. Under current plans, Insitu will continue to build its long-range UAV, the ScanEagle, while Boeing will provide systems integration, payload, and features to allow it to interoperate with other aircraft, ground stations, and sensors.[93] Under this arrangement, ScanEagle has already been deployed with the U.S. Marines to Iraq.[94] More partnerships and teaming arrangements are likely, even among established firms specializing in UAVs and larger defense prime contractors.[95] Joint ventures and vertical integration can sometimes help solve technical barriers to innovation—but they also help build political clout for the UAV industry.

As the military starts to acquire significant numbers of some UAVs, political support for additional UAV acquisition will be reinforced.

Employment at General Atomics has already grown tenfold in about a decade, making the firm a more important political player. DARPA projects and other R&D investments, although small, also garner support from vocal congressional constituencies including small businesses, universities, and startup firms.

The prime defense contractors' efforts are even more extensive. Primes must both demonstrate their technical competency and deploy their formidable lobbying resources to ensure that UAVs eventually appear in the numbers promised by the NCW vision. Boeing representatives, for example, have a conscious political strategy, using the term "system" rather than "vehicle" when discussing UAVs; the company plans to leverage its expertise in systems integration as a selling point. And perhaps that strategy has already enjoyed at least a superficial success: the Department of Defense announced in July 2005 that it prefers the name "UAS" for Unmanned Aerial System in place of the established term, UAV.[96] Beyond the name change, though, Boeing hopes to build a coalition of supporters by promoting unmanned vehicles as part of the network, interoperable with other battlefield systems produced by Boeing and other defense companies. Perhaps UAVs can complement rather than compete against other platforms for resources, roles, and missions under network-centric warfare.

UAV investment will need particularly strong political support. Unmanned systems, especially if they promise to be successful enough to take up more than niche tasks in the network, naturally face steep resistance from supporters of manned aircraft. Neither the community of aviators nor the manufactures of existing manned equipment (e.g., Lockheed Martin, maker of the JSF) will fade quietly. They will fight pressure to build greater numbers of UAVs insofar as UAVs threaten to take resources from their own programs. But given the limited number of manned programs planned, the emerging community of UAV manufacturers should be able to push their case using lobbyists from firms and industry associations. With the prospects for more procurement funding over the next several years, we may be witnessing the emergence of a "virtuous" cycle of political support to military innovation: the interest of transformation visionaries in unmanned aerial systems attracts the interest of firms and politicians, whose efforts to support the burgeoning UAV programs then attract wider support from within the military. In transformational military investment, everyone tries to follow the money.

CHAPTER FIVE

COMMUNICATIONS

The core idea of network-centric transformation is that the military can take advantage of modern communications technology to change the way that it fights. Network-centric warfare is meant to improve military effectiveness specifically by replacing existing military communications with a new approach. Single-purpose communications systems serving the needs of individual weapons or particular types of military units will gradually disappear as multipurpose communications networks enter service. Implementing network-centric warfare obviously will require the acquisition of at least some new communications equipment, and many proponents clearly believe that implementing network-centric warfare will require more changes in military communications than in any other area of technology.[1]

If legacy communications systems could handle the volume of data now made available from myriad sensors, could provide the Common Operational Picture (COP) to tactical forces, could enable collaborative problem-solving during high-speed operations, and could otherwise facilitate network-centric rather than platform-centric military operations, then perhaps the United States would already have a transformed military. But even though the after-action reports from Operation Enduring Freedom and Operation Iraqi Freedom are filled with indications of progress toward developing a network-centric military—and with indi-cations of the promised increase in military effectiveness—the United States remains in the early stages of transformation.[2]

Key programs are still in the system-definition and product-develop-ment phases. In the communications sector, these programs constitute the Global Information Grid (GIG), "a collection of programs and initia-tives aimed at building a secure network and set of information capabili-ties modeled on the Internet."[3] The list includes mechanisms for moving data, such as Transformational Satellites and the Joint Tactical Radio System (JTRS). It also includes services and applications to manage and exploit the data flow, such as the Cooperative Engagement Capability (CEC) and the Warfighter Information Network-Tactical (WIN-T). For military transformation to reach fruition, the U.S. military needs to collaborate with the defense industry in pursuit of military innovation, developing and procuring network-centric communications systems.

The requirements for the new systems are near the limit of current technical capabilities. For example, the Government Accountability Office reported in March 2004—several years into the JTRS devel-opment effort—that none of the program's "20 critical hardware and software technologies are mature according to best practice standards."[4] Moreover, the product development schedule for JTRS is quite short, raising the prospect that JTRS will be plagued by the well-known prob-lems of concurrent development, including cost overruns and failure to meet the initial performance specifications.[5]

But despite the demanding requirements that transformation poses for scientists and engineers in the communications sector, the technological trajectory on which they must work should be familiar. The following analysis of the military communications sector shows that transforma-tion depends on sustaining innovations. Established firms are therefore likely to be able to overcome the technological hurdles, given sufficient funding and time.

The difficult task for transformation advocates is to marshal the resources required to implement their vision of military innovation, and for that they need political savvy and a strong coalition of supporters. The communications infrastructure that will underpin network-centric warfare is so complicated and has so many components that the major development projects can involve a broad group of firms.[6] But because the communications projects all aggregate into the Global Information Grid, the various programs are less likely to cannibalize each other's funds, and the aggregate network-related spending has relatively high visibility in the budget process. The GIG encourages the major players in military communications to cooperate to define the technical standards that should enable various types of hardware and software to link up into a "system of systems"; the same firms also work closely with the military services to figure out how the network can be used operationally.[7] Those consultations provide excellent forums to strengthen the lobbying coalition supporting transformation.

We expect that the acquisition of the technology for the new military communications network will proceed relatively smoothly, because transformation calls for sustaining innovation in the communications sector. Moreover, because the network builds on a technical architecture that requires cooperation from many firms, each of which wields considerable political influence in its own right, a natural political coalition will stimulate Congressional interest and log rolling to support the investment. Some programs almost certainly will face technical problems, although it is hard to predict which specific ones will founder. Some programs' organizational approaches will prove more effective than others' at maneuvering through the Congressional appropriations process and managing the relationship between profit-driven firms and their military customers. But the technological, bureaucratic, and political factors in the communications sector and the history of transformation efforts thus far generally match the pattern predicted by the political economy theory of military-technological innovation.

NETWORK-CENTRIC WARFARE AND COMMUNICATIONS INNOVATION

According to a Department of Defense draft Management Initiative Decision on the GIG, "In the same manner that the World Wide Web is transforming industries and societies on a global scale, the GIG will support the transformation of warfighting."[8] The key concepts that define network-centric warfare, specifically including distributed warfighting and effects-based operations, in broad terms depend on two different types of communications systems.[9]

Distributed warfighting will depend on small units using new types of communications equipment to increase tactical situational awareness, often in real time; meanwhile, effects-based operations will rely on a different type of network connectivity that generally covers longer distances with less fine-grained information. Tactical engagements in the future will require sharing a great deal of local information. Friendly forces will be able to react to a Common Operational Picture by maneuvering in swarms. They will be able to mass fires and allocate precision strikes against particular enemy targets from the best-positioned friendly units. They will be able to call for help from other nearby units when a particular node's relatively simple single-purpose capabilities need another kind of weapon to overcome the adversary through a combined-arms solution. Information must be shared on the local network at very high speed, and the network will ideally allow for transmission of processed data on friendly and enemy positions and some degree of collaborative mission planning (e.g., chat rooms and digital white boards). The emphasis of the local network is on timely information sharing, battle management, and portability and miniaturization of the network infrastructure.

Above the local level, communications needs are different. Some local information, particularly on the outcome of the fight, needs to be shared with higher levels in the chain of command. But for most purposes, the higher echelon needs less detail and less real-time updating, although ideally the network will give commanders the opportunity to "drill down" to see more detailed local information when they need it. At the same time, in order to improve combat effectiveness, the tactical commander needs to take advantage of communications links to understand his contribution to the political effect of the military operation (to implement effects-based operations) and to access maps and weather information, as well as still or video pictures of key mission objectives and other databases. The long-range messages involved in this reachback have different characteristics, often travel via satellite, and deal with different physics than the intense, very high-speed messages needed for tactical engagements. Distributed warfighting and reachback therefore tend to involve different communications systems, although both types of system will be connected to the GIG.[10]

Neither the local nor the long-range connections required for network-centric warfare can be readily implemented with the communications systems used by today's military. Any communications system can be broken down analytically into a series of layers, each of which is responsible for a different aspect of the networking process, from establishing the physical connection (e.g., via radio using a particular

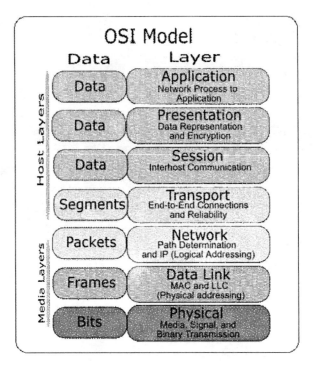

FIGURE 5.1 THE OSI MODEL FOR COMMUNICATIONS NETWORKS

This version of the well-known model that appeared in Wikipedia. Source: JB Hewitt, http://
en.wikipedia.org/wiki/Image:OSI-model-jb.png

waveform) to determining the meaning of messages and checking and
correcting for errors in the transmission process (one version of this well-
known chart is reproduced as figure 5.1).[11] Legacy systems tend to look
very different from network-centric systems, when they are broken down
according to this model.

In the caricature legacy system, everything from the physical layer to the
presentation layer is hardwired into each piece of communications equipment.[12] Radios that establish physical connections at a given frequency also
have unique design characteristics at higher layers, so they only work with
a particular transport layer algorithm to figure out whether interference has
corrupted a transmission and with a particular presentation layer protocol
to interpret a given pattern of data as a comprehensible message. That close
integration across layers allowed designers of legacy systems to tailor performance for specific tasks—generally for the needs of a specific military service or, more likely, a particular community within a service. But the self-
contained designs hamper interoperability between systems and prevent

modern battle-management systems from combining data from multiple sources in real time to achieve the best possible view of the battlespace.

Furthermore, many legacy systems are optimized for voice communications rather than for transmitting data, and they often are limited to exchanging data with specific partners, planned well in advance. The session and network layers of a modern network would allow a node to 'log in.' entering (and leaving) a conversation as it passed through an area of the battlespace, but a typical legacy system cannot handle this "dynamic allocation" of network addresses. Nor are most legacy systems designed to relay and route messages automatically among nodes to get around terrain obstacles, jamming, or other service interruptions.[13]

In sum, legacy communications systems were designed for discrete tasks across specific, planned connections. They were not designed as "networks," and they most certainly were not designed to handle the volume of data and the number of nodes envisioned by transformation advocates.[14]

The next generation of systems, now progressing through systems definition and development, builds more explicitly on the network model. For example, the Assistant Secretary of Defense for Networks and Information Integration decided in 2003 that future military communications systems should all be based on Internet Protocol version 6 (Ipv6).[15] That version sets certain broad requirements, especially at the transport, network, and data link layers, that should help systems to interoperate, to allocate addresses dynamically, and to route data across the network. IPv6 will not prove optimal for the specific requirements of every military task, but the premise of network-centric warfare is that the added capabilities of the improved network will more than compensate for shortfalls in any particular system.

Specifically, IPv6 cannot guarantee extremely high communications speeds required for some real-time tactical engagements, so some equipment will require an exception from the general rule. But even in those cases—for example, cooperative defense against high-speed anti-ship cruise missiles—the real-time, tactical communications systems should pass some information up to the Common Operational Picture and should use some data from slower situational awareness networks, when it makes sense.[16] Programs like the Single Integrated Air Picture (SIAP) are working to define interfaces where data flows between system-specific capabilities and the "system of systems"—that is, to define the connections between different tiers of the overall network that use different hardware and software platforms.[17]

The idea in the current generation of acquisition projects for military communications equiment is to explicitly divide physical connections (radios) from transmission protocols and data formats (communications software) from applications dealing with battle management, command and control.[18] Ideally, the warfighter will not need to know how the network transmits data, and information may cross multiple types of physical connections along its route. Communications projects can now be grouped (loosely) into acquisition efforts to build the network backbone and efforts to define the messages that will be sent. The former task includes, for example, Transformational Satellite Communications System for reachback, JTRS for the IP-based network to enable the Common Operational Picture, and the Data Distribution System (DDS) for real-time transfer of local data during engagements. The latter task includes, for example, the joint SIAP for the air battle and the Army's Force XXI Battle Command, Brigade and Below (FBCB2) system for command and control, as well as situational awareness.[19] Of course, these data-shipping and protocol definition tasks overlap and interact, making communications acquisition management more complicated than ever. High-level coordinating concepts such as the Navy's FORCEnet and the Air Force's C2 Constellation have been established to try to manage the complexity.[20] Overall, implementing network-centric warfare calls for innovative hardware, software, and organization: new systems that separate the lower (phsyical) from the higher (network) communications layers, and different systems for local high-speed, situational awareness, and reachback communications needs.

THE INDUSTRIAL LANDSCAPE OF THE COMMUNICATIONS SECTOR

A diverse range of companies participates in the communications sector, including all of the familiar names of defense-industry prime contractors. Most of the large companies have capabilities to make products for several levels of the seven-layer model of network communications, notably including BAe Systems, General Dynamics, Northrop Grumman, and Raytheon. Several large companies specialize in communications, although they also play in other avionics markets: Harris, Honeywell, ITT, and Rockwell Collins are longtime competitors, while L3 Communications has combined many smaller firms into a mid-sized military communications specialist with diverse activities. Meanwhile, the customers' strong interest in network-centric warfare has also attracted attention from defense primes that have not traditionally been involved with communications systems, and Boeing and Lockheed Martin each now head major projects that leverage expertise in program management and software development. Finally, a few smaller, niche players have allied with larger defense companies to focus on particular networking tasks (e.g., a small group of radio engineers that has joined SAIC), some strong international suppliers are reaching into the U.S. market (e.g., Thales), and several larger companies from outside the defense industry act mainly as merchant suppliers of components to the defense primes (Cisco Systems and Sun Microsystems, for example). And a truly comprehensive view of the market would also include satellite firms, although satellites, ground stations, and communications terminals are in most cases supplied by firms already listed above.[21]

One way to develop a rough roster of established firms in the communications sector—and some commercial IT firms that are interested in selling in the defense marketplace—is to consider the consortia that have formed to develop standards for network-centric warfare.[22] The Network Centric Operations Industry Consortium is an industry-led project to develop network standards that involved twenty-eight member companies from all parts of the communications sector when it launched in the fall of 2004 (see table 5.1).[23] The idea is that the open-architecture network definitions will help to ensure interoperability.[24] The group's primary tasks fall at the network and transport layers of the standard communications model, where it is trying to define standards into which participant companies can fit their lower-level (physical and data link layer) and higher-level (presentation and application layer) proprietary designs to compete for specific military acquisition programs. Firms that specialize in the lower and higher layers obviously have a strong interest in understanding (and trying to influence) the core standards promulgated by the consortium, so they have joined along with the network-services companies.[25]

The membership of the SIAP project team offers a similar, government-led snapshot of the major defense networking firms. Again, most of the big suppliers participated in the SIAP Systems Engineering team: Boeing, Lockheed Martin, Northrop Grumman, and Raytheon. For that standards definition project, however, they were joined by a group of the military's special technical advisers that maintain substantial technical expertise but are barred from producing systems in competition with private industry: MITRE, JHU Applied Physics Laboratory, the Software Engineering Institute, and the Center for Naval Analyses.[26] Finally, in-house military labo-

TABLE 5.1 FOUNDING MEMBERS OF THE NETWORK CENTRIC
OPERATIONS INDUSTRIAL CONSORTIUM

BAe Systems	Ericsson	Innerwall	Rockwell Collins
Boeing	Factiva	L-3 Communications	Saab
CACI	Finmeccanica	Lockheen Martin	SAIC
Carillo Business Technologies	General Dynamics	Microsoft	Smiths Aerospace
Cisco Systems	HP	Northrop Grumman	Sun Microsystems
EADS	Honeywell	Oracle	Thales
EMC Corporation	IBM	Raytheon	Themis

ratories like the Navy's SPAWAR Systems Center and the Naval Surface
Warfare Center-Dahlgren consulted regularly with the project. A similar
cast of technical advisers and military laboratories along with the "usual
suspects" from industry are also involved in high-level communications
projects for the Air Force and the Army (e.g., the C2 Constellation).[27]

Especially for the big defense companies, various communications capabilities are often squirreled away in different divisions of the firm, making it hard to track the likely competitors in any particular market niche
without deep experience in the communications sector. Even then, many
industry participants have trouble, because the modern defense industry
agglomerations of technical and manufacturing skill came together as the
result of mergers and acquisitions. In addition, companies rarely fully integrated their internal operations, adding to the confusion. In fact, this lack
of full-scale internal integration sometimes allows different divisions of
the major companies to appear on opposing teams in competitions for
the next generation of military communications.[28] In other cases, unique
industrial capabilities allow a company to contribute one of its key products as a sole-source supplier to all of the teams competing for a contract.

For simplicity in considering contemporary military innovation in the
communications sector (the transformation to network-centric warfare),
we will focus the rest of this chapter on tactical communications (leaving
out satellite communications and issues pertaining to reachback). The discussion will emphasize a few projects on the transformation agenda, notably JTRS, which now includes networking (since JTRS radios have been
made "routers" as well as data shippers), and the SIAP (especially as it per-
tains to debates over the future direction of the Cooperative Engagement
Capability). Even though the discussion is limited to those few systems,

TABLE 5.2 MAJOR PARTICIPANTS IN JTRS CLUSTER 1 AND
THE COOPERATIVE ENGAGEMENT CAPABILITY.

JTRS Cluster 1

Prime contractor:	*Boeing*	*Anaheim, CA*
Teammates:	Northrop Grumman	Carson, CA
	Mission Systems	
	Rockwell Collins	Cedar Rapids, IA
	BAe Systems	Wayne, NJ
	Harris RF Communications	Rochester, NY

Cooperative Engagement
  Capability

Prime contractor:	*Raytheon Systems*	*St. Petersburg, FL*
	Command, Control,	
	Communications, and	
	Data Systems	
	Other Raytheon groups	Dallas, TX, and
		McKinney, TX
		Laurel, MD
	Johns Hopkins Applied	
	Physics Laboratory	

the relevant industrial landscape remains vast. Table 5.2 shows the major participants in JTRS Cluster 1 (the part of the program that is furthest along, which involves radios primarily for the Army)[29] and in CEC.

PERFORMANCE METRICS FOR NETWORK-CENTRIC WARFARE COMMUNICATIONS

Most military and political leaders expect that transformation will require heavy investment in new communications equipment. In theory, network-centric warfare will eventually simplify platforms and munitions, because they will rely on the network rather than organic capabilities. In a sense, the fate of other programs associated with transformation, such as various UAV systems, is tied directly to decisions made in the communications sector. The upper limits of UAV capabilities as both intelligence, surveillance, and reconnaissance platforms and communications relays hinge on the balance between capabilities that must be resident on the platform and those that will reside on the network. As NCW is implemented, the unit cost of platforms and munitions may drop, but only if investment in communications increases.[30]

Network-centric warfare not only calls for more communications equipment to be installed on each platform—platforms need to transmit and receive much more data than ever before—but it also requires continuous, real-time networking—for example, to provide updates to the tactical Common Operational Picture. Consequently, transformation advocates expect that the type of equipment that they need to buy will be substantially different from the equipment that they have bought in the past.

The defense industry, which makes its living by responding to its military customer's needs, has a huge incentive to figure out the details of the new pattern of demand: what are the performance characteristics of new communications systems that will attract significant sums of money from the government buyer? If the established defense industry can satisfy the technological demands for the new systems, then its unique ability to work closely with the military and to understand the military's evolving doctrine will help smooth the acquisition process, and the defense industry's political support will spur transformation. The first step to understanding the prospects for military innovation is to consider the type of technological change envisioned for the new doctrine: established firms flourish by providing sustaining innovations, which improve performance along familiar trajectories, but they often struggle with disruptive innovations, which emphasize new ways of measuring systems' quality.

Throughput

At the tactical level, network-centric warfare requires all friendly units to send and receive the data that can be compiled into a very detailed Common Operational Picture. Historically, military units in contact with the enemy developed their own knowledge of the local conditions: for example, the topography, the numbers and location of the enemy forces, before the availability of reserves that might provide support during the fight. As weapons' engagement ranges have increased, the area that each commander needs to understand has expanded, and the number of different commanders who are interested in any given area has also increased. The wider area of interest requires more data to be transferred and involves more nodes in sending and receiving that data. The two effects compound each other in posing problems for communications.[31] Similarly, the introduction of over-the-horizon sensors, the number of which will be expanded substantially in network-centric operations, has also increased the amount of data to be sent and the number of nodes to manage. Commanders always want better information, and they need to transmit and receive more data to get it. Developing the COP requires large communications pipes.

Even on a very small scale, different soldiers, ships, or airplanes have different sightlines, and each is constantly challenged to transmit what he knows to his buddies. Infantry squads in the past relied on shouts and hand signals, but if individuals can carry small radios or handheld digital assistants, as they will in the transformed force, they will be able to communicate better.[32] Network-centric warfare specifically hopes to capitalize on data fusion from multiple sensors to get a more accurate picture of the battlespace. If one friendly unit loses sight of an adversary because its view is blocked by a hill or an atmospheric effect, another may still be able to provide the tracking data. Stealthy enemies will often register fleetingly on sensor displays, but their position and trajectory may be confirmed by adding up a series of such views from a variety of sensors—as long as a data processor can receive inputs from all of the sensors in a timely fashion. And then the data processor needs to send the information that it calculates, the COP, back out to all of the forces that contributed to the composite picture.[33]

The amount of information that a communications network can handle is its maximum throughput, and network-centric warfare calls for a vast increase in this measure at the tactical level. Throughput is actually a combination of two physical factors: bandwidth, the size of the "pipe" across which the data is transmitted, and efficiency, the amount of information that can be squeezed through a given size of pipe per unit of time.[34]

In commercial and peacetime communications, bandwidth is relatively easy to come by, and the term is frequently bandied about in nontechnical discussions of the Internet: many people are familiar with comparisons between dialup modem connections, cable modems, and workplace T1 Internet connections; the general feeling is that higher bandwidth is what is needed to get faster Internet downloads. Outside the military, the thinking is, "if you need a faster connection, buy a bigger pipe."[35] This thinking has affected the military, too. Investment in the Global Information Grid includes a program to expand fiber optic capacity among military bases, the GIG-Bandwidth Expansion. And the Navy's fleet commands, for example, agreed in 2003 that their top technology priority would be more communications bandwidth for ships at sea.[36]

For most military tasks, however, tactical and operational communications cannot rely on a fixed infrastructure, and the size of the pipe is constrained. In mobile communications, bandwidth depends on the waveform used by a particular radio.[37] Higher frequency transmissions can carry more information, but only for limited distances.[38] Widening the pipe would require transmitting across a broader frequency range, but the military cannot costlessly use more of the frequency spectrum for each broadcast. For example, military transmissions "hop" across various frequencies to avoid enemy jamming attempts, and fewer alternate frequencies can be available if each transmission uses broader bandwidth.[39] The next generation communications system, JTRS, will include a "Wideband Networking Waveform," a new physical layer protocol that should ease bandwidth constraints to some extent.[40] Ultimately, though, JTRS will still face the physical constraints inherent in antenna technology and the limited radio spectrum available.[41]

What the military commanders really want, though, is more data throughput, which transformational communications systems can supply by increasing transmission efficiency, even if increasing bandwidth is not easy.[42] Better network software may be able to prioritize transmissions, reduce their vulnerability to errors that would require resending, and compress the data into shorter messages that still include the key information.[43]

Transmission efficiency improved during the course of the Cold War. Old communications systems tied up a frequency whether they were sending any real data or not. The next step in improving efficiency, embodied in systems like Link 11 and Link 16 that are now widely used, arranged for groups of radios to talk to each other by taking turns using the same frequency. The systems are based on a library of allowed messages that can be transmitted through the pipe during a standard time slot; each radio in the system, one after the other, is allocated a time slot in which it has the opportunity to send a message to all the others.[44] These legacy systems have great difficulty dynamically allocating time slots to new participants in the network, their data transmission rates slow down as the number of network participants increases, and they cannot efficiently send large volumes of data because their packet sizes are constrained by the message-queuing mechanism.[45] Current communications systems are not optimized for transmission efficiency, but the idea of improving radios by making data flow more efficiently is not new.

JTRS is expected to improve performance on this metric by a substantial margin. The internal workings of JTRS are based on a packet-switched network (IPv6) rather than Link 16's structured architecture:

instead of taking turns sending messages, JTRS users will pump packets of data onto the network whenever they have something to send.[46] Each radio that receives a packet will be able to tell from its header whether it needs to be sent on further through the network; once a packet reaches its destination, its header will explain how it can be combined with other packets into a complete message. Under this system, users do not need to wait their turn to send messages, and they do not need to wait for an entire cycle through the network to send additional packets of a multipacket message.[47] Moreover, each JTRS box will include an "intelligent router" to help manage the network's data-transmission load. Packets will be sent through pipes that have room for them, and ideally, the network load will be balanced: each link will be used, and none will be overwhelmed as long as alternative routes through the network are available.[48]

On the other hand, the shift to a packet-switched network in some ways will actually hinder the drive for network efficiency. Because the packets that make up a message may take different routes through the network and so will not necessarily arrive at their destination in the same order that they were sent, the packets' headers have to contain a good deal of information—both the message's destination and directions for reassembling it from the packets. For short messages, adding headers will significantly increase the total amount sent through the pipes, actually reducing transmission efficiency.[49]

The transition to a packet-switched network architecture is based on an implicit calculation about efficiency in the network layer of the seven-layer OSI model. It presumes that the benefits of eliminating waste when a network member has nothing to send in its allocated time slot and of routing messages intelligently will outweigh the costs of the packet headers. This premise makes sense: as network-centric warfare adds more nodes to the network, the old Link 16 architecture will require each node to wait a longer time for its turn to transmit—that is, efficiency is likely to drop unless the network layer shifts from time-division to packet switching.

Future military communications investment will also attempt to take advantage of other ways to increase throughput. For example, incorporating faster computers and better software into radios will allow them to take advantage of new data-compression algorithms to concentrate more information into a packet of a given size.[50] These opportunities to improve throughput could in principle be implemented using any physical-layer radio system. In practice, the military will buy some upgrades for Link 16 in the short term, but transformation advocates expect to focus all of their long-term investment on systems like JTRS.[51]

JTRS requires a major change in networking technology, which might even be described as a "radical" innovation for defense suppliers familiar with the old style of military communications. As a result, developing the new technology for JTRS demands considerable investment of resources, and between invention of new equipment may not proceed smoothly.[52] At the component level, replacing structured time-division networking with intelligent routers or other technological improvements may require the use of products whose quality is assessed with performance metrics not previously important for military communications. Suppliers that understand commercial Internet performance may be well positioned to sell such components to defense communications prime contractors.[53] But at the systems level, the new technology for military communications requires sustaining innovation: trying to expand bandwidth, improve transmission efficiency, and, ultimately, increase data throughput is nothing new for defense suppliers.

LATENCY

Many military tasks that rely on communications are time-sensitive. For example, real-time control of the unmanned portions of the Army's Future Combat System will depend on high-rate communications.[54] Similarly, sensor data about the location of a mobile target needs to be processed and transmitted to a friendly shooter who can take advantage of the information before the enemy unit can move and hide.[55] Delays in transmission increase uncertainty about the target's location, making the intelligence less valuable. Similarly, a network-based air defense against incoming cruise missiles, whether defending a land target or a carrier battle group, relies on high-speed communications to enable composite tracking: if missiles are incoming very fast, even slight transmission delays can introduce enough uncertainty about their location to prevent a battle-management system from computing the right fire-control solution and cuing the appropriate air-defense missile or close-in air-defense gun.[56] The bigger the role in tactical engagements assigned to the Common Operational Picture, the more crucial it is that the communications network not delay the transfer of data. Latency is the measure of the in-transit delay associated with sending data from one node to others in the network.

One traditional way to reduce latency is to increase throughput: using a pipe that can handle more data at a time and reducing the amount of data per message that needs to be sent will reduce the length of time until the recipient has the entire message. But some of the solutions to data throughput problems actually introduce problems with latency.

The most obvious way that some modern communications systems increase latency is by processing the data before it can be transmitted. Even fast computers take time to apply compression algorithms before sending and decompression algorithms after receiving a message. Encryption similarly adds a layer of processing to the overall communications process. But with modern computers getting faster and faster, the latency cost of data processing is dropping to less and less significant levels.

The desire to incorporate data from more and more nodes in the network subtly introduces latency into the COP through two mechanisms. First, unless communications equipment is truly standardized in the future (an unlikely prospect), different types of nodes will transmit using different waveforms. JTRS is designed as a "software radio," meaning that its waveforms will be programmable rather than hard-wired, and JTRS will send and receive many different waveforms. Once JTRS is deployed, various nodes will be able to share access to the same network. But even if a JTRS can act as a translator as well as a router, repackaging packets into different waveforms will require processing time.[57] Even if all nodes eventually carry the same basic radio, JTRS, each "cluster" of JTRS production is tailored to its primary users (ground, maritime, air, and special forces)—meaning that each has a different antenna shape and carries software for different waveforms.[58] Even an all-JTRS network will still require translation, if it has diverse members.

Second, expanding the network will tend to increase the number of "jumps" a packet has to make between its origin and its destination. The common tactical picture involves collaboration among nodes that are nearby each other—nodes that can use high-frequency transmissions (relatively high bandwidth) and that are close enough that the time it takes for a radio wave to cover the distance is negligible. However one of the advantages touted for composite tracking in the COP is that it will combine data from nodes that cannot "see" each other directly due to terrain obstacles—nodes that see different aspects of the enemy forces. These nodes will be able to communicate through network relays. Each relay introduces some latency as the router does its job. In a complex system with many nodes, even a relatively small delay at each router can add up into a tactically significant delay in the overall network.

In each of these two cases, the alternative to accepting some latency is to accept some degradation of the quality of the network. Fewer participants would mean faster service but fewer views contributing to the data fusion that produces the COP. Fewer participants in the network would also reduce the ability of simple, single-purpose nodes to rely on the network for support during combat. The optimal tradeoff between low latency and other values of network-centric warfare depends on the particular mission under consideration. Systems engineering of each node will presumably place a different emphasis on reducing latency, depending on the node's primary mission, and the node's network interface could be designed appropriately. The concept of network-centric warfare is built on a "network of networks," some of which will be lower latency than others.

The most time-critical tasks that hope to benefit from network-centric warfare—air defense against high-speed antiship cruise missiles and ballistic missile defense—will likely operate with their own, dedicated networks. Even though the military plans to standardize its communications on IPv6, those applications that demand the lowest latency cannot use that standard. While a packet-switched network under the right conditions can transmit data extremely rapidly, that architecture cannot guarantee any particular level of latency. At the time that a packet is sent into the network, it is impossible to know what route the packet will travel to its recipient or how many times the packet will have to be resent through clogged pipes. For applications like the Cooperative Engagement Capability, which requires that transmissions not exceed a certain (very low) level of latency in order to give the battle management system time to react to the incoming missiles, the unknown transmission time is not acceptable.[59]

The developers of CEC solved their unique communications problems by developing a special radio, the Data Distribution System. DDS is designed for an extremely demanding combat environment that dictates the essential features of the radio: low latency, high resistance to jamming, and low probability of intercept.[60] DDS is a very high-powered, frequency-hopping, highly directional radio, meaning that it can transmit a large amount of data very quickly to one other member of the CEC network at a time. The Cooperative Engagement Processor chooses which of its communications partners most needs updated information and makes pairwise contact with that partner; particularly important partners can be scheduled for more frequent interaction. The system also sends out high-priority information first in each frame (the packet of information sent before the directional antenna slews to the next pairwise partner), so the least important information is dropped if there is more to send than fits in a single frame. Using the DDS, CEC transmits raw data from powerful air defense search radars (notably the SPY-1 radar on Aegis-equipped ships, although other sensors can contribute data, too), and the Cooperative Engagement Processor on each node of the CEC network uses all of the data available to the whole network to calculate the best possible composite tracks of incoming missiles' locations and trajectories.[61] The accuracy of those tracks fundamentally depends on the CEC systems' design to minimize latency.

The CEC architecture, while technically sophisticated, is still limited. The network is self-forming and new nodes can join the network without advance planning (unlike the structured requirements of Link 16). But managing the pairwise communications gets extremely complex as the number of nodes increases, and network management overhead starts to increase latency.[62] Even though new software versions try only to send new sensor data that will add to the quality of the overall network's composite tracks, the pairwise system still sends more data than it needs to: at the time that a node decides whether to transmit its new, raw data, it cannot know what new data the other nodes have received, either from their own sensors or through their DDS pairwise contacts with other members of the network.[63] And the highly directional, heavy antenna of the DDS, with its high power consumption, is difficult to adapt to platforms other than ships.[64] Given these problems, CEC is not yet a perfect solution for cooperative air defense nor can it underpin the Single Integrated Air Picture without substantial modification.[65]

Solipsys, a startup company that splintered off the Johns Hopkins University Applied Physics Laboratory, has proposed an alternative to CEC called the Tactical Component Network (TCN) that aims to solve some of CEC's technical problems and to provide a better SIAP.[66] The TCN works on a hub-and-spoke principle. Each platform in the network collects its own sensor data and compares it to an image of the battlespace received from a centralized processing hub. Any local information on enemy position and trajectory that is better than the hub's estimate is transmitted to the core, but most raw data need not be sent. The central processor then updates the COP for each of the spokes. Because much less raw data is transferred and because data need not be relayed through pair-wise connections, TCN consumes much less bandwidth than CEC. With its lower bandwidth demand, TCN can use a simpler radio system such as satellite telephones that use the Iridium constellation of low-earth-orbit satellites. The "I-phones" are much smaller and lighter, consume less power, and have a less complicated antenna that can be installed on a wider variety of platforms than the DDS.[67] A round-trip data transit through Iridium takes less than a second;[68] however, that delay is still longer than the ideally functioning DDS system.[69] The TCN design arguably eliminates bandwidth (or throughput) as a communications constraint on the COP, perhaps at some latency cost. Advocates of TCN and CEC each have their arguments and rebuttals against the competing system.

Yet the terms of the debate are defined by familiar performance metrics. The goal of low-latency communications and the need to trade off latency against other performance metrics like throughput, quality of service, and network security are not new to the military environment. CEC and TCN are implemented using very different architectures, software programs, and hardware components. But both systems—and, in fact, all of the communications systems that might provide network-centric warfare's Common Operational Picture (specifically, the SIAP)—call for sustaining innovation.

INTEROPERABILITY

In modern warfare, different kinds of forces need to cooperate to achieve military objectives—that is, the military relies on the interoperability of its units and equipment to fight as a system rather than as a bunch of individuals. The cooperation can be achieved only if the military has prepared suitable doctrine known to all of the different forces, has trained its forces to work together, and has acquired weapons designed with the right physical characteristics. Just within the material realm of equipment design and procurement, interoperability includes everything from ensuring that munitions work with the platforms that carry them to ensuring that data can flow across communications networks from one unit to another. Over the past several decades, debates about military reform have increasingly focused on communications interoperability.[70]

Transformation calls for a significant expansion of interoperability, as all military nodes are expected to contribute to the same network. [71] Forces from all of the services will mingle within sectors of the battlespace, and each small unit will be able to rely on support from the friendly units that can best contribute to its operational effectiveness, breaking through layers of service hierarchy and interservice rivalry. In the fluid engagements of the future, the network will require not only new breadth of access—links between more different kinds of platforms—but also more dynamic access, as maneuvering units enter or leave the tactical network as they become more or less relevant to each other's areas of operations and mission objectives. The need for new equipment to realize the full potential of interoperability is particularly acute at the tactical level.[72]

The idea that better communications interoperability can improve military effectiveness is certainly not new. For example, the wide distribution of radios to American ground forces and pilots in World War II is said to have significantly aided the advance in 1944–45 by facilitating close air support.[73] And anecdotes abound of mission failures due to poor communication—and of narrow escapes using unorthodox techniques to send messages. For example, a number of stories circulate about an Army officer who supposedly used a personal credit card and a pay phone to call his division headquarters at Fort Bragg, NC, during the 1983 invasion of Grenada, because that was the only way that he could contact Navy ships off the coast. The details of the various accounts differ—was the officer calling for close air support or to prevent a possible friendly fire incident because the Army and Marines ashore did not know if they were shelling each other?[74] But everyone remembers some version of the story as an important reason to improve communications interoperability, and the story contributed to the political support for the Goldwater-Nichols defense reform in 1986.[75]

The problem with calls for increased communications interoperability has been that different forces really do have different system requirements for their core missions. If high-resolution images or extensive data on many targets are to be sent through the network, then a high-throughput physical connection will be required. But those connections tend to work best at short range and when few terrain obstacles interrupt the line of sight; for longer range or terrain flexibility, radios need to use lower frequencies with their inherent bandwidth constraints. The alternative is to transmit via relays and network routers, which require more complex and expensive communications systems based on technologies that were invented relatively recently. Meanwhile, above the physical layer, protocols designed for voice, video, and data cannot directly substitute for each other without substantial sacrifice of efficiency.

Moreover, different operational tasks require different levels of secrecy or jam-resistance, which may undermine communications interoperability. Forces engaged in high-intensity combat are more willing to risk interception (if not decryption) of their signals than stealthy special forces, because the enemy already knows that the conventional forces are in the vicinity. Overall, different throughput, quality of service, and security needs imply different optimal technical solutions for communications systems.[76] The decision to optimize system design tradeoffs on performance metrics other than interoperability has not necessarily been an accidental one or an unintended consequence of bad defense management and organization.

JTRS, the next-generation tactical communications system, will offer a vast improvement in communications interoperability through its waveform translation service, even if it will not enable full interoperability throughout the military network. Even with the widespread deployment of JTRS, the physical and operational needs of each community within each service will still differ.[77] The different clusters of JTRS development and production will therefore incorporate at least three different types of antennas, each of which is optimized for a different set of waveforms. Each set of hardware can physically transmit only a limited range of waveforms, even if the software part of the radio is truly waveform independent. Fortunately, the capabilities of the different antennas will overlap: two JTRS boxes with different antennas will be able to connect to each other, while each can talk to nodes that could not contact the other JTRS box directly.[78] JTRS routers can thus act as sophisticated relays within the network. Furthermore, as JTRS spreads through the military, most tactical communications will be standardized on the Wideband Networking Waveform, yet another increment of improved interoperability.[79]

Creating a tactical network for the military demands a new focus on communications interoperability, but that new focus does not require any conceptual breakthrough. New standards call for sustaining innovation, following in the footsteps of World War II tactical aviators and others who fought communications barriers among and within the services. Technical breakthroughs will overcome some physical barriers that inhibit design of fully interoperable data links, and systematic workarounds will replace ad hoc solutions to other problems. Still other barriers will not be overcome at all, despite the wishes of doctrine writers and transformation visionaries. These sustaining technological innovations are a normal part of the business plans of the established defense industry.

However, the quest for network interoperability has at least one component that is less familiar to designers of military communications systems. The hardest task in efforts to increase interoperability will be to develop systems that allow a node (of any type) to enter or leave the tactical network without planning in advance.[80] The military's traditional structured time-division communications systems (e.g., Link 16) are essentially incapable of the dynamic network management called for in the plans for NCW. Just as getting away from structured time-division communications will be a difficult step that will be required to improve throughput, it is also a difficult step in increasing military network interoperability. This step may contribute an element of disruptive innovation to transformational communications, perhaps offering an opportunity for limited participation by nontraditional suppliers in the future defense industry. But NCW mostly demands sustaining innovation on the interoperability performance metric.

QUALITY OF SERVICE

Implementation of network-centric warfare will require a significant increase in the quality of service provided by military communications systems, especially if platforms designed for NCW are simple, single-purpose nodes that depend on the network for functions that platforms currently provide themselves. More than ever before, the military's requirements-generation process is demanding that communications systems guarantee a particular level of connectivity: the network must be available when nodes need to transmit and receive, and must be robust enough to overcome atmospheric interference, able to correct for "normal" errors in transmission, resistant to enemy jamming attempts, and "self-healing" when enemy activity disrupts a particular route or relay.[81] Civilian Internet users get frustrated when they get a busy signal from a dial-up service provider; military users potentially face much greater costs from service interruptions.

NCW advocates plan to address the need for improved quality of service in several ways. First, NCW calls for distributing communications terminals more widely through the force structure, allowing a substantial increase in the number of links in the network. Ideally, every node will be able to contact every other node rather than relying on a relatively vulnerable hierarchy of links via headquarters and centralized communications relays. Replacing the current force's communications hubs with relatively inexpensive UAV relays will facilitate this process. Second, JTRS will improve on the innovative frequency-hopping strategies implemented in previous generations of military radios like the Army's SINCGARS.[82] If jamming or interference blocks one transmission, the network should be able to move around the problem. Third, the standardization of military communications protocols on IPv6 will take advantage of a system that was developed explicitly to respond to potential service interruptions. The dynamic routing of packets through the Internet is intended to find a path through congested lines—or through a network in which the enemy has destroyed some links.

All of these strategies for improving quality of service entail sustaining innovations. This aspect of the modern military's communications problem is not very different from the problem faced by the designers of the SAGE air defense network in the 1950s and the various iterations of the command and control network for U.S. strategic nuclear forces.[83] Those systems initially relied on redundancy because they were supposed to guarantee that a message could get through even after a Soviet first strike had destroyed some of the United States. The invention of packet switching radically improved the performance of their redundant links. That well-understood architecture—now ubiquitous in the commercial Internet—can adapt and maintain connectivity in a hostile environment. As discussed above, the Internet Protocol's high quality of service sometimes comes with somewhat lower throughput and higher latency, and that tradeoff has limited the spread of the architecture in previous generations of military communications. But the idea that increasing the quality of service of military communications is a crucial selling point for new technologies is not new to the established defense industry.

Security

Information dominance is one of the principal goals of military transformation. If the enemy gains access to the network, it may be able to know at least as much as friendly forces or, worse still, to disrupt communications links or corrupt data flows and storage. Even if the enemy's understanding of the information on the network is imperfect, a security breach surely will reduce the friendly information advantage, reducing the effectiveness of the networked force. Moreover, the simple fact that all friendly forces will frequently transmit and receive messages from the network may give away their positions: enemies may exploit the expanded reliance on communications through simple triangulation even if they cannot decrypt the messages that they intercept.[84] Transformation therefore demands a new focus on network security, including stronger codes, radio links that are more difficult for the enemy to intercept, and new techniques that prevent enemies from broadcasting false data onto the network.

Security technologies and strategies are among the most zealously guarded military secrets, so it is hard to know very much about the investment in innovation for this aspect of transformation. One simple technique for reducing the probability of interception of a radio signal is to aim the transmission upward; the American military has used satellite links for secure transmissions for decades to take advantage of this well-known fact, and NCW's tactical networks may use UAV relays for this same reason.[85] CEC's DDS radio uses a highly directional antenna for its pairwise contacts to achieve the same result.[86] Presumably, designers of future communications systems will capitalize on these and other techniques to the fullest extent possible. And presumably, they are prepared to make appropriate tradeoffs and to evaluate innovative proposals to improve network security, because this performance metric is well established in military communications. Nontraditional suppliers of communications equipment and software, no matter how innovative, that cannot meet demanding information assurance standards necessary for military operations will either be left on the outside or left to partner with long-standing communications suppliers. Again, NCW relies on sustaining innovation in network security.

SUSTAINING INNOVATION IN THE COMMUNICATIONS SECTOR

Implementing network-centric warfare will require significant technological progress in the communications sector. Under at least two circumstances, NCW might actually reduce rather than increase military effectiveness if forces were equipped with poor communications systems. First, current and legacy generations of equipment were generally not designed to function as a network, and true networking will require higher throughput, lower latency, broader interoperability, enhanced quality of service, and increased network security; scientists and engineers need to find ways to relax the constraints that have forced difficult tradeoffs among the various communications sector performance metrics. During the long transition period from legacy communications systems to the

GIG, planners and strategists must take into account the limitations of the emerging system; otherwise they risk operational failures.

Second, if the most strenuous demands of transformation advocates are eventually satisfied, the vulnerability of nodes—whether weapon or sensor platforms—will increase if networks are not sufficiently robust and secure. In theory, purpose-designed network-centric nodes will be both less capable of operating autonomously from the network and optimized to perform a single function. Network failures will leave such nodes vulnerable to adversaries when they are not integrated with the entire systems—through either technical failures or adversary tactics. So, for example, a small ship intended to serve in a network in one capacity, such as antisubmarine warfare, might be vulnerable to attack from the air if it is disconnected from the other parts of the network assigned to provide air defense. This characteristic of equipment designed for NCW radically increases the importance of network quality of service.

Despite the difficulty of the task ahead for communications suppliers, almost all of the demand for innovation in this sector calls for improvements on well-known performance metrics. Although the vision suggests a few new ways of measuring communications performance—notably true dynamic access to the network in which nodes can join and leave a given tactical network as required by the flow of the battle—the overwhelming majority of the improvements that the doctrine-writers want to see in new systems are sustaining innovations. Established suppliers of military communications equipment should be able to evaluate proposals, invest in promising new technologies, and develop the new systems to implement NCW. As a result, on technical grounds, established military communications suppliers should be at least as capable as any other type of firm in their efforts to supply equipment for this military innovation.

BUILDING THE POLITICAL COALITION FOR NCW COMMUNICATIONS

Military communications suppliers are eager to help implement the NCW vision. The constraint on military innovation in this sector is not a demand for disruptive innovation that would make the established firms ambivalent about the required investment; instead, the constraint is the weak political support for any defense spending on communications equipment.

In the past, the military has been more successful convincing Congress to allocate large sums of money to programs to develop and procure platforms, especially high-profile weapon systems, than persuading Congress to spend on munitions, support systems, and communications equipment. The facilities that assemble fighter aircraft and warships each employ thousands of workers in a particular location, so the ups and downs of platform acquisition in the defense budget have a huge effect on the local business cycle—and on local politicians' prospects for reelection. Moreover, it is relatively easy to explain how a new weapon system will respond to a particular threat or will improve the military's capability to execute some part of the national security strategy of the United States. Finally, the military services believe that once they get their platforms, they will be able to convince Congress to pay for the mission systems later but that the reverse would not necessarily be the case: showing a destroyer with an empty vertical launch tube is a powerful argument to buy more missiles, but showing a missile on shore waiting to go to sea just looks like a prudent stockpiling strategy.[87] The same arguments have limited political support for communications equipment acquisition.

The political environment appears to be changing to favor investment in communications equipment, laying the groundwork for a major military innovation. On the military side of the customer-supplier relationship, responsibility for acquisition of communications equipment is increasingly centralized. The Department of Defense, because of its leaders' vision of network-centric warfare, is trying to create a powerful advocate for spending on this sector. A single Joint Program Executive Office (JPEO) was created for JTRS in the spring of 2004 with "acquisition oversight" to make tradeoffs within the JTRS project, prioritizing system design elements and determining the level of investment to be committed to each of the various JTRS clusters.[88] So far, the separate services are still responsible for actual procurement of radios and their integration onto service-specific platforms, but the civilian hierarchy in the Department of Defense has clearly given strong new support to communications spending.[89] The uniformed military leadership has also created a new advocate for network-centric communications systems at the highest level of its requirements-generation process: a Functional Capabilities Board will try to help programs like JTRS compete with politically powerful platforms for a share of the defense acquisition budget.[90]

Further, as the DoD, the services, and important Congressional supporters buy into network-centric warfare, the modern equivalent of empty vertical launch tubes for missiles or aircraft carriers without fighter wings will be platforms built without sufficient attention to the problem of connectivity. Weapons systems that cannot benefit from information and knowledge acquired and processed externally and that cannot share their own situational awareness with other friendly forces in the battlespace with be less effective and will cry out for additional investment.

By itself, the centralization of the buyers of communications systems would not be likely to provide sufficient clout to drive a major military innovation. For example, a number of reorganizations in recent years have tried to overcome obstacles to communications interoperability—with little effect. The services, backed by their industry supporters, have maintained the primacy of other performance metrics in setting the parameters for programs to develop communications systems, despite the pressure of the new rules.[91]

However, network-centric warfare will change the reservoir of political support from industry. NCW calls for bigger investment than ever before in communications equipment, which will attract more industrial players, and it apparently requires a new level of technical cooperation among firms to develop standards and protocols. New industry organizations, notably including the Network Centric Operations Industry Consortium, have developed in parallel to the reorganization of the acquisition community. The consortia are likely to discourage companies from undercutting each other's contributions to the overall NCW program. These consortia might play a role in transformation analogous to institutions that have held cartels together in the past despite well-known economic incentives for individual cartel-members to cheat. Fundamentally, cartels are hard to manage, because the small group of industry players cannot talk to each other enough to build mutual trust, especially given that laws prohibit open collusion. In the military communications context, it is only a small step from a consortium that allows firms to discuss conceptual approaches and technical standards to a consortium that helps its members overcome competitive pressures and cooperate on lobbying strategy.[92] All of the consortium members can get a piece of the action by supporting the group efforts, and the overall technological trajectory—dominated by sustaining innovation—will not necessarily drive any of the current suppliers out of business. As a result, large defense firms may add political grit behind the military's budget request to Congress for funds for the acquisition of a true military network.[93]

SYSTEMS INTEGRATION AND PUBLIC–PRIVATE PARTNERSHIP

The focus on connectivity and interoperability implied by network-centric warfare has increased the casual use of the term "systems integration" among defense experts. Using more precise definitions, the critical step to implement transformation is "system-of-systems" integration, which includes connectivity but also goes beyond. It includes the analysis of alternatives to allocate military tasks among the various platforms available and the specification of technical requirements for future military equipment.

Systems integration (SI) is actually required for all major military innovations: doctrine-writers' visions need to be translated into specific requirements for the development and procurement of new equipment. The military's buyers need to know what to buy, from whom to buy it, and what price to pay. But technology development is not a core competency of the military, at least not to the extent that it is a core competency of the kind of technology-oriented private firms that meet the customer's demand for most innovations. The military needs the means to make sure that the technological requirements derived from the wishes of its operational experts are attainable with a reasonable investment of time and resources. Operational requirements also need to be translated from "statements of objectives" into specific project plans for which the acquisition community can write contracts. To fill those needs, DoD and the services must have access to the core competency of organizations dedicated to specialized systems integration and technology management.

Despite the increased attention brought by the prospect of an IT-RMA, military systems integration is not new. Many organizations including laboratories owned by the military services, federally funded research and development centers (FFRDCs), and private, for-profit systems integration firms have long helped the military integrate systems at the weapons, platform, and system-of-systems levels. Modern systems integration techniques were developed in the Cold War American defense establishment.[1] They were aggressively applied, largely successfully, to develop technology for that conflict.

Unfortunately, the current relationship between integrators and their military customers is fragile, and ignorance of the political and economic dynamics of defense acquisition could undermine vital systems integration organizations. As manufacturing prime contractors (e.g., Boeing, Lockheed Martin, and Northrop Grumman) press to do more of the systems integration task on ever-larger "transformational" projects, the risks and costs of conflicts of interest and management failures escalate. By contrast, the successful niche systems integration providers like FFRDCs can provide technical advice and management assistance that minimizes the appearance of conflicts of interest, the overhead cost of managing complex systems development, and the military's vulnerability to unrealistic technological proposals.

To implement transformation, the military commands charged with developing doctrine and acquisition requirements should work more closely with systems integrators. Transformation opens the potential for the emergence of new niche systems integration providers and for established producers to play new roles. But overwhelmingly, with respect to systems integration, the transformation calls for sustaining innovation. The implication is that established organizations are prepared with the right sort of public–private partnership among the military, technical advisers, and manufacturers to pursue military innovation.

TYPES OF SYSTEMS INTEGRATION

Systems integration is a more complex task than many defense analysts realize. A basic definition of SI emphasizes interoperability—the requirement that each military system work in concert with other systems, on the basis of sufficient communication across well-defined interfaces. Network-centric warfare concepts obviously stress such intersystem compatibility; casual discussions of systems integration in the context of transformation, in fact, often refer only to interoperability requirements.[2] However, ensuring interoperability is only one part of the systems integrators' task. They are responsible for a number of roles during the overall acquisition process, beginning with translating objectives derived from military doctrine into technical requirements suitable for launching acquisition programs. The key part of this process is making tradeoffs of capabilities among various systems. Later in the acquisition process, systems integrators must maintain control of technical standards and interfaces (ensuring interoperability), manage cooperation among contractors and subcontractors, test products and their subcomponents, and support users' efforts to customize and modernize products as missions and technologies evolve.

An entire military operational force can be thought of as a system composed of multiple subsystems, each of which is itself complex. As different subsystems (e.g., aircraft, ships, or ground vehicles) interact more and more intensely in modern warfare, a "system of systems" has emerged.[3] Today's systems integrators, then, must decide, given a set of desired capabilities, which component of the system of systems should perform each of them. For network-centric warfare, systems integration should define the nodes that make up the network, the capabilities that will be essential for each type of node, and the number of nodes that must participate in various operations.

Systems integration is required at several levels of military acquisition, all of which involve making choices between technical alternatives and establishing links between disparate equipment so that heterogeneous parts can operate together. First, at the "lowest" level, *weapon-system integration* combines various components, often supplied by subcontractors, into a single product (e.g., a surface-to-air missile or a fire-control radar).[4] Certain key facilities owned by the prime defense contractors specialize in this type of systems integration (such as Raytheon in Tucson, Arizona, for missiles, or Northrop Grumman in Linthicum, Maryland, for radars). Second, *platform integration* combines various types of equipment (weapons, propulsion, sensors, communications, etc.) into mission-capable assemblages. This second process is not necessarily more or less complex than weapon-system integration, nor does it necessarily add more or less value; different types of systems integration must be analyzed on a case-by-case basis. But again, some prime contractors (Lockheed Martin Aeronautics in Fort Worth, Texas, or General Dynamics' Bath Ironworks in Bath, Maine) mainly concentrate on platform integration.

The real emphasis in transformation—and the level of systems integration that is now most ardently pursued by defense-oriented organizations—is *system-of-systems integration,* or *architecture systems integration.* It connects different types of platforms so as to facilitate cooperative military operations; it constitutes the technical counterpart to the military services' operational expertise (knowledge of how to fight). It essentially translates doctrinal statements of objectives into sets of requirements that can be written into the acquisition community's contracts with industry. It involves broad tradeoffs among different technical approaches—for example, hardware-versus-software solutions, or a decision on whether to transmit raw or processed data across the network. Historically, system-of-systems integration has been accomplished by organizations within the military services (e.g., laboratories that support systems commands, like the Naval Surface Warfare Center, Dahlgren Division) or closely allied to them (specialty organizations, including FFRDCs like the MITRE Corporation). Network-centric warfare's emphasis on simplified platforms, distributed capabilities, and interconnection of military assets via advanced communications networks will force the acquisition community to rely more than ever on first-class system-of-systems integration.[5]

Military-oriented SI skill is based on advanced, interdisciplinary technical knowledge—sufficient understanding of all of the systems and subsystems to make optimizing tradeoffs. It also requires a detailed grasp of military goals and operations as well as a reservoir of trust that bridges military, economic, and political interests.[6] Some SI organizations also have some production capabilities (which may be either an advantage or a liability to the integration process), but systems integration is a separate task from platform building and from subsystem development and manufacturing.

Systems integration is an independent sector of the defense industrial base, but one with porous boundaries that sometimes allow members of other sectors (e.g., platform builders) access. Different combinations of SI capabilities are found in traditional defense industry prime contractors, specialized systems integration houses, FFRDCs and other quasi-public organizations, and the military laboratories. Because all these organizational types understand the crucial role of systems integration in transformation, most are maneuvering to establish their credibility as systems integrators; for example, prime contractors justify acquisitions on the grounds that they contribute to a "systems integration capability," and military laboratories rewrite mission statements to emphasize systems integration.[7]

Organizations that can provide SI services have a key, early role in implementing transformation. The overall definition of the network-centric system of systems will set the objectives for projects in other sectors of the defense industry (e.g., shipbuilding). Specifically, the first steps toward transformation involved military efforts to define the doctrinal vision. Since then, systems integrators have worked to determine what capabilities are necessary for each type of node in the network in light of the technical, operational, and economic implications of how capabilities are distributed. Systems integrators also stay involved, in an oversight role, through the production and even deployment of equipment to make sure that their architecture definitions are followed and that evolutionary changes and updates to equipment remain faithful to the system-of-systems vision. This job is one for which the massive, complex Cold War defense effort left the United States well prepared. Organizations that specialize in system-of-systems integration were established as part of the ballistic missile and air defense programs as early as the 1950s, and in cooperation, they also played vital roles in developing equipment for anti-submarine warfare, missile defense, and other system-of-systems missions.

WHO DOES SYSTEMS INTEGRATION?

Many organizations have at least some expertise that might contribute to system-of-systems integration (for a list of examples focusing on the Navy, see table 6.1).

As the customer for equipment, the U.S. military must define projects' objectives, but the actual technical system-of-systems integration task is very difficult for the military itself to accomplish. The acquisition community's core competencies are in understanding government regulations and monitoring suppliers' compliance with cost, schedule, and other contractual terms. Acquisition agents are usually not expert in state-of-the-art technologies and the innovative capabilities of various

TABLE 6.1 EXAMPLES OF NCW-RELATED SYSTEM-OF-SYSTEMS INTEGRATION ORGANIZATIONS

	Government	Private, Non-Profit	Private, For-Profit
Analysis	System Commands (SPAWAR, NAVSEA, NAVAIR)	Center for Naval Analysis, Institute for Defense Analysis, RAND	ANSER, TASC, Booz-Allen
Scientific Research	Naval Research Laboratory, SPAWAR Systems Center, San Diego*	APL, Lincoln Laboratory, Software Engineering Institute	
Technical Support	SPAWAR Systems Center, San Diego*	APL, MITRE, Aerospace Corporation	SAIC, SYNTEK
Production			Lockheed Martin Naval Electronics and Surveillance Systems, Raytheon Command Control Communications and Information Systems
Testing and Fleet Support	SPAWAR Systems Center, San Diego*		

* Each of the Navy's acquisition system commands has related technical organizations equivalent to the SPAWAR Systems Center—for example, the Naval Air Warfare Center, China Lake, and the Naval Surface Warfare Center, Dahlgren.

firms, even if they have a historical legacy of technical skill. In the Navy, for example, the old technical bureaus were phased out during the second half of the Cold War, and technical tasks were increasingly outsourced to private industry. The struggle now is for the remaining naval officers and civilians in the acquisition organizations to keep track of ties to many different private firms with many different areas of expertise.[8]

The difference between procedural and technical skills is a frequent source of inter- and intra-organizational tension in the military acquisition community. The military's systems commands, which are the primary acquisition organizations, can still draw on expertise from subsidiary laboratories, which maintain important niche capabilities, research expertise, and key physical assets (e.g., model basins) required to develop and test new designs. Unfortunately, the relationship between science-oriented military laboratories and regulation-oriented systems commands is often tense. Scientists often feel that the continuity of their research and their technical skills are undermined by frequent "cherry-picking" of researchers out of the laboratory and into the system command itself.[9] For their part, systems command personnel tend to believe that scientists should support their immediate needs for technical advice and technologies rather than pursue research projects that may or may not pay off.[10]

This difficult interface between "pure" science and system acquisition is a challenge for all forms of technical advisory organization—not just for the military's in-house laboratories—but the difficulty is magnified within the military chain of command. The internal technical capabilities of each military service are, on the one hand, constrained by civil-service rules, which prevent them from competing effectively for top scientists and engineers.[11] On the other hand, the same rules protect internal technical staff from competitive and budgetary threats. As a result, the operational part of each service often perceives its laboratories and technical advisers as less cooperative than the highly responsive scientists and engineers in private defense industry, who can be induced to work hard for the military through appropriate contractual compensation. As a result, the operational force often fails to support the research laboratories aggressively.[12]

Warfighters do support the laboratory system, but only in a particular way that undermines the labs' ability to conduct analyses of alternatives and make high-level tradeoffs among technical approaches. The Navy's system centers, for example, are very good at fleet support. But those close ties to the fleet's needs for quick fixes before particular missions leave port do not comport with the standardization and interface stewardship role of the systems integrator. The skills that enable fast fixes in the field—especially of particular systems or subsystems—are not the same as the skills that produce thoughtful optimization of the system of systems.[13]

The military's in-house laboratories emphasize testing system performance, confirming that prototypes meet specifications, and determining which of several proposals from contractors best meets military acquisition criteria. This emphasis permeates these organizations so strongly that several scientists in military laboratories that we interviewed even defined systems integration precisely in terms of testing performance and interoperability.[14] While they understand the importance of technical advice during the up-front analysis of alternatives, before criteria for evaluating prototypes and delivered equipment are even defined, laboratory personnel particularly value feedback from testing physical systems in improving their ability to define requirements for subsequent projects.[15] In sum, while in-house laboratories can offer some components of SI skills, they cannot currently offer the complete package, especially at the system-of-systems level. Expanding laboratories' capabilities would require major systemic change.

Prime contractors are an alternative group of organizations with SI capabilities. Especially in recent years, in response to the NCW vision's emphasis on high-level systems integration, traditional prime contractors that specialize in platform design and production have begun to offer architecture systems integration services. Firms with core competencies in electronics and network-oriented activities are also angling for platform integration work, arguing that inter-platform integration (interoperability) is becoming an ever more important part of the design of the platforms themselves.

Prime contractors have focused for years on understanding the unique demands of the military customer, hiring retired military officers for important positions in their strategic planning departments. Private firms are also largely exempt from civil-service rules, allowing them the flexibility to hire top technical talent when necessary;[16] for scientists who crave equity compensation, private firms can also offer stock options.[17] When technical teams develop internal rapport that generates extra value from synergies or experience, private firms have incentives to support such built-up human capital. Managing technical personnel is a core competency of technology-dependent private firms, including the defense industry prime contractors.[18]

However, platform systems integration and system-of-systems integration are not the same task, and it is not clear that developing skill at one helps very much in developing skill at the other. Platform integrators may improve their performance through any of a number of different activities: repeated design or prototype development experience; production experience; and maintenance of close relationships with applied technical laboratories, basic science research establishments, academic institutions, or the operational user community.[19] Platform-builders' unique advantage is in linking systems engineering capability with intricate knowledge of the manufacturing process, allowing them to consider opportunities for gains in production efficiency during the design process. Naturally, prime contractors emphasize the importance of production capability in their discussions of systems integration—just as military laboratories emphasize the importance of full-scale system testing. However, while this advantage surely carries weight, it is likely to be relatively small in the defense sector, where production runs are often short and very-close-tolerance production processes are often craft-like, minimizing the potential for major savings. Such production issues should consequently receive a relatively low weighting in the system-of-systems integration trade space, although system-of-systems specialists should strive to consider platform makers' concerns when they do their overall analyses and define requirements. System-of-systems concerns about platforms' interfaces with the network should take precedence in transformation planning and acquisition.

Moreover, the potential for conflicts of interest—or at least for the *appearance* of conflicts of interest, a more stringent standard that has been deemed appropriate for government organizations—mandates a separation between architecture systems integration and production in the defense industry. Production prime contractors have the technical capability to scan subcontractors' products, including the offerings of innovative commercial firms, for likely partners and subcontractors—that is, they can perform one of the key technical and management tasks of a systems integrator. They also can make technical decisions about interfaces, network standards, and other requirements definitions, and they are increasingly using their expertise to compete for technical advisory and systems engineering contracts in addition to their traditional role as platform systems integrators.[20] By vertically integrating so as to combine platform and components-oriented design and production organizations, large prime contractors might provide technical SI services with minimal transaction costs.[21] But the idea of expanding the roles of established prime contractors faces a crucial nontechnical barrier: lack of trust. Manufacturers certainly test their products before delivery to the customer, but the customer also needs an independent ability to verify product performance, just as military laboratories emphasize. In addition, the customer might reasonably fear that a manufacturer's tradeoff analysis might be biased in favor of the sort of alternatives that the manufacturer is expert at making. More subtly, the prime's analysis of alternatives might (unintentionally) be skewed by the production contractors' technical understanding of particular systems and solutions.

This conflict of interest problem was first manifest in the defense industry in a 1959 Congressional investigation of the relationship between

TRW's satellite and missile production businesses and the TRW-owned Space Technology Laboratory (STL). STL played a technical direction role in Air Force development and production projects, including some for which TRW had submitted proposals. Neither protectors of the government trust nor members of the defense sector that competed with TRW on those space-systems contracts would accept the situation, even though no specific malfeasance was uncovered or even alleged. STL was essentially split off from TRW to become Aerospace Corporation, an independent, nonprofit, nonproduction, systems integration specialist, later designated an FFRDC.[22]

That organizational innovation, which spread with the establishment of other FFRDCs and the similarly organized "university applied research centers" (UARCs), allowed the military's acquisition organizations to outsource the technical advisory role during the Cold War in a way that was protected from conflict-of-interest scandals.[23] FFRDCs now offer a third potential source for system-of-systems integration capabilities required for transformation. Some FFRDCs, like MIT's Lincoln Laboratory, specialize in particular kinds of military-oriented research (advanced electronics, in that case), comparable in some ways to the in-house military laboratories but more closely tied to frontier academic research. While the core tasks of various FFRDCs overlap to some extent, Aerospace Corporation (space systems), MITRE (air defense), and APL (naval systems) are the ones that specialize in architecture systems integration.[24]

Like in-house laboratories and prime contractors, FFRDCs have advantages and disadvantages as systems integration service providers. The historical strength of FFRDCs has been their reputation for high-quality, objective advice. Through flexibility in salary negotiations and their quasi-academic status, FFRDCs have been able to attract high-quality personnel. Their promise not to compete for production contracts and to provide equal access to all contractors while safeguarding proprietary information has given them unique, independent technical capabilities.[25] However, they have frequently been criticized as inefficient and relatively expensive; while leaders of FFRDCs frequently claim that their nonprofit status allows them to charge less than a hypothetical for-profit adviser with equivalent technical skills, many others (notably leaders of for-profit firms, like SAIC) allege that the lack of a profit motive in FFRDC work leads to inefficient performance and the potential for featherbedding.[26] Legislation currently limits the budgetary

resources available to FFRDCs, and for a number of years a law pre-
vented the establishment of any new FFRDCs.[27] The fiscal controversy
limits the ability of FFRDCs to expand to provide full-service system-
of-systems integration support to military transformation, despite their
evident technical and organizational advantages.

For-profit firms that agreed not to engage in any production might be
able to offer the benefits of FFRDCs while avoiding the controversies
linked to nonprofit status. Small engineering companies like SYNTEK
can offer technical advice to the military with a credible promise not to
engage in production, but it is difficult to imagine such a firm nurturing
a major laboratory with an independent research capability and agenda,
at least under current procurement rules. Without direct access to such
scientific assets, it is reasonable to question the ability of a consultancy
to maintain top-level system-of-systems integration skills.[28] Larger for-
profit firms like SAIC—which owns Bellcore, the former research arm
of the Regional Bell Operating Companies (a partial descendant of Bell
Laboratories)—offer to fill this niche, but to cover the overhead cost
of such laboratories they resist pressure to abstain from all production
work.[29] Although for-profit firms in the defense industry have learned
to form teams to develop major systems and sometimes even to join
a team on one contract with a firm against which they are competing
for another contract, real questions persist about how much proprietary
data the for-profit contractors are willing to share with one another. A
promise not to engage in production would allay some of the fears that
prevent platform firms from becoming architecture systems integrators,
but major for-profit advisory firms are still limited by customers' and
competitors' skepticism about their true, long-term independence.

PERFORMANCE METRICS FOR SYSTEMS INTEGRATION

Project managers have trouble choosing sources for technical advice
and deciding how much investment in up-front systems integration is
enough. To help rate the quality of various possibilities, Carnegie Mellon
University's Software Engineering Institute (SEI), a research FFRDC,
has developed an evaluation system for several computer-related skills,
including software engineering and systems engineering. The ratings
assigned according to the SEI "Capabilities Maturity Models" are based
on a business' commitment to follow certain procedures designed to

manage complex projects: specifically, they emphasize maintaining control of documentation and interfaces to ensure system-wide performance as components and subsystems are improved in parallel. These software-oriented procedures are at least related to the broader SI task, and they may provide a useful model for further work defining metrics for overall systems integration capabilities.[30]

For a broad discussion of the relationship between systems integration and transformation, however, such detailed metrics for evaluating systems integrators are not necessary. The key question is how the military services can best stimulate system-of-systems integration to implement military innovation.

TECHNICAL AWARENESS

The foundation of systems integration is familiarity with the technical state of the art in the wide range of disciplines that contribute to the components of the system. Systems integrators must be able to set reasonable, achievable goals for the developers and manufacturers of system components even as they "black box" the detailed design work for those components. If one component maker has a problem that it can solve only at great expense but that could be solved much more easily by changing the requirements of a different component or by altering the interface standard in a way that would cost other component manufacturers less, it is the responsibility of the systems integrator to understand and implement the necessary tradeoff among the various component specifications. The more the systems integrator knows about the subsystems, the better it will be able to perform. Systems integrators can obtain this technical knowledge in many ways, including systematically and continuously training and educating critical engineers, hiring personnel from subsystem contractors, and seconding employees to other organizations to work in all phases of component design and production.[31]

Transformation is unlikely to change the role of technical awareness as a performance metric for systems integration. To the extent that network-centric warfare draws on unfamiliar component systems, it may strain the technical awareness of established SI organizations. For example, emerging unmanned-vehicle technologies may take over a number of tasks previously assigned to manned systems, requiring systems integrators to be familiar with the state of the art in unmanned vehicles if they are to make tradeoffs between manned and unmanned systems.

However, the systems integrator need not have the capability actually to design and build either the manned or the unmanned systems. The specific technical knowledge is not the core competency for the systems integrator; the sine qua non of systems integration is, instead, the ability to gain access to that knowledge, by working with subsystem contractors, academic experts, or in-house researchers.

Developing new sources and kinds of technical awareness may be the core competency of a systems integrator, but it is only natural that the less familiar the component technologies of a particular project are to a systems integrator, the less effective that integrator will be. Even the organizations with the broadest architecture systems integration capability have specialties—Aerospace Corporation in space systems, for example, or MITRE in command and control. It is not obvious, though, that network-centric warfare demands new specialties. Instead, it seems to involve the advanced application of a combination of established ones— for example, reliance on space systems for surveillance and communications relay, on intensive exploitation of command and control networks and battle-management computation. If a new focus on the network characterizes the SI task for network-centric warfare, MITRE, APL, and for-profit firms like Logicon and SAIC appear to have the necessary technical awareness. Perhaps the Software Engineering Institute's foray into integration provides the basis for a transition from a pure research FFRDC into a research and systems integration combination (akin to APL) that specializes in network technology.[32] And Internet technology is hardly foreign to the military's specialty SI suppliers. Although the commercial Internet has burgeoned well beyond its defense origin, its core began as the Arpanet, a program of the Defense Advanced Research Projects Agency (DARPA). The Arpanet in fact has been cited as a classic example of the military's "systems approach" to advanced technology.[33]

The variety of substantive technical awareness among the established systems integration organizations offers an opportunity to the U.S. military acquisition system. Various systems integrators might offer competing technical proposals, each offering its best system solution to network-centric warfare challenges and pointing out flaws in alternative proposals. American pluralist government is built on the principle that the clash of ideas yields the best policy solutions; that clash of ideas might help compensate for each existing organization's implicit biases in favor of its technical specialties. APL might point out any pitfalls of Aerospace Corporation's space-based solutions, while Aerospace could illuminate the risks inherent in APL's hypothetical networking approach. Still, it remains the responsibility of the customer to evaluate competing claims and put together a composite view of systems integration advice. The transformational systems integration solution is already building on sustaining innovation in technical awareness.

PROJECT-MANAGEMENT SKILL

Efforts to control costs have been a continuous feature of defense policy, even if efficiency has rarely if ever been the main goal of a military acquisition program. Projects always need to meet military requirements and to satisfy political constraints.[34] Yet warfighters would always like to acquire more systems; technologists always can use additional resources to push the performance envelope further; and politicians always have non-defense priorities, including lowering taxes. Because all three groups also try to plan their expenditures as part of the budgeting process, they need estimates of the cost of the product and its development and delivery schedule that are as accurate as possible.

For complex acquisitions with numerous, heterogeneous components—a system of systems—reliable estimates are difficult to come by, because of the vast amounts of information that must be managed to describe the current and projected states of progress. Participants also have incentives to hide certain information from oversight. Sometimes they believe setbacks to be temporary (that they will get back on schedule, the promised performance trajectory, or the estimated cost projection before they have to report problems); sometimes they fear that full disclosure will aid competitors or lead to pressure to renegotiate fees and expropriate profits. Managers learn to report data in favorable ways that can give a biased picture of progress: they aim to protect ongoing projects from scrutiny without actually lying or submitting false claims.[35] They also enthusiastically embrace acquisition reform efforts and management fads that promise to reduce costs in the future—after enough investment has been sunk into the project to lock it into the political landscape, whether or not the efficiency benefits of the reform ever actually materialize.[36]

System-of-systems integrators have the expertise to manage projects as well as possible in the face of these constraints.[37] The better that a given systems integrator performs the project management task—setting accurate schedules, projecting attainable technical goals, and minimizing transaction costs among the many organizations that have to contribute to a systems contract—the greater the incentive the buyer has to hire that systems integrator. Project management skill is a key performance metric for SI organizations.

Transformation calls for sustaining innovation in project management. Ultimately, for network-centric warfare to be useful to the warfighter, a number of different programs (for example, ships, aircraft, unmanned vehicles, munitions, and sensors) need to deliver compatible systems to the fleet in the correct order; the schedules need to be timed so that the various deployment dates form the network. From early in the program, Congressional Representatives worried that the Littoral Combat Ships' hull design would not be sufficiently coordinated with the separate efforts to develop the small ships' mission modules—and the Defense authorization bill for fiscal year 2006 included explicit guidance about improving project management and schedule control.[38] The prompt response from the LCS modules' program manager was to promise rapid delivery of the first mission module and additional attention to scheduling needs.[39] This management strategy directly builds on skills developed for Cold War programs like the Polaris fleet ballistic missile program, which required tremendous innovation in missiles and guidance, in communications and navigation, and in submarine platforms. Polaris faced the same sort of management and scheduling problems as LCS and other programs for network-centric warfare. System-of-systems integration was effectively invented precisely for the purpose of managing such massive, heterogeneous acquisitions.[40]

Network-centric warfare may require integration of an even broader array of components, making the system-of-systems integration task even more difficult. But systems integrators are already applying modern information technology to manage complex subcontractor networks, to scan for technological leads that might contribute innovative solutions to military problems, and to interact with potential new suppliers, innovating to support this core task.

At the platform integration level, the project management task under transformation will be little changed from its previous incarnations. Whether any given platform integrator is well positioned to participate in transformation will depend on the demand for its technical skills—whether network-centric warfare calls for sustaining or disruptive innovation in that sector of the defense industry. The platform-integration task will continue to include management of subcontractor relationships and the detailed design of military systems. In sectors dominated by sustaining innovations, platform integrators' databases of successful subcontractors and procedures for working with the social and political constraints of the government contracting environment will contribute to successful acquisition programs. Despite acquisition reform advocates' appropriation of phrasing from transformation advocates—the "revolution in acquisition affairs" or "revolution in business affairs"—the quest for acquisition reform is separate from military transformation.

At the architecture systems integration level, innovators' biggest challenge in project management will stem from the need to integrate the plans and schedules of several powerful customer organizations.[41] The core project management task will not change much. System-of-systems integrators will have to integrate some new technical tasks into military systems development, but the disruptive innovations, if any, will fall at the platform or component level rather than that of organizational and management techniques for the system-of-systems project. Transformation requires that high-level systems integration evolve along a familiar performance trajectory, contributing as much efficiency and scheduling accuracy to major systems acquisition as possible. The sustaining nature of that innovation suggests that transformation will not change the core composition of the system-of-systems integration sector.

Perceived Independence

The key role of a system-of-systems integrator in defining the technical requirements of various system components (and hence of the system as a whole) requires that it be able to make tradeoffs in the interest of system performance rather than in the interest of the organizations that design or make the system. The architecture systems integration task is tremendously complicated; military systems have multiple goals, including maximizing warfighting performance, sustaining political support for the acquisition program and the national security strategy, and minimizing expenditure of resources for acquisition, maintenance, training, and operations.[42] That complexity, along with the requisite technical expertise, effectively guarantees that detailed decisions in system-of-systems integration will not be completely transparent to military customers, Congressional appropriators, or the defense industry primes and subcontractors that supply components of the system. All of those groups must trust that the systems integrator has considered and protected their interests in making its architecture-definition decisions. Any organizations that feel that their trust has been violated are in a position to create a scandal by complaining publicly; they are constrained only by the understanding that complaining too often or too loudly can subvert the entire process of providing for the national defense.[43] Fear of scandals and the need to minimize the appearance of bias in system definition drove the creation of the Cold War system-of-systems integration organizations, specifically including the FFRDCs.

The difficulty in maintaining independence for architecture systems integration is compounded by the pecuniary incentives in defense acquisition. Like all organizations, systems integrators have an incentive to favor solutions that maximize their own organizational rewards, maintaining and exploiting their positions connecting customers and producers in the organizational network of the military-industrial complex.[44] This bias may be purely tacit, such as that by which scientists propose certain types of technical solutions based on their particular expertise, thereby reinforcing the value of that particular expertise. It may also be structural: profits in the defense industry have disproportionately accrued to production rather than research or technical advisory organizations, in large part because profits are formally and informally fixed at a certain percentage of project revenue, and the bulk of the acquisition spending is concentrated during the procurement rather than the systems-development phases.[45] Further, in the post–Cold War threat environment, wherein the United States faces no peer competitor, firms having "critical masses" of workers (generally production rather than technical organizations) have been able to add considerable political weight to their pleas for financial support from Congressional appropriators.[46] Consequently, the financial prospects for pure system-of-systems integrators are weak, and they face pressure from shareholders to merge with production-oriented firms, so that the vertically integrated combination can make more profit.

Freedom to choose optimal technical solutions is constantly threatened at the margin by the bureaucratic interests of the services and the political power of platform producers. Because this pressure is well known, trust from the customers that the systems integrators will protect the military's interests, and not simply their own material interests, is also threatened.

Bias is built into the very makeup of most established systems integration houses. They originally served particular customers, and the needs of each customer were well known.[47] Lack of bias in this context meant that within their own issue domains they might reasonably be expected to play the honest broker. In turf battles with external forces, however, they should be expected to favor particular types of solutions. Thus Aerospace Corporation might be unbiased in telling the Air Force about how to organize and equip its own space capabilities but less so when arguing for space-based solutions as opposed to terrestrial approaches proposed by other government entities.[48]

By and large, the FFRDC/UARC system of nonproduction technical advisers functioned successfully during the Cold War.[49] The contractual relationships of FFRDCs and UARCs with the government commit them not to engage in production. Some degree of tension inevitably remains between the producer firms and the FFRDCs, which insist that they need to engage in prototype building that is quite similar to production in order to maintain their SI skills. Such tension seems particularly likely to escalate in the software industry, where the development and production phases of a code-writing project frequently overlap.

APL, for example, has been criticized for mixing production with systems integration, specifically in a dispute over the best technology for the Navy's Cooperative Engagement Capability.[50] Solipsys, a software firm founded in the late-1990s by disenchanted former employees of APL, created a rival system, the Tactical Component Network (TCN). Solipsys feared that the Navy would not give TCN a fair hearing, at least in part because APL is both the technical adviser to the Navy and the developer of CEC.[51] Regardless of the technical merits of CEC versus TCN, and here opinions vary widely,[52] the controversy would have been less bitter if APL were not exposed to charges that it might favor one solution over the other because it developed that alternative. And the ultimate solution to the conflict raises even more questions: Raytheon, the manufacturer of CEC, bought Solipsys. Raytheon now emphasizes several other Solipsys products in its advertising, and the public hears much less about the possible role of TCN in the ongoing Single Integrated Air Picture program into which future generations of CEC will be incorporated.[53] Even if the acquisition authorities find a way to make the technically correct decision, conflict-of-interest claims may arise, and the likely outcome will be extra oversight of the SIAP program, which will increase costs and undermine political support for military innovation.

Scandals alleging "waste, fraud, and abuse" and cost and schedule failures have derailed military investment in the past, and conflicts of interest might be a threat to the move toward network-centric warfare. The peaks in the major cycles of the U.S. Cold War defense budget were associated with procurement scandals, which at least superficially played a role in reversing the defense budget trend. Even if, at the time, structural factors like the changing threat environment or the completion of a generational change in key equipment were bringing the procurement cycle to an end, calls to rein in defense-acquisition abuses were a proximate cause of the downturn in the defense budget.[54] Buying the equipment for network-centric warfare will require sustained high levels of acquisition spending, and a scandal would threaten that investment.

Military transformation relies on sustaining innovation to meet the metric of "perceived independence" for system-of-systems integration performance. Some of the technical advisers for whom lack of bias was a key core competency during the Cold War have actually begun to stray from that trajectory, under pressure to defend sunk investment in particular technical approaches. The best way to implement network-centric warfare would be to return to the well-known "lack of bias" performance trajectory as soon as possible, while suitable organizations still exist with core competencies to proceed with system-of-systems integration.

CUSTOMER UNDERSTANDING

The success of each system-of-systems integrator depends on how deeply it understands the military environment. The integration organization's architecture definitions and project-management decisions must serve its customer's true goals, which can be difficult to articulate in a simple, program-specific, "statement of objectives." The military, with all its communities (e.g., the Navy's three, led by aviators, submariners, and surface warfare officers), is a complicated institution with a long history, unique traditions, and organizational biases developed over generations of operational experience.[55] For example, Navy-oriented systems integrators like APL, SYNTEK, and Lockheed Martin Naval Electronics and Surveillance Systems have built up a great deal of tacit knowledge about how and why the Navy operates, knowledge without which they would not be trusted to perform system-of-systems integration. Customer understanding is important for any organization, but it is a uniquely vital performance metric for architecture systems integration organizations.

Customer understanding is a moving target; long experience alone is insufficient. A systems integrator must commit itself to invest continuously in its military-operational knowledge base. It must monitor lessons learned from recent exercises and operational deployments, as well as changes in military doctrine and national grand strategy, in order to maintain the "right" kind of technical awareness.[56] Ideally, members of the SI organization should participate in war games and exercises wherein the military tests new operational concepts and introduces virtual prototypes of future platforms and subsystems. SI experts also can learn by deploying with warfighters to see their solutions in action. Teaming in various forms can only help personnel and organizations develop a greater appreciation for mutual idiosyncrasies. A large part of customer understanding is the maintenance over time of interorganizational relationships that transcend individuals and projects.

The need to make tradeoffs and provide analyses of alternatives that may threaten existing programs and the short-term plans of system-of-systems integrators' customers puts SI organizations in a delicate position. Individual services are wary of criticism and fear losing ground in budgetary competition with other services, just as individual platform-makers may resent the oversight that an independent systems integrator exercises on a particular project, even while understanding the contribution that oversight and systems integration generally make to the overall success of investment in national defense. This requirement is another reason why it is difficult for government agencies to perform systems integration in-house: subordinate project managers in the systems commands might not risk criticizing their bosses' preferred programs (or the "pet rocks" of even higher ranking officials).[57] Quasi-public FFRDCs face similar pressure not to criticize their customers too much, but individual employees' support and promotion prospects do not come through as direct a chain of command from the potential targets of their technical advice and criticism. The position of for-profit systems integration houses is similar to that of the FFRDCs: they may be more responsive to short-term budget pressures from sponsoring organizations than FFRDCs are, but they may have more independence than FFRDCs to seek alternative customers if a relationship with a particular contracting command temporarily sours.

Unfortunately, customer understanding might also reinforce institutional inertia. In many ways, it is analogous to bureaucratic "capture," which can lead a regulator to see things from the perspective of industry rather than the public interest. In this case, too much customer understanding might turn a systems integrator into a knee-jerk supporter of its client military service. Yet these dangers cannot be avoided by creating firewalls or by artificially introducing change from the outside. Rather, both the customer and the SI organization must self-consciously distinguish between customer understanding for the sake of overall success and collaboration for the sake of blocking change or protecting institutional interests. In short, the systems integrator must be free (and protected) to resolve tradeoffs in ways that may harm short-term customer interests but guard the long-term health of the organization as a whole. Appeals to the public interest and hopes that bureaucrats and businessmen will "do the right thing" by themselves are weak reeds on which to rest military innovation, but even the best government organization is at the mercy of technical constraints and the need for close customer understanding. Fortunately, fear of public scandals and competition from other systems integration organizations ultimately prevent at least egregious violations of the public trust.

At the architecture systems integration level, transformation's biggest challenge lies in the fact that the system of systems crosses many organizational boundaries. Communities within the services have strong, independent identities, ideas about how wars should be fought, and priorities for setting schedules and allocating funding. Each service, in turn, tries to influence the course of transformation—and to influence the definition of the system of systems by pushing preferred lists of program objectives and by defending and funding particular programs that the overall systems integrator must then integrate into the network-centric force structure. Architecture systems integrators will have to understand and balance the conflicting motivations of the several customers, each of which can tolerate only a few "big ideas" in its organizational identity.[58] These considerations suggest that a truly joint systems approach may require establishment of a single, joint acquisition agency to which a single system-of-systems integrator could be attached. However, added organizational layers between integrators and their service customers, who will actually operate military systems, might degrade customer understanding, reducing the effectiveness of analysis of alternatives. Adopting a single buyer for transformational systems might also threaten the diversity of approaches that interservice rivalry could otherwise provide. A single buyer might also be shut out of the real discussions of how operators want to use their new equipment (its ties to the operational parts of the military services would be even more distant than each service's current systems commands), reducing acquisition's contribution to military effectiveness.

Ultimately, new layers of organization rarely solve interorganizational boundary issues, so the key issue for system-of-systems integration organizations remains how to accomplish the task of sustaining innovation on the customer understanding performance metric.

EMPHASIZING SYSTEM-OF-SYSTEMS INTEGRATION

Modern military innovation relies on a set of institutions to connect political, economic, and technical concerns in an ever more complex environment. System-of-systems integration is the key to that process for the ongoing transformation agenda. Military innovation cannot be implemented without a renewed public–private partnership based on mutual understanding and trust between the military's warfighters and doctrine-writers and the technical specialists in system-of-systems integration, who manage the interface with for-profit defense manufacturers.

Certain established SI houses, like APL and MITRE, clearly have expertise that is closely related to present plans for network-centric warfare, and they should play major parts in the network-centric defense industry. Similarly, some of the production-oriented prime contractors have high-level systems integration groups that on technical awareness and project management grounds might join the nucleus of competitive SI suppliers. However, in the face of commitments to the lack-of-bias and customer-understanding performance metrics, prime contractors' skills are better applied in the service of platform rather than architecture systems integration.[59] Given the predominance of sustaining innovations in systems integration, the key step in preparing the defense industrial base for network-centric warfare is not to try to change the cast of characters but to update and focus the technical emphasis of the military's own acquisition community.

Transformation does not require the government to invite platform-making prime contractors into the systems integration sector. The primes want "in" for self-serving reasons. They perceive that systems integration is the locus of greatest responsibility in the future defense industry. Moreover, as political pressure builds in support of transformation, and systems that are not perceived as transformational (like the Army's Crusader self-propelled howitzer) become vulnerable to cancellation, prime contractors are looking for ways to link their activities to transformation. The logic for the primes is the same as it always has been: if a particular kind of acquisition reform is popular, your programs should be "demonstrators" of the new technique. If systems analysis and PERT charts are the way to show budget and schedule control, your programs should use them; if network-centric warfare is the future operational concept, your programs should emphasize their connections to the network, and your firm should emphasize its systems integration skills.

Acting as a systems integration agent might be the best protection of all for a prime contractor's business base. Production firms in the defense sector might be expected to complain about outside SI houses' role on particular projects, because the adviser's job includes raising awkward criticisms of the prime contractors' technical approaches and production skills. One way to avoid such criticism would be to make systems integration part of the prime's job. However, given the importance of independence for quality systems integration and the fact that up-front technical advice and coordination will help to keep transformation programs on schedule and budget, production contractors should find it in their interest to support outside SI organizations.[60]

On the other hand, it remains very difficult for the military to choose its technical advisers for system-of-systems integration, because performance metrics for systems integration are difficult to tie to the traditional framework for defense contracting. No top-down metric that is developed for SI skill will be able to substitute for organizational competition. The various systems integration organizations can offer a diversity of technical approaches and system-of-systems proposals, and they can offer technical commentary on and critiques of each other's proposals, giving the military customer enough advice to make informed choices early in the transformation process.

Competition among systems integrators is especially important since the consolidation of the defense industrial base through mergers in the 1990s. Competition for production contracts is now limited. Moreover, the overhead cost of maintaining multiple production lines for each weapon system is now unacceptably high, as total production runs for each highly sophisticated system are shorter than production runs of comparably advanced projects in the Industrial Age of mass production. However, competition among technical advisory organizations—each with a different design philosophy or technical focus—is relatively inexpensive to sustain, and those dedicated systems integrators should be able to help monitor technical efficiency during the production phase of the acquisition process. Exploiting competition among dedicated SI organizations should be a relatively low-cost response to the tension between budgetary pressure and the high resource demand of investing in military transformation. In the end, however, the buck must stop somewhere. Competition among systems integration organizations may keep everyone honest and allow ideas to be triaged, but the military itself must sort through competing claims and make decisions.

Alternatively, a team combining the relevant technical groups from the established systems integrators might be able to offer a comprehensive technical base for network-centric systems integration. Ten FFRDCs and national laboratories combined to provide technical support to the Ballistic Missile Defense Organization through a teaming arrangement called the Phase One Evaluation Team (POET).[61] On the one hand, the POET clearly provided access to an exceptional breadth of technical talent.[62] On the other hand, the participant organizations retained their traditional customers, missions, and cultures; they may not have invested their best resources in, or devoted their full attention to, the missile defense effort.[63] An SI team for network-centric warfare would gain similar advantages and face similar limitations.

To apply the full resources of the established systems integrators to the new challenges of network-centric warfare, it might be advantageous to create a new systems integrator with a new organizational identity. But it would not be necessary to create such an organization from scratch; it would be very costly to replicate the investment in human capital that has already been made by established organizations. When MITRE was created as the systems integrator for the SAGE air defense system in the late 1950s, its core was formed from Division Six of Lincoln Laboratory, which chose at that point to focus on research rather than systems integration. MITRE then proceeded to expand its technical awareness into new areas, integrating air defense missiles like the BOMARC into the SAGE system initially designed to cue fighter interceptors.[64] Today, it might be possible to blend various technical groups spun off by the established organizations and form a new FFRDC. The new institution would maintain its capabilities on familiar performance metrics but would do so in the service of a new organizational mission.[65]

In the current policy environment, the balance is tipping away from dedicated systems integration houses like FFRDCs and toward prime contractors that build platforms. Reversing that trend and creating a POET-like team for network-centric systems integration would provide at least minimal protection from scandal that might derail the information-technology revolution in military affairs. Despite the questions that some have raised about whether the POET optimized technical support for missile defense, a POET-like team for network-centric warfare might make important strides toward improving the technical future of the American way of war.

Major acquisition projects or groups of related projects during the Cold War often spawned new procurement and advisory organizations. Advocates of network-centric warfare frequently note that the current acquisition system is organized on a platform-by-platform basis, which naturally deemphasizes crucial network investment. The potential problem is very much akin to the barriers to investment in missile defense through traditional acquisition channels that led in the 1980s to the creation of the Strategic Defense Initiative Office, predecessor of the Ballistic Missile Defense Office and now called the Missile Defense Agency. Advocates of missile defense feared that the services' bureaucratic standard operating procedures would always underemphasize investment in missile defense compared to the services' traditional priorities. Similarly, the military network may need an acquisition organization that will develop a bureaucratic interest in acting as the budgetary advocate for transformation. Perhaps, if it were given a stronger acquisition role, a bigger staff, and better technical support, the Pentagon's Office of Force Transformation could serve this purpose. If it ever were, its first step would surely be to sort out its relationship to top-notch system-of-systems integration expertise. No matter who is in charge of the buying, the first step will be public–private partnership for systems integration.

CHAPTER SEVEN

MILITARY INNOVATION
AND THE DEFENSE INDUSTRY

Since the terrorist attacks of September 11, 2001, the busy U.S. military has contributed to the global war on terror, chased Taliban remnants and al-Qaeda militants in Afghanistan, and occupied Iraq in the midst of a violent insurgency. There seems little prospect that the military will be relieved of these responsibilities soon. Army, Marine, and special forces units are barely able to keep pace with their deployment schedules, and their equipment is being worn down. Despite large increases in overall military spending, the cost of operations has forced planners to economize in other areas, and pressure is mounting to contain investment spending on long-range acquisition programs.

During this period of high operational tempo, civilian and military leaders have remained committed to military innovation, and some argue that the national security challenges facing the United States today reinforce the logic of transformation. Secretary of Defense Donald Rumsfeld has repeatedly stated that the war on terror requires military transformation. The website of DoD's Office of Force Transformation links to dozens of articles claiming that various emerging technologies and concepts derived from network-centric warfare are helping fight the wars in Afghanistan and Iraq.[1]

Furthermore, transformation advocates claim that building innovative military capabilities will help allow the United States to sustain its military strength in the long term. Some influential voices within the U.S. national security community believe that China may emerge as a peer competitor to the United States. Network-centric warfare might be particularly well suited to respond to China's force modernization programs, especially in maritime systems,[2] so military transformation is touted as a way to deter an enormous, increasingly wealthy, technologically sophisticated country from becoming an enemy across the Pacific Ocean. Others argue that military technology is spreading to both friends and foes, who may buy advanced, militarily useful technology in global markets and who may emulate American equipment rather than paying high costs to develop indigenous weapons from scratch.[3] According to these analysts, the United States needs to aggressively innovate just to maintain its international position in the face of technological globalization. In the most optimistic visions, the so-called military-after-next will enable the United States to maintain its lead in military effectiveness over potential rivals, using smaller, lightly manned, widely dispersed forces that may even cost less to acquire and maintain than traditional, platform-centric systems.

We have not written this volume to advocate military transformation in general or the specific variant represented by network-centric warfare. But we do explain why the theory that technological change in society requires a comparable change in military affairs is wrong. Military visionaries develop new military doctrines for their own reasons—reasons that have been well chronicled in the literature on military innovation—and their visions are only sometimes closely integrated to the grand strategy set by the political leadership, the international threat environment, and the trajectory of technology in civilian markets.[4] This book is primarily about the visionaries' next task, following their invention of a new doctrinal concept: implementing military innovation by mobilizing political support, scientific and engineering effort, and the production capabilities of the defense industry. Military innovation does not necessarily follow perforce from social change; instead, it depends on the alignment of military, corporate, and Congressional interests.

In the modern United States, the acquisition of new technologies will play a critical role in the implementation of network-centric warfare. If the President, Department of Defense, and the uniformed military services want a network-centric future, they must send appropriate signals to industry to produce the necessary sustaining and disruptive innovations. They must also harness the industry's political influence to help convince Congress to invest more heavily in military innovation. These conclusions and those that follow have been derived directly from our theory of military innovation explained in chapter 2, the evidence presented in our three case studies, and the analysis of public-private partnership in systems integration in chapter 6.

THE DEFENSE INDUSTRY AND MILITARY TRANSFORMATION

Close analysis does not uphold the oft-expressed view that military transformation requires reshaping or even replacing the established defense industry. Only a particular kind of technological innovation transforms the industrial landscape: disruptive innovation, which introduces new performance metrics—performance that customers want but that established firms are not conceptually prepared to provide.[5] Broadly speaking, the demand for innovative military systems to implement network-centric warfare does not introduce the widespread potential for disruptive innovation. The type of innovation implicit in the new military doctrine varies by sector of the defense industry, but in most sectors, transformation requires sustaining innovation.

Contrary to many analysts' intuitive belief that the RMA should draw from a general information technology revolution that would bring new suppliers of computers and communications equipment into the defense industrial base, the biggest changes in the defense industry are likely to concentrate in the platform-building sectors like shipbuilding. The Navy's transformation vision, Sea Power 21, includes a focus on smaller, simpler, single-purpose ships—likely introducing some new performance metrics to the military shipbuilding industry. Not surprisingly, according to our theory, nontraditional firms (small shipyards, foreign builders, and systems integrators) are involved at the core of programs like the Littoral Combat Ship.

But in the sectors that transformation advocates usually like to discuss—the UAV industry and the rapidly expanding communications and systems integration areas—our analysis challenges the conventional wisdom. In those sectors, the military wants huge improvements of performance measured by traditional standards—like throughput and quality of service in the communications sector. Established suppliers that are expertly responsive to the military's unique language for describing operations, complex culture, and rule-laden acquisition environment are already very well positioned to provide such sustaining innovations.

Calls to purge the term "defense industrial base" from our lexicon in favor of simply "industrial base" do not do justice to the unique characteristics of the firms that provide weapons and systems to the U.S. military. Defense firms have numerous competencies that are not found elsewhere within the American economy. Merely having the administrative mechanisms in place to deal with the complexities of Defense Federal Acquisition Regulations, for example, constitutes a core competency that cannot be duplicated easily by most commercial firms that might be lured into the defense business. Even acquisition reforms will not change the importance of these competencies; the "revolution in business affairs" advocated by Clinton-era officials only went so far toward making federal contracting similar to its civilian counterpart.[6] Congressional representatives, and, indeed, the federal workforce as a whole, demand a higher level of transparency, fairness, and accountability than is compatible with commercial business practices.

It is nonetheless likely the government's acquisition system will evolve as part of military transformation. Most of these changes will involve tinkering at the margins—with changes in the Advanced Concept Technology Demonstrations system or export controls and dual-use technology regulations, for example. The next several years may even see a major acquisition reform effort by Congress: the DoD leadership has pushed for numerous reforms to both its internal procedures and its relationship with the private sector. In the end, however, the basic premises that have led the United States to today's complex acquisition system are integral to our Constitution and entire political system.[7] No acquisition-reform magic will wipe away the importance of the established defense industry's detailed understanding of the military market.

DEFENSE SECTORS

It is less helpful to discuss the defense industrial base as whole than it is to focus on specific sectors that provide particular types of capabilities. Many of our findings are sector-specific.

SHIPBUILDING

The network-centric vision, if fully realized, suggests that the nature of nodes—the platforms from which the military operates—must change. The Navy may soon buy more ships like the LCS that are designed to operate in a highly complex, fully networked system of systems. Under NCW, warships will no longer serve as multipurpose vessels operating independently. Each platform will instead be a specialized component of larger system that will include other types of platforms (both weapons and sensors). But not all of the qualities that make an individual ship's capabilities attractive to warfighters will change with the implementation of NCW: the emphasis on simple, affordable, single-purpose ships will involve some disruptive innovation, but the continued reliance on speed, stealth, and battlegroup cooperation all involve sustaining innovations. Even concepts like modularity, which will allow individual LCS hulls to be rapidly reconfigured with different payloads to adapt to the mission at hand, will involve primarily sustaining innovation in naval architecture and ship construction.

The NCW vision must be tempered by the reality that large, multipurpose warships are unlikely to disappear from the fleet anytime soon. Even the most strident transformation advocates acknowledge that their views do not envision changing the nature and composition of the entire military. The defense budget is highly unlikely to allow for sufficient recapitalization and modernization to change the entire fleet. Drawing on analogies to the level of transformation achieved by Nazi Germany's armed forces that enabled the adoption of blitzkrieg tactics, transformation proponents suggest that roughly 10–15 percent of the current force needs to be transformed.[8] Potentially innovative shipbuilding programs, even if they focus on affordability, remain very expensive, which will limit the rate at which new ship classes are introduced.

The Navy's development and procurement programs drive its relationship with the defense industry. The LCS program has attracted some nontraditional suppliers to bring an emphasis on certain new performance metrics. But as in all sectors of the defense industry, established military shipyards enjoy many advantages over their commercial and international competitors. They have a longstanding and relatively successful business relationship with the Navy and the other services dating back decades. They have invested heavily in understanding the needs of the Navy, both by hiring retired naval officers and by closely monitoring the decision-making processes in Washington. Finally, they maintain large and active lobbying organizations including the American Shipbuilding Association (ASA) to remind the public of their view of the benefits of preserving existing firms (and their facilities). All this suggests that smaller firms like Austal, Bollinger, and Marinette Marine will generally participate in the production of transformational naval ships as partners with larger shipyards or platform integrators rather than as prime contractors themselves. The teams that are currently working on the LCS program probably represent the wave of the future for naval shipbuilding.

Unmanned Aerial Vehicles

The vision of network-centric warfare relies heavily on UAVs both as nodes (e.g., as carriers of various sensors and, increasingly, weapons) and as communications relays to link various components together into the Global Information Grid. The performance metrics that will establish what constitutes a successful UAV and which firms will best be able to produce such craft are still emerging: many experts still struggle to articulate what distinguishes UAVs from other possible ways of accomplishing military missions.

There seems little reason to believe that new firms will suddenly develop disruptive technologies for UAVs. A relatively large number of firms are developing and producing UAVs today, and even more have produced UAV prototypes and demonstrators in the recent past. The firms on the list include some of the largest of the established defense prime contractors like Boeing and Northrop Grumman. Other firms that currently produce UAVs, like General Atomics and AAI, are working hard to build a trusted relationship with their customers and to augment their political influence in Congress. Startup firms, by contrast, mostly hope to succeed through joint ventures with or outright acquisition by these established companies. Most of the smaller UAV entrepreneurs know that they do not understand the military very well, and few UAV-technology enthusiasts are inclined to learn the military culture and the federal acquisition regulations.

Yet the possibility of disruptive innovation remains, because the performance metrics for UAVs are not well established or well understood. In theory, over time new standards might emerge that will undermine the existing positions of today's market leaders. Moreover, some of today's

UAV manufacturers have had rocky relations with their customers. The current generation of UAVs, specifically including the Global Hawk and the Predator, has proven more expensive and harder to operate than some advocates expected. On the other hand, the military's initial operational experiences with UAVs in Afghanistan and Iraq have reinforced the visionaries' view that UAVs will be a vital component of network-centric warfare. In short, the military has finally bought a first generation of UAVs in large enough numbers to establish a set of meaningful customer–supplier relations. But the relationships between the military buyers and suppliers like Northrop Grumman and General Atomics are not yet firmly entrenched.

Unlike shipyards, which employ thousands of workers in a small number of highly visible locations, small UAV manufacturing plants cannot capture the full attention of Congress by themselves. A few Congressional leaders such as Senator John Warner (R-VA) have paid attention because they believe in the operational possibilities of UAVs, not because contracts bring home pork to demanding constituencies. But successful UAVs presented as components of the network-centric system of systems could attract powerful political support from defense industry prime contractors. The key hurdle on which military innovation in the UAV sector depends is building the relationships among technology entrepreneurs, prime contractors, and the military-acquisition organizations.

COMMUNICATIONS

Communications have always been critical to military operations. Electronic communications emerged with the use of the telegraph in the mid-nineteenth century, the first wireless signals in World War 1, and widely deployed radio and radar during the interwar years. Network-centric operations will increase the volume of communications required for both ordinary operations and high-intensity combat. In addition, combat support operations demand bandwidth as well—for everything from traditional logistics management to telephones and Internet access that link deployed soldiers to their families back in the United States, helping to preserve morale.

Most if not all of the standard measures of success for military communications will remain important as transformation proceeds. NCW demands vigorous investment and technological progress on familiar performance metrics like throughput, latency, interoperability, quality of service, and network security. At the same time, it introduces no new performance metrics, with the possible exception of dynamic access that will allow nodes to gracefully enter and exit tactical networks in real time. With this array of technological demand, the large and diverse military communications sector will remain as before for the most part.

The biggest change to the communications landscape is the new level of investment that NCW advocates propose. Communications' higher profile will attract interest from a stronger political coalition. Meanwhile, the technical complexity of the military networking project suggests a way for many suppliers to cooperate on both technical and political action. Private consortia that have been created to set standards for the military network are also perfect forums for allocating tasks and coordinating lobbying strategies. The government's low profile in the current effort to set technical standards for network-centric communications interoperability reduces the opportunity for Congressional oversight and may actually help the military's transformation advocates to build political support for their expensive military innovation project.

SYSTEMS INTEGRATION

For network-centric warfare, system-of-systems integration—rather than simple development of platforms and even networks per se—must be a high priority. Before the defense industry can design and build nodes and networks, the systems' requirements need to be defined: what does each node need to accomplish on its own, and what functionality should be distributed through the network? Systems integrators analyze alternatives, make necessary tradeoffs between cost and performance, and sequence decisions so that early architectural choices do not limit the future expansion and adaptation of the system of systems.

Responsibility for integration and the requisite financial support is not easy to find on the organization charts of the Department of Defense and the military services. Where a tradition of systems integration does survive, buried deep in laboratories far from the top of the command hierarchy, its definition has generally become skewed toward relatively simple performance testing. In-house capabilities for full-scale system-of-systems integration have been weakened by years of cutbacks and retirements. Even more disheartening, systems integration, especially at the system-of-systems level, is poorly understood. Some immediately equate systems integration with interoperability, which is as much a performance metric for communications systems as it is a goal of the overall architecture design for network-centric warfare. Nearly all program officers recognize the importance of connecting their particular systems to the whole, ensuring interoperability, but few program managers have the resources, technical know-how, authority, and organizational clout to ensure that sound decisions about system-design tradeoffs are made.

There are many obstacles to investing in systems integration. In Congress, systems integration has weak political support, because systems integration projects do not employ as many people as platform programs. Systems integration often also has weak support from industry, because, under traditional business models, industry profits come from production rather than front-end requirements definition, research, and development. Systems integrators may even have an adversarial relationship with platform builders on specific programs, because when they do their job right, systems integrators critique contractor performance, and they sometimes propose tradeoffs that lead to cuts in particular acquisition programs. When a systems integrator is also a part of a vertically integrated firm with multiple divisions, the government should fear that it might not receive optimal systems integration solutions. As an official from one of its competitors put it, "when you ask General Dynamics a question, you may well receive a General Dynamics answer."

Ideally, individual services and the Department of Defense as a whole are both responsible for buying adequate systems integration expertise—certainly if their leaders want to promote a significant, perhaps revolutionary, round of military innovation. However, it is difficult to decide how much funding for systems integrators is enough. A variety of firms and types of firms play roles in systems integration, each of which may be able to contribute some expertise, competing or cooperating with other systems integration organizations. Alternatively, leaders of the transformation initiative may prefer to create a new organization to harness expertise in system-of-systems integration for network-centric warfare. Regardless of the specific format, the system-of-systems integrators must be involved in a wide range of acquisition programs—from ships to UAVs—to make and enforce key decisions regarding architecture, tradeoffs, and interface standards.

SUMMARY

In sum, to understand the implications of transformation for entire defense industry, the analysis must begin with a firm grasp of what capabilities underpin network-centric warfare. Only then can insights about whether those capabilities require sustaining or disruptive innovations help to predict the impact of transformation on particular sectors of the defense industry. In the aggregate, our analysis of several of the key capabilities associated with network-centric warfare suggests that there will be much less change in the defense industrial base than has often been assumed.

THE THEORY OF MILITARY INNOVATION

The previous literature on military innovation has been largely concerned with the sources and motivations for military innovation. More to the point, most of it has dealt with doctrinal innovation rather than the technological innovation needed to implement new strategies and doctrines. We fill a gap in the national security literature by proposing a theory of military-technological innovation.

Turning the spotlight on technology and equipment does not mean we discount the importance of doctrinal changes or that we hope to resuscitate technologically determinist theories of military power. In fact, we specifically argue against the technological determinism implied by popular theories of revolutions in military affairs, which hold that major socio-economic transitions such as the beginning of the commercial "Information Age" necessarily cause revolutionary changes in military power. Our theory explains why military leaders' doctrinal visions must drive any potential Revolutions in Military Affairs. The defense economy (the defense industrial base) is separate from the commercial economy; it has its own, trusted channels for customer–supplier relationships that cannot readily be replaced by new ties to commercial suppliers; and the fundamental influence of politics on military investment decisions—in place of the purely financial calculations that drive the investment decisions of commercial buyers—draws sharp distinctions between the motivations for revolutionary change in the military and the commercial economy.

In a nutshell, our theory shows how new ideas about how the military will fight are translated into technical requirements and, ultimately, materiel produced by the defense industry. The need to buy equipment to implement new doctrine imposes political, economic, and technical

constraints on the military, determines which types of doctrinal innovation will be easier or more difficult to implement, and implies that
certain implementation strategies used by policy entrepreneurs will be
more successful than others.

In a mixed economy with severe ideological constraints on public
ownership (such as the United States), the production of military equipment is left largely to the private sector, although it is overseen by a
large, complicated bureaucracy backed by innumerable rules and regulations. At a minimum, private defense firms must be willing partners with
DoD and the military services in the quest for new systems. More than
that, the military relies on the political support of the defense industry
to help convince Congress to invest in military innovation.

Although Congress is generally sympathetic to new technologies,
members are even more sensitive to employment levels and federal
expenditures in key districts. Congressional politics and the military's
comfort level with traditional defense contractors favor maintaining
their longstanding relationships that are based on a powerful confluence
of money and electoral politics. If the transition to NCW threatens
established sectors of the defense industrial base, Congress will make it
politically difficult to move forward with the new programs necessary to
achieve a network-centric future.

Framing military innovation as a challenge to entrenched interest
groups can also make it more difficult for the government to find expert,
reliable advice about technical choices: technical advisory organizations by
themselves are politically weak, and they need the help of more-powerful
manufacturers in order to gain voice in the political process. Those manufacturers, therefore, cannot be defined as adversaries of innovation. Given
appropriate incentives, the defense industry can support transformation,
which can be implemented with sustaining innovations and joint ventures
that combine startups' disruptive innovations with established firms' customer understanding. The best way to implement military innovation is to
avoid promising to bankrupt longstanding suppliers of military equipment.

TRANSFORMING THE AMERICAN MILITARY

Today, network-centric warfare is part of the daily national-security dis-
course in the military, Congress, and even in the occasional newspaper
or magazine article. Even as the demands of the wars in Afghanistan and
Iraq and the global war on terror have forced the Defense Department

and the military services to concentrate on operational demands and military readiness, the transformation process has continued. After some early hesitation—Congress imposed a statutory requirement in 2001 that the military provide a clear working definition of network-centric warfare—the military and Congress have increasingly accepted the concepts. But getting the terminology right is not enough.

For transformation to succeed in the long run, military leaders must persuade Congress to invest enough in so-called transformation programs. This focus is especially difficult in wartime, because the time and attention of the acquisition community is dedicated to getting the troops the supplies and equipment necessary to fight: munitions, repairs and maintenance, effective armor for HumVees and other vehicles, increased pay for combatants, and so forth. But only a commitment from the leadership will enable the acquisition community to find time and personnel resources for transformation. Ideally, the DoD and the Services will deconflict the needs of the current force from the needs of the transformed military.[9]

Military innovation also requires setting reasonable goals for technology development, protecting investment from both overoptimistic technological entrepreneurs and from short-term pressures to transition technology into the current force. Some senior decision-makers may seek to attain the technological promise of the RMA prematurely—making it impossible to maintain interface control and system-wide documentation and diverting resources from planning for an optimal NCW system. On the other hand, entrepreneurs are too willing to rely on future benefits of innovation, promising dramatic reductions in program costs that may never be achieved. Overselling may threaten established but not-yet-in-production programs when test failures or developmental delays cost the taxpayers money and the services time. Already the rush to deploy Predators and Global Hawks, first to Afghanistan and then to Iraq, before they had even completed operational tests and evaluation has proved to be a double-edged sword: while both platforms demonstrated their usefulness, they also were plagued by failures that have led some to question the future of UAVs more generally.

Program difficulties that lead to program cancellations or sharply decreased funding may breed resistance to innovation among business leaders. After all, the abrupt cancellation of the Seawolf submarine cost General Dynamics' Electric Boat a lot of money. Virtually the entire range of Navy contractors felt betrayed by the Navy's management and ultimate cancellation of the Arsenal Ship program. Today some grumble about the fate of another stillborn surface combatant program, DD-21, even though the official line is that the DD(X) family of ships will incorporate much of the work done on the DD-21 project. Several industry executives we met with argued that the Navy has botched its UAV programs by failing to move from prototypes to production, by demanding unreasonable performance from immature technologies, and by authorizing studies rather than buying real prototypes. Abrupt decisions—what might sometimes even be viewed from contractors' perspectives as imperious management of the business–government relationship by the civilian and military leadership in the Department of Defense—can undermine the sense of partnership between the military and the defense industry.

But public–private partnership is essential to set the requirements for the development of the right kinds of new technologies and to convince Congress to invest in military innovation, with its technological and political uncertainty. Congress has generally supported the idea of transformation, because new technology is generally politically popular in the United States. But many transformational programs like the Littoral Combat Ship and the Joint Tactical Radio System have faced close scrutiny during the Congressional authorization and appropriations processes. The programs have to overcome difficult technical problems and competition for resources from the plethora of existing programs that come complete with vocal service, industry, and public constituencies. Even the budget increase after September 11 has not relieved pressure to divert resources from investment for the future into current consumption by operational forces. In this uncertain budgetary environment, political, organizational, and bureaucratic strategies matter.

Decisions about military innovation should not be ceded to any one group, because military commanders, politicians, salesmen, and scientists and engineers each have their own blinders that would skew program priorities if they were not balanced by the influence of the other groups. Military acquisition is fraught with political, economic, and technological pitfalls, any one of which can block the implementation of a new doctrinal vision. To understand how militaries change, how socioeconomic changes and new technologies affect real military power, and how military innovations come to fruition, we need a theory of military innovation that addresses politics, economics, and technology. This book has provided just such a theory.

PREFACE

1. U.S. Office of Force Transformation, *Elements of Defense Transformation*, no date, http://www.oft.osd.mil, accessed June 6, 2005.
2. U.S. Office of Force Transformation, *The Implementation of Network-Centric Warfare*, no date, p. 6, http://www.oft.osd.mil, accessed June 6, 2005.
3. *Implementation of Network-Centric Warfare*, p. 3.
4. *Implementation of Network-Centric Warfare*, pp. 4–5.
5. In addition to Vice Admiral Cebrowski and others in uniform, civilian Department of Defense leadership think along these lines. See, for example, Office of the Under Secretary of Defense (Industrial Policy), *Transforming the Defense Industrial Base: A Roadmap* (February 2003), http://www.acq.osd.mil/ip/docs/transforming_the_defense_ind_base-report_only.pdf. Some nongovernmental analysts agree. See James R. Schlesinger and Murray Weidenbaum, *Defense Restructuring and the Future of the U.S. Defense Industrial Base: A Report of the CSIS Senior Policy Panel on the U.S. Defense Industrial Base* (Washington, D.C.: Center for Strategic and International Studies, March, 1998), http://www.csis.org/polmil/dibreport.html.
6. Tim Weiner, "Pentagon Envisioning a Costly Internet for War," *New York Times*, November 13, 2004.

1. Buying Transformation

1. Arthur K. Cebrowski and John J. Garstka, "Network-Centric Warfare: Its Origin and its Future," U.S. Naval Institute *Proceedings*, January 1998, pp. 28–35.
2. Republicans and Democrats dispute which specific variant of the broad military strategy of primacy the United States should adopt, but they seem to have reached a new political consensus in favor of maintaining and exploiting American hegemony. Barry Posen, "Command of the Commons: The Military Foundation of U.S. Hegemony," *International Security* 28, no. 1 (Summer 2003): 5–6.
3. For prominent, early examples of thinking about revolutions in military affairs, see Andrew F. Krepinevich, "Cavalry to Computer: The Pattern of Military Revolutions," *The National Interest*, no. 37 (Fall 1994): 30–43; Martin van Creveld, *The Transformation of War* (New York: Free Press, 1991), esp. chapter 7 and the postscript.
4. James Q. Wilson, "Innovation in Organization: Notes Toward a Theory," in James D. Thompson, ed., *Organizational Design and Research: Approaches to Organizational Design* (Pittsburgh: University of Pittsburgh Press, 1966), p. 198.
5. Office of the Under Secretary of Defense (Industrial Policy), *Transforming the Defense Industrial Base: A Roadmap* (February 2003), http://www.acq.osd.mil/ip/docs/transforming_the_defense_ind_base-report_only.pdf.
6. A recent overview of thinking about future of war can be found in the set of papers written for the National Intelligence Council's 2020 Project workshop on the "Changing Nature of Warfare" in Washington, DC, 25 May 2004. The papers are available at http://www.cia.gov/nic/NIC_2020_2004_05_25_intro.html.
7. Mary Kaldor, *New and Old Wars: Organized Violence in a Global Era* (Stanford: Stanford University Press, 1999).
8. Robert D. Kaplan, *The Coming Anarchy: Shattering the Dreams of the Post-Cold War* (New York: Random House, 2000).
9. Michael T. Klare, *Resource Wars: The New Landscape of Global Conflict* (New York: Metropolitan Books, 2001), chapter 5.
10. Jeremy Shapiro, "Information and War: Is It a Revolution?" in Zalmay M. Khalilzad and John P. White, eds., *Strategic Appraisal: The Changing Role of Information Warfare* (Santa Monica: RAND Corp., 1999) pp. 113–53; Robert Tomes and Peter Dombrowski, "Arguments for a Renewed RMA Debate," *National Security Studies Quarterly* 7, no. 3 (Summer 2001): 109–22; Stephen Biddle, "The Past as Prologue: Assessing Theories of Future Warfare," *Security Studies* 8, no. 1 (Autumn 1998): 1–74.
11. Geoffrey L. Herrera, "Inventing the Railroad & Rifle Revolution: Information, Military Innovation and the Rise of Germany," *Journal of Strategic Studies* 27, no. 2 (June 2004): 243–71.

12. Manuel Castells, *The Information Age: Economy, Society, and Culture*, vols. 1–3 (Malden, MA: Blackwells Publishers, 2000); Bruce Abramson, *Digital Phoenix: Why the Information Economy Collapsed and How It Will Rise Again*, (Cambridge: MIT Press, 2005); James N. Rosenau, *Turbulence in World Politics* (Princeton: Princeton University Press, 1990).

13. James R. Markusen, "The Boundaries of Multinational Enterprises and the Theory of International Trade," *Journal of Economic Perspectives* 9, no. 2 (Spring 1995): 169–89; Michael Lewis, *The New New Thing: A Silicon Valley Story* (New York: Norton, 1999).

14. Everett Ehrlich, "Virtual Political Reality," *Washington Post Weekly Edition*, December 22, 2003–January 4, 2004, p. 22.

15. Kevin Kelly, *New Rules for the New Economy: 10 Radical Strategies for a Connected World* (New York: Penguin Books, 1999).

16. Kenneth Flamm, *Creating the Computer: Government, Industry, and High Technology* (Washington: Brookings Institution, 1988), p. 208; Kenneth Flamm, *Targeting the Computer: Government Support and International Competition* (Washington: Brookings Institution, 1987), pp. 88, 125.

17. Emily O. Goldman, "International Competition and Military Effectiveness," Paper presented at the Annual Meeting of the International Studies Association, Montreal, Canada, March 19, 2004.

18. William H. McNeill, *The Pursuit of Power: Technology, Armed Force, and Society since A.D. 1000* (Chicago: The University of Chicago Press, 1982), esp. chapters 6, 7, and 8 on the Industrial Revolution. Other historical accounts emphasize that causality often runs in the opposite direction, too: military revolutions can profoundly shape society. Geoffrey Parker, *The Military Revolution: Military Innovation and the Rise of the West, 1500–1800* (New York: Cambridge University Press, 1996); MacGregor Knox and Williamson Murray, eds., *The Dynamics of Military Revolution, 1300–2050* (New York: Cambridge University Press, 2001).

19. Alvin and Heidi Toffler, *War and Anti-War: Survival at the Dawn of the 21st Century* (Boston: Little, Brown, 1993), p. 32.

20. Paul K. Davis, "Uncertainty-Sensitive Planning," in Stuart Johnson, Martin Libicki, and Gregory F. Treverton, eds., *New Challenges, New Tools for Defense Decisionmaking*, MR-1576-RC (Santa Monica: RAND Corporation, 2003): 131–55.

21. Hans Binnendijk, "Introduction," in Hans Binnendijk, ed., *Transforming America's Military* (Washington: National Defense University Press, 2002), p. xvii.

22. Robert Tomes, *US Military Innovation and Strategy after Vietnam: The 'New American Way of War' 1973-2003* (London: Routledge, 2006). Barry Posen has described the emergence of a new American military format that he named TEST: Total Exploitation of Science and Technology. He also dates the American shift from a mass mobilization / heavy force format to the first stirrings of the network-centric force format to the military's response to the aftermath of the Vietnam War and the difficult experience of Israeli

armor in the 1973 war. For the early decisions, see Paul Herbert, "Deciding What Has to Be Done: General William E. DePuy and the 1976 Edition of FM 100–5, Operations," *Leavenworth Papers*, no. 16 (1988).

23. Kevin Kelly, *New Rules*.

24. Cebrowski and Garstka, "Network-Centric Warfare: Its Origin and Its Future."

25. Joint Vision 2020 is available at www.dtic.mil/jv2020/.

26. For the Army's vision statement, see http://www.army.mil/armyvision. For useful overviews, see Edward F. Bruner, *Army Transformation and Modernization: Overview and Issues for Congress*, RS20787 (Washington: Congressional Research Service, Library of Congress, April 4, 2001); and Bruce R. Nardulli and Thomas L. McNaugher, "The Army: Toward the Objective Force," in Binnendijk, ed., *Transforming America's Military*, pp. 101–28.

27. The U.S. Air Force's *Vision 2020* can be found at http://www.af.mil/vision/. The quotation is from *The Aerospace Force: Defending America in the 21st Century*, p. iii, http://www.af.mil/lib/taf.pdf. For overviews of Air Force transformation issues, see Christopher Bolkom, *Air Force Transformation and Modernization: Overview and Issues for Congress*, RS20787 (Washington: Congressional Research Service, Library of Congress, June 1, 2001); David Ochmanek, "The Air Force: The Next Round," in Binnendijk, ed., *Transforming America's Military*, pp. 159–90.

28. Andrew L. Ross and Peter J. Dombrowski, "Transforming the Navy: Punching a Featherbed," *Naval War College Review* 56, no. 3 (Summer 2003).

29. That NCW is no longer merely a service vision was illustrated early on by the Department of Defense report to Congress on NCW: Department of Defense, *Network Centric Warfare* (Washington: Department of Defense, July 27, 2001), http://www.c3i.osd.mil/NCW/. See also Hunter Keeter, "Cebrowski: Joint Philosophy Fosters Network Centric Warfare," *Defense Daily*, April 12, 2002, p. 8.

30. Clay Wilson, *Network Centric Warfare: Background and Oversight Issues for Congress* RL32411 (Washington: Congressional Research Service, June 2, 2004), p. CRS 1.

31. U.S. Office of Force Transformation, *The Implementation of Network-Centric Warfare*, no date, http://www.oft.osd.mil, accessed June 6, 2005; Navy Warfare Development Command [hereafter NWDC], *Network Centric Operations: A Capstone Concept for Naval Operations in the Information Age* (Newport, R.I., draft dated June 19, 2001), p. 1. The growing literature on NCW includes David S. Alberts, John J. Garstka, and Frederick P. Stein, *Network Centric Warfare: Developing and Leveraging Information Superiority*, 2nd ed. (Washington: C4ISR Cooperative Research Program, 1999); Cebrowski and Garstka, "Network-Centric Warfare: Its Origin and Future;" Committee on Network-Centric Naval Forces, Naval Studies Board, *Network-Centric Naval Forces: A Transition Strategy for Enhancing Operational Capabilities* (Washington: National Academy Press, 2000); William D. O'Neil, "The Naval Services: Network-Centric Warfare," in Binnendijk, ed., *Transform-*

ing America's Military, pp. 129–58; and Edward P. Smith, "Network-Centric Warfare: What's the Point?" *Naval War College Review* 54, no. 1 (Winter 2001): 59–75.

32. Sea-based forces generally translate to rapidly deployable or "expeditionary" forces when taken out of the Navy context, and the other services openly rely on the Navy's proposed Sea Basing plans (part of the Navy's Sea Power 21 initiative) to support their own plans for network-centric warfare.

33. Robert Holzer, "Massive Sensor Grid May Reshape U.S. Navy Tactics," *Defense News*, May 14, 2001, pp. 1, 4.

34. Scott C. Truver, "Tomorrow's U.S. Fleet," U.S. Naval Institute *Proceedings*, March 2001, p. 103.

35. William A. Owens with Ed Offley, *Lifting the Fog of War* (New York: Farrar, Straus and Giroux, 2000).

36. NWDC, "Network Centric Operations," p. 9.

37. Kenneth Pollack, *Arabs at War: Military Effectiveness, 1948–1991* (Lincoln: University of Nebraska Press, 2002): 557–61, 575–78.

38. NWDC, "Network Centric Operations," p. 11.

39. http://www.nwdc.navy.mil/Concepts/AA.asp; NWDC, "Network Centric Operations," p. 10.

40. NWDC, "Network Centric Operations," pp. 4–5.

41. Ronald O'Rourke, "Defense Transformation: Background and Oversight Issues for Congress," *CRS Report for Congress*, Updated April 4, 2005, p. 4.

42. There are, of course, other theories of military innovation. For a cultural interpretation, see Elizabeth Kier, *Imagining War: French and British Military Doctrine Between the Wars* (Princeton: Princeton University Press, 1997). Matthew Evangelista argues that technology push from scientists determines investment and doctrinal innovation in his *Innovation and the Arms Race: How the United States and the Soviet Union Develop New Military Technologies* (Ithaca: Cornell University Press, 1988).

43. Barry R. Posen, *The Sources of Military Doctrine: France, Britain, and Germany Between the Wars* (Ithaca, N.Y.: Cornell University Press, 1984). According to Posen, failure of the civilians to intervene often leads to political-military disintegration, with potentially disastrous consequences in times of crisis or war.

44. Peter J. Boyer, "A Different War," *New Yorker*, July 1, 2002, pp. 54–67; Frank Hoffman, "Goldwater-Nichols After a Decade," in Willamson Murray, ed., *The Emerging Strategic Environment: Challenges of the Twenty-first Century* (Westport, CT: Praeger, 1999): 156–82; Sharon Weiner, "The Politics of Resource Allocation in the Post–Cold War Pentagon," *Security Studies* 5, no. 4 (Summer 1996): 125–42.

45. Harvey M. Sapolsky and Eugene Gholz, "The Defense Industry's New Cycle," *Regulation* 24, no. 3 (Winter 2001–2002): 44–49.

46. Stephen Peter Rosen, *Winning the Next War: Innovation and the Modern Military* (Ithaca: Cornell University Press, 1991).

47. Karen Walker, "Joint Forces Command to Shape C2 Programs," *Defense News*, April 11, 2005, p. 1.

48. Christopher P. Cavas, "U.S. Navy Picks Two LCS Teams," *Defense News*, May 31, 2004, p. 1.

49. Hunter Keeter, "NAVSEA Makes 'Fundamental Changes,' Effective Nov. 1," *Defense Daily*, October 29, 2003.

50. Owen R. Coté Jr., *The Politics of Innovative Military Doctrine: The U.S. Navy and Fleet Ballistic Missiles* (Ph.D. diss., Massachusetts Institute of Technology, 1995).

51. In practice some of the "open" debate may be open only within the classified community. "Open" in this context means available for critique and improvement by other military communities.

52. Clark A. Murdoch, lead investigator, *Beyond Goldwater-Nichols: Defense Reform for a New Strategic Era*, Phase 1 Report, (Washington: Center for Strategic and International Studies, March 2004), p. 36.

53. Transformation is frequently used to justify the acquisition of new systems, as a quick perusal of the web sites for most military development projects will suggest. See also O'Rourke, "Defense Transformation," pp. 15–16; 37–38.

2. IMPLEMENTING MILITARY INNOVATION

1. U.S. Department of Defense, Office of Force Transformation, *Military Transformation: A Strategic Approach* (Washington: Fall 2003), pp. 8, 14, 26–27.

2. Barry R. Posen, *The Sources of Military Doctrine: France, Britain, and Germany Between the Wars* (Ithaca: Cornell University Press, 1984).

3. Steven Peter Rosen, *Winning the Next War: Innovation and the Modern Military* (Ithaca: Cornell University Press, 1991); Elizabeth Kier, *Imagining War: French and British Military Doctrine Between the Wars* (Princeton: Princeton University Press, 1997); Deborah D. Avant, *Political Institutions and Military Change: Lessons from Peripheral Wars* (Ithaca: Cornell University Press, 1994).

4. Keith J. Costa, "Cebrowski Cites Progress in Work to Transform the Pentagon," *Inside the Pentagon*, August 5, 2004, p. 13; Thomas G. Mahnken and James R. FitzSimmonds, *The Limits of Transformation: Officer Attitudes Toward the Revolution in Military Affairs*, Newport Paper no. 17 (Newport, R.I.: Naval War College Press, 2003).

5. With current communications, command, and control systems, missions with poor central coordination tend to fail. For example, one of the biggest problems in Operation Anaconda, a major battle in eastern Afghanistan in March 2002, was the assumption that current technology was sufficient to provide enough situational awareness and command and control synchronization to allow the battle to be directed by senior generals located off the coast of Oman, more than 1,000 miles from the battlespace. Sean Naylor,

Not a Good Day to Die: The Untold Story of Operation Anaconda (New York: Berkley Publishing Group, 2005), esp. pp. 318–23, 333–38.

6. David Talbot, "How Tech Failed in Iraq," *Technology Review*, November 2004, pp. 36–44.

7. The importance of close public-private relationships to implementing controversial innovations has a long history. See, for example, Kurt Hackemer, *The U.S. Navy and the Origins of the Military-Industrial Complex, 1847–1883* (Annapolis: Naval Institute Press, 2001).

8. Clayton M. Christensen, *The Innovator's Dilemma: When New Technologies Cause Great Firms to Fail* (Boston: Harvard Business School Press, 1997). Our theory of military innovation extends and improves Christensen's general story. His business-oriented theory assumes that an innovative firm's customers are private businesses or consumers. We adapt his distinction between sustaining and disruptive technological changes to the military and government acquisition environment.

9. Eugene Gholz and Harvey M. Sapolsky, "Restructuring the U.S. Defense Industry," *International Security* 24, no. 3 (Winter 1999–2000): 5–51. See also table 6.11 of the Defense Department's budget "Green Book," available at http://www.defenselink.mil/comptroller/defbudget/fy2005.

10. Thomas L. McNaugher, *New Weapons, Old Politics: America's Military Procurement Muddle* (Washington: Brookings Institution, 1989). In those few areas where public organizations continued to dominate defense production—notably, in the design and manufacture of nuclear weapons, which the government kept in-house because of the extreme sensitivity of the task—the military sometimes fell victim to "technology push" from ambitious scientists (who often were as interested in basic physics as they were in responding to real military needs). Matthew Evangelista, *Innovation and the Arms Race: How the United States and the Soviet Union Develop New Military Technologies* (Ithaca: Cornell University Press, 1988). See also Sybil Francis, "Save the Labs?" *Breakthroughs* 4, no. 1 (Spring 1995): 18–22. For network-centric systems, the military buyers do not have to work with those government-owned suppliers; they work with the mainstream of the defense industrial base, so a different dynamic governs the innovation process.

11. Gholz and Sapolsky, "Restructuring the U.S. Defense Industry."

12. Harvey M. Sapolsky, "Science and Politics of Defense Analysis," in Hamilton Cravens, ed., *The Social Sciences Go to Washington: The Politics of Knowledge in the Postmodern Age* (New Brunswick: Rutgers University Press, 2004), pp. 67–77; Michael E. Brown, *Flying Blind: Politics of the U.S. Strategic Bomber Program* (Ithaca, N.Y.: Cornell University Press, 1992); Eugene Gholz, "The Curtiss-Wright Corporation and Cold War-Era Defense Procurement: A Challenge to Military-Industrial Complex Theory," *Journal of Cold War Studies* 2, no. 1 (Winter 2000): 35–75.

13. Gholz and Sapolsky, "Restructuring the Defense Industry."

14. James M. Utterback, *Mastering the Dynamics of Innovation* (Boston: Harvard Business School Press, 1994); Christensen, *The Innovator's Dilemma.*

15. Matthew Evangelista argues that technological push explains the Cold War nuclear arms race: scientists developed new nuclear weapons technologies, and then, like entrepreneurs in commercial businesses, were faced with the need to sell their innovative concepts to the military customer. As Evangelista put it, "a new weapon starts with a technological idea rather than a response to a specific threat or as a means to fulfill a long-standing mission" (p. x). The weapon was later justified to decision-makers and budgeteers using external factors such as threat perceptions. But unlike commercial entrepreneurs, the scientists knew exactly whom they had to convince to buy the weapons, and they developed long-term relationships with the appropriate decision-makers. Evangelista, *Innovation and the Arms Race.*

16. John Sutton, *Sunk Costs and Market Structure: Price Competition, Advertising, and the Evolution of Concentration* (Cambridge: MIT Press, 1991), pp. 7–8, 11.

17. Linda R. Cohen and Roger G. Noll, "Government Support for R&D," in Linda R. Cohen and Roger G. Noll, eds., *The Technology Pork Barrel* (Washington: Brookings Institution, 1991), p. 25.

18. Even in the 1990s and early 2000s, when military acquisition officials began to frequently talk about the return on investment (ROI) that they hoped to earn through funding research and development projects, the buyers could not directly measure *economic* benefits from acquiring military systems. In the defense industry, the officials that control the taxpayers' money being invested in R&D seek strategic and political benefits, and for all their talk about ROI, numbers do not drive their investment decisions.

19. William P. Rogerson, "Economic Incentives and Defense Procurement," *Journal of Economic Perspectives* 8, no. 4 (Autumn 1994): 65–90.

20. Carl H. Builder, *The Masks of War* (Baltimore: Johns Hopkins University Press, 1989), pp. 101–14.

21. Richard P. Hallion, "A Troubling Past: Air Force Fighter Acquisition since 1945," *Airpower Journal* (March 1990): 4–23.

22. Samuel P. Huntington, *The Soldier and the State: The Theory and the Politics of Civil-Military Relations* (Cambridge: Harvard University Press, 1957), pp. 415–21.

23. Harvey M. Sapolsky, Eugene Gholz, and Allen Kaufman, "Security Lessons from the Cold War," *Foreign Affairs* 78, no. 4 (July/August 1999): 77–89.

24. Sharon Weiner, "The Politics of Resource Allocation in the Post–Cold War Pentagon," *Security Studies* 5, no. 4 (Summer 1996): 125–42.

25. Arnold Kanter, *Defense Politics: A Budgetary Perspective* (Chicago: University of Chicago Press, 1979).

26. Thomas P. Hughes, *Rescuing Prometheus: Four Monumental Projects that Changed the Modern World* (New York: Vintage Books, 1998).

27. The debates during the summer of 2005 about two major shipbuilding programs—the Navy's DD(X) destroyer and the Coast Guard's Deepwater system—are good examples of the military's problems convincing Congress to

follow military investment priorities and of the importance of lobbying support and good public-affairs work in defense acquisition. See Christopher
P. Cavas, "Fuzzy Visions Plague Deepwater, DD(X)," *Defense News*, August
22, 2005, p. 1.

28. Gholz and Sapolsky, "Restructuring the U.S. Defense Industry."

29. Gordon Adams, *The Iron Triangle: The Politics of Defense Contracting* (New
York: Council on Economic Priorities, 1981).

30. Alan V. Deardorff and Richard L. Hall, "Explaining the Role of Interest
Groups in United States Trade Policy," University of Michigan School of
Public Policy Discussion Paper no. 415, November 11, 1997; Richard L.
Hall, *Participation in Congress* (New Haven: Yale University Press, 1996);
Kenneth R. Mayer, *The Political Economy of Defense Contracting* (New
Haven: Yale University Press, 1991).

31. Eugene Gholz and Harvey M. Sapolsky, "The Defense Budget's New Cycle,"
Regulation 24, no. 3 (Winter 2001–2): 44–49.

32. Jacques S. Gansler, "The Defense Industry's Role in Military R&D Decision
Making," in Franklin A. Long and Judith Reppy, eds., *The Genesis of New
Weapons: Decision Making for Military R&D* (New York: Pergamon Press,
1980), pp. 45–46.

33. Clayton M. Christensen and Michael E. Raynor, *The Innovator's Solution:
Creating and Sustaining Successful Growth* (Boston: Harvard Business School
Press, 2003), pp. 116–21, 152–53.

34. Author interview with a defense industry representative, July, 2001.

35. Leslie Wayne, "An Office and a Gentleman," *New York Times*, June 19,
2005, sec. 3, p. 1.

36. Admiral William Owens, author of *Lifting the Fog of War* (with Ed Offley), is
an example of a high-ranking officer. For hopeful efforts at less exalted rank,
see Col. Douglas A. MacGregor, *Breaking the Phalanx* (Westport: Praeger
Publishers, 1997), and Capt. Edward Smith Jr., "Network-Centric Warfare:
What's the Point?" *Naval War College Review* 54, no. 1 (Winter 2001). All
of the cited authors consult formally or informally with military doctrine-
writing organizations.

37. For a recent example, a senior Air Force acquisition official apparently
steered contracts to Boeing at the same time that she was negotiating a
lucrative contract for post-government employment with the firm. She was
caught, and in the ensuing scandal, she went to jail. Several Boeing contracts were at least delayed if not cancelled. Dominic Gates, "Boeing Rolls
Out Tanker Despite Air of Scandal," *Seattle Times*, June 17, 2005, p. D1;
R. Jeffrey Smith, "E-mails Detail Air Force Push for Boeing Deal; Pentagon Official Called Proposed Lease of Tankers a 'Bailout,' Study Finds,"
Washington Post, June 7, 2005, p. A1. This case of outright malfeasance is
unusually extreme.

38. Steven Kelman, *Procurement and Public Management: The Fear of Discretion
and the Quality of Government Performance* (Washington: AEI Press, 1990);
Steven L. Schooner, "Fear of Oversight: The Fundamental Failure of Busi-

ness-Like Government," *American University Law Review* 50, no. 3 (2001): 627-723.

39. Ann Markusen, "The Economics of Defence Industry Mergers and Divestitures," *Economic Affairs* 17, no. 4 (December 1997): 28-32; Jacques S. Gansler, *Defense Conversion: Transforming the Arsenal of Democracy* (Cambridge: MIT Press, 1995); John A. Alic, L.M. Branscomb, A.B. Carter, and G.L. Epstein, *Beyond Spinoff: Military and Commercial Technologies in a Changing World* (Boston: Harvard Business School Press, 1992).

40. Robert Perry, "American Styles of Military R&D," in Franklin Long and Judith Reppy, eds., *The Genesis of New Weapons* (New York: Pergamon, 1980).

41. Brown, *Flying Blind*, pp. 23–25, 316–27, 337–42.

42. McNaugher, *New Weapons, Old Politics*, pp. 124–33.

43. Boeing has struggled to repair its relationship to the Air Force in the wake of the Darleen Druyun scandal (see note 35), and Boeing's relationships with other services has suffered, too. Paul L. Francis, Director of Acquisition and Sourcing Management, Testimony Before the Subcommittee on Tactical Air and Land Forces, Committee on Armed Services, House of Representatives, "Defense Acquisitions: The Army's Future Combat Systems' Features, Risks, and Alternatives," GAO-04–635T, April 1, 2004. Similar feelings of betrayal have posed problems in the past, e.g. for Curtiss-Wright and for Grumman. Gholz, "Curtiss-Wright Corporation and Cold War-Era Procurement"; George M. Skurla and William H. Gregory, *Inside the Iron Works: How Grumman's Glory Days Faded* (Annapolis: Naval Institute Press, 2004).

44. Christensen, *The Innovator's Dilemma*, pp. xiv-xvii. For applications of this framework to defense planning, see Capt. Terry C. Pierce, "Jointness Is Killing Naval Innovation," U.S. Naval Institute *Proceedings*, October 2001, pp. 68–71; and Fred E. Saalfeld and John F. Petrik, "Disruptive Technologies: A Concept for Moving Innovative Military Technologies Rapidly to Warfighters," *Armed Forces Journal International* (May 2001): 48–52.

45. Christensen, *The Innovator's Dilemma*, p. xv.

46. This part of Christensen's theory builds on Eric von Hippel, *The Sources of Innovation* (New York: Oxford University Press, 1988).

47. Christensen and Raynor, *The Innovator's Solution*, pp. 103–7, 109–17, 190, 194.

48. Christensen, *The Innovator's Dilemma*, p. 189. Of course, not all new technologies that perform poorly in mainstream markets and find customers in nearby niche markets qualify as disruptive innovations. Some new products never improve their performance enough to dominate the initial mainstream market, in which case they simply qualify as normal innovations in neighboring markets.

49. Harvey M. Sapolsky, "On the Theory of Military Innovation," *Breakthroughs* 9, no. 1 (Spring 2000): 39.

50. This pattern was followed with the widespread introduction of missiles into the military arsenal—a disruptive innovation in the defense industry of

the 1960s. See G. R. Simonson, "Missiles and Creative Destruction in the American Aircraft Industry, 1956–1961," in G. R. Simonson, ed., *The History of the American Aircraft Industry: An Anthology* (Cambridge: MIT Press, 1968), pp. 230, 241.

51. One of his early steps in 2000 was to commission a study by these authors under the leadership of Andrew Ross. The results of this study were published as Peter Dombrowski, Eugene Gholz, and Andrew L. Ross, *Military Transformation and the Defense Industry After Next: The Defense Industrial Implications of Network-centric Warfare*, Newport Paper 18 (Newport: Naval War College Press, 2002).

52. See, for example, James R. Schlesinger and Murray Weidenbaum, *Defense Restructuring and the Future of the U.S. Defense Industrial Base: A Report of the CSIS Senior Policy Panel on The U.S. Defense Industrial Base*, Center for Strategic and International Studies, March, 1998, http://www.csis.org/pol-mil/dibreport.html.

53. Vago Muradian, "Do Big U.S. Programs Stifle Innovation?" *Defense News*, May 10, 2004, p. 1.

54. Office of the Under Secretary of Defense (Industrial Policy), *Transforming the Defense Industrial Base: A Roadmap* (February 2003), http://www.acq.osd.mil/ip/docs/transforming_the_defense_ind_base-report_only.pdf.

55. Office of the Under Secretary of Defense (Industrial Policy), *Annual Industrial Capabilities Report to Congress*, February, 2004, http://www.acq.osd.mil/ip/docs/ind-cap-annual-report-to-congress_2004.pdf.

3. Small Ships

1. John Hattendorf, *The Evolution of the U.S. Navy's Maritime Strategy, 1977–1986* (Newport: Naval War College Press, 2004).

2. David T. Burbach, Marc Devore, Harvey M. Sapolsky, and Stephen Van Evera, "Weighing the U.S. Navy," *Defense Analysis* 17, no. 3 (December 2001): 259–65.

3. Edward Rhodes, " ' . . . From the Sea' and Back Again: Naval Power in the Second American Century," *Naval War College Review* (Spring 1999): 13–54.

4. On the origins of the Streetfighter concept, see Greg Jaffe, "Debate Surrounding Small Ship Poses Fundamental Questions for U.S. Navy," *The Wall Street Journal*, July 11, 2001.

5. Rear Admiral Charles Hamilton, USN, and Rear Admiral Donald Loren, USN, "It's All in the Family," U.S. Naval Institute *Proceedings* 128, no. 8 (August 2002): 68–70.

6. Christopher J. Castelli, "Chief of Naval Operations Backs Idea of Smaller Warships, Carriers," *Inside the Navy*, April 4, 2005.

7. Malina Brown, "Magnus: Navy Should Stop Leasing, Start Building High-Speed Vessels," *Inside the Navy*, April 12, 2004; Jason Ma, "Joint-Service

High-Speed Connector Team Develops Draft CONOPS," *Inside the Navy*, February 2, 2004.

8. For a comprehensive description and analysis of the LCS program, see Robert O. Work, *Naval Transformation and the Littoral Combat Ship: A Report of the Center for Strategic and Budgetary Assessments* (Washington: Center for Strategic and Budgetary Assessments, February 2004).

9. On the DD(X) familial relationship, see http://peoships.crane.navy.mil/lcs/family.htm.

10. Vice Admiral Michael Mullen, USN, Deputy Chief of Naval Operations for Resources, Requirements, and Assessments (N8), as quoted in Hunter Keefer, "Navy Six Months from Refining Industry Roles in LCS Concept," *Defense Daily*, July 18, 2002, p. 6.

11. John T. Bennett, "CNA Report Endorses LCS-Heavy 2020 Fleet, Beefed-up Pacific Presence," *Inside the Navy*, February 14, 2005.

12. Christopher J. Castelli, "Acquisition Chief Promulgates Views on LCS Acquisition Strategy," *Inside the Navy*, August 22, 2005. The U.S. Navy maintains an "LCS Homepage" that tracks the program's status: http://peoships.crane.navy.mil/lcs/default.htm.

13. Christopher P. Cavas, "U.S. Navy Picks Two LCS Teams," *Defense News*, May 31, 2004, p. 1.

14. Many transformation advocates certainly expect changes in the shipbuilding industry. Geoff Fein, "Future Naval Force Will Require Industry to Change, Commander Says," *Defense Daily*, June 8, 2005.

15. Jonathan Rauch, "The New Old Economy: Oil, Computers, and the Reinvention of the Earth," *Atlantic Monthly*, January 2001, pp. 35–49.

16. Author interview with a defense industry representative, November 2000.

17. Christopher P. Cavas, "Northrop's $463 Million Bet," *Defense News*, May 17, 2004, p. 1.

18. For more extended discussions of shipyard ownership consolidation, see Ronald O'Rourke, *Navy Shipbuilding: Recent Shipyard Mergers—Background and Issues for Congress*, RL31400 (Washington: Congressional Research Service, Library of Congress, May 3, 2002).

19. On the overall health of the American shipbuilding industry, especially as it relates to national security, see U.S. Department of Commerce, *National Security Assessment of the U.S. Shipbuilding and Repair Industry* (Washington: U.S. Department of Commerce, Bureau of Export Administration, Office of Strategic Industries and Economic Security, May 2001).

20. Thomas C. Hone, "Force Planning Cycles: The Modern Navy as an Illustrative Case of a Frustrating Trend," *Defense Analysis* 9, no. 1 (April 1993): 31–42.

21. A 2005 study by the Office of Force Transformation put forward a range of potential fleet sizes, including some proposals that called for significant growth in numbers. Bennett, "CNA Report."

22. Lisa Troshinsky, "Navy Won't Get 375 Ships, CBO Analyst Predicts," *Aerospace Daily*, February 5, 2004, p. 1.

23. Christopher P. Cavas, "U.S. Navy Sets 30-Year Plan," *Defense News*, March 28, 2005, p. 1; Sandra I. Erwin, "Heavy Seas Ahead," *Government Executive* 37, no. 12 (July 15, 2005): 68.

24. Harvey M. Sapolsky, "Equipping the Armed Forces," in George Edwards and W. Earl Walker, eds., *National Security and the U.S. Constitution* (Baltimore: Johns Hopkins University Press, 1988), pp. 121–35; Thomas McNaugher, *New Weapons, Old Politics: America's Military Procurement Muddle* (Washington: Brookings Institution, 1989), pp. 45–47, 120, 132–33.

25. This tendency toward complexity may also apply to NCW-friendly platforms including LCS, even though simplicity and affordability are key selling points for transformational systems. The interaction between political and technological uncertainty may be one limit on the ability of NCW advocates to get their vision adopted by the acquisition community.

26. Ronald O'Rourke, *Navy CVNX Aircraft Carrier Program: Background and Issues for Congress*, RS20643 (Washington: Congressional Research Service, Library of Congress, May 23, 2002). Northrop Grumman, which calls itself "an RMA firm," has expressed a preference for modifying Ingalls' Wasp-class amphibious ships rather than developing a new design for the LHA replacement (LHA-R). See Christopher J. Castelli, "Northrop Exec: Repeating Existing LHD Design Is Most Cost Effective," *Inside the Navy* (April 1, 2002), p. 12.

27. For the LCS, see Geoff Fein, "Team Effort Leads Lockheed Martin LCS Design," *Defense Daily*, May 2, 2005.

28. Geoffrey Wood, "The Rise of Unconventional Naval Platforms," *Military Technology*, May 2002, pp. 58–63.

29. James A. King, "Stealth Means Survivability," U.S. Naval Institute *Proceedings* 127, no. 12 (December 2001): pp. 80–83.

30. For an overall assessment of the operational and tactical utility of stealthy vessels see, Congressional Budget Office, *Transforming the Navy's Surface Combatant Force* (Washington: Congressional Budget Office, March 2003), chapter 2.

31. Keeter, "Navy Six Months from Refining Industry Roles in LCS Concept," p. 6.

32. Wayne Hughes, *Fleet Tactics and Coastal Combat*, 2nd edition (Annapolis: Naval Institute Press, 1999).

33. Author interviews with civilian employees of the U.S. Navy, June 2002.

34. Renae Merle, "Navy Plans to Buy Fewer Ships," *Washington Post*, September 7, 2004, p. E01; William Matthews, "U.S. House Passes Cost-Containment Measures," *Defense News*, June 6, 2005, p. 1.

35. Dave Ahearn, "Clark Delivers Stout Defense of Navy Shipbuilding Program," *Navy News Now*, February 10, 2004.

36. Ronald O'Rourke, "Transformation and the Navy's Tough Choices Ahead: What Are the Options for Policy Makers?" *Naval War College Review* 54, no. 1 (Winter 2001): 90–106.

37. Geoff Fein, "Future Naval Force."

38. Jacques S. Gansler, *Affording Defense* (Cambridge: MIT Press, 1991), pp. 141–214.

39. McNaugher, *New Weapons, Old Politics*, pp. 132–33; James H. Lebovic, *Foregone Conclusions: U.S. Acquisition in the Post–Cold War Transition* (Boulder: Westview Press, 1996).

40. Leslie Wayne, "Navy of Tomorrow, Mired in Yesterday's Politics," *New York Times*, April 19, 2005.

41. Eugene Gholz and Harvey M. Sapolsky, "Restructuring the U.S. Defense Industry," *International Security* 24, no. 3 (Winter 1999–2000): 5–51.

42. Author interviews with defense industry representatives, February 2001 and March 2002.

43. General Dynamics' program manager for the LCS at one point actually suggested that later ships in the LCS class might be built at Bath Iron Works. Jason Ma, "Navy, Industry Advertise Maturity and Low Risk of LCS Selections," *Inside the Navy*, May 31, 2004.

44. Lorenzo Cortes, "Appropriations Conferees Fully Fund LCS and DD(X) Procurement Funding for FY '05," *Defense Daily*, July 22, 2004; Lorenzo Cortes, "Navy Official Identifies Potential LCS Seaframe Price, Module Price Not Defined Yet," *Defense Daily*, February 26, 2004. For the $250 million figure, see Cavas, "Navy Picks Two," p. 8.

45. Randy Woods, "Navy Briefing Estimates Littoral Ships Could Cost $542 Million Each," *Inside the Navy*, July 22, 2002, p. 1.

46. Of course, complex communication systems that are particularly robust, redundant, secure, etc.—all traditional military network-performance metrics—may require complex naval architecture to install, especially if stealth remains an important performance metric for ships.

47. Richard A. Stubbing, *The Defense Game* (New York: Harper and Row, 1986).

48. In the LCS context, see Geoff Fein, "Lockheed Martin's LCS Takes Advantage of Existing Technologies," *Defense Daily*, April 29, 2005.

49. David W. Munns, "Navy Opts for Speed, Innovation in LCS Design Winners: Variety in Lockheed, General Dynamics Proposals May Provide Future Tradeoffs," Navy League of the United States website, http://www.navyleague.org/sea_power/jul_04_30.php.

50. Navy leaders have drawn a similar comparison between modularity of small ship designs and mission-specific configuration of aircraft carrier air wings. Lorenzo Cortes, "Admirals Compare LCS Concept to Carrier Air Wings," *Defense Daily*, June 17, 2004.

51. Geoff Fein, "LCS Would Be Revolutionary Change for the Navy, Ship's First Commander Says," *Defense Daily*, July 7, 2005; "Littoral Combat Ship," http://www.globalsecurity.org/military/systems/ship/lcs.htm.

52. Author interview with a defense industry representative, May 2002.

53. Of course, commercial vessels normally operate on a "point-to-point" basis and are not designed or intended to survive when severely damaged.

54. Jason Ma, "As Navy Loses Technical Experts, Role of Contractors Increases," *Inside the Navy*, May 9, 2005.

55. During author interviews with representatives of most of the Big Six, engineers and strategic planners seemed eager to demonstrate how well their current programs fit transformation and NCW requirements. They also asked numerous variants of the "So, what does NCW really mean?" question. In short, they had discovered the importance of the vision and wanted to understand what its adoption would mean for their own businesses. By contrast, smaller and commercial yards demonstrated much less knowledge of transformation. Their executives sometimes merely listened politely to our descriptions of NCW and naval transformation.

56. Harvey M. Sapolsky and Eugene Gholz, "The Defense Industry's New Cycle," *Regulation* 24, no. 3 (Winter 2001–2): 44–49.

57. See, for example, the brochure of the American Shipbuilding Association, "The American Shipbuilding Industry: Seapower" (Washington: ASA, 2004), http://americanshipbuilding.com/asa_brochure.pdf.

58. Malina Brown, "Young Building Case to Persuade Lawmakers to Repeal DD(X), LCS Cuts," *Inside the Navy*, June 21, 2004.

59. Ahearn, "Clark Delivers Stout Defense of Navy Shipbuilding Program."

60. Edward Rhodes, "Do Bureaucratic Politics Matter? Some Disconfirming Findings from the Case of the U.S. Navy," *World Politics* 47, no. 1 (October 1994): 1–41. In the context of current Navy plans and military transformation, see Christopher P. Cavas, "New USN Chief Sets Tight Deadlines for Studies," *Defense News*, August 15, 2005, p. 12; Geoff Fein, "Amid Concern Over Shipbuilding, Navy Facing Backlog of 40 Ships," *Defense Daily*, March 22, 2005.

61. Lorenzo Cortes, "Navy Official Says LCS Number Not Set," *Defense Daily*, June 24, 2004.

62. Ronald O'Rourke, "Navy Littoral Combat Ship (LCS): Background and Issues for Congress," *CRS Report for Congress*, RS21305 (Washington: Congressional Research Service, Library of Congress, June 24, 2005).

63. Allan R. Millett, "Why the Army and the Marine Corps Should Be Friends," *Parameters* 24, no. 4 (Winter 1994–95): 30–40.

64. Malina Brown, "Young Building Case."

65. Washington, D.C., probably has the only public transportation system in the world where billboard advertising touts warships and multi-billion-dollar weapon systems, as if subway riders should call the sponsors to place an order right away. Of course, Washington, D.C., commuters actually do include people who make decisions on buying weapons—they just make the purchases in their official capacity rather than as private citizens. Malina Brown, "In Littoral Ship Contest, Lockheed Seeks Edge with Media Blitz," *Inside the Navy*, May 24, 2004.

66. Jason Ma, "Navy, Industry Advertise Maturity;" Malina Brown, "Lockheed Aims to Rally Support for Littoral Ship on Capitol Hill," *Inside the Navy*, June 7, 2004.

67. Geoff Fein, "Navy Facing Backlog."

68. Ronald O'Rourke, "Navy DD(X), CG(X), and LCS Ship Acquisition

Programs: Oversight Issues and Options for Congress," *CRS Report for Congress*, RL32109 (Washington: Congressional Research Service, Library of Congress, updated June 24, 2005), pp. 79–82.

69. Halter Marine was acquired by Vision Technologies Kinetics, Inc., a subsidiary of Singapore Technologies Engineering, Ltd., from Friede Goldman Halter, Inc., in July 2002. It is now known as VT–Halter Marine Group.

70. Author interview with defense industry representative, February 2001.

71. For discussion in the context of a specific (failed) program that was widely perceived as innovative in many of the senses of network-centric warfare, see Robert S. Leonard, Jeffrey A. Drezner, and Geoffrey Sommer, *The Arsenal Ship: Acquisition Process Experience* (Santa Monica: RAND, 1999).

72. Author interview with defense industry representative, January, 2001.

73. Cavas, "Navy Picks Two," p. 8. However, Lockheed Martin Maritime Systems and Sensors has extensive naval experience as the prime contractor for the Aegis air defense system, and it is also an equal partner with Northrop Grumman in Integrated Coast Guard Systems, the prime contractor for the Coast Guard's massive Deepwater modernization program. For related analysis of the teams, see Ronald O'Rourke, *Navy DD(X) Future Surface Combatant Program: Background and Issues for Congress*, RS21059 (Washington: Congressional Research Service, Library of Congress, May 10, 2002).

4. Unmanned Aerial Vehicles

1. Unmanned vehicles include unmanned ground vehicles (UGVs), unmanned underwater vehicles (UUVs), unmanned surface vehicles (USVs), and unmanned aerial vehicles (UAVs). Unmanned combat aerial vehicles (UCAVs) are a subcategory of UAVs.

2. David B. Glade II, "Unmanned Aerial Vehicles," in William C. Martel, ed., *The Technological Arsenal: Emerging Defense Capabilities* (Washington: Smithsonian Institution Press, 2001), pp. 173–95.

3. George Cahlink, "War of Machines," *Government Executive*, July 15, 2004.

4. Elizabeth Bone and Christopher Bolkcom, *Unmanned Aerial Vehicles: Background and Issues for Congress* (Washington: Congressional Research Service, Library of Congress, April 25, 2003), p. 1.

5. Defense Science Board, *Unmanned Aerial Vehicles and Uninhabited Combat Aerial Vehicles* (Washington: Defense Science Board, February 2004), pp. iii–iv.

6. Jeff Mustin, "Future Employment of Unmanned Aerial Vehicles," *Aerospace Power Journal* 16, no. 2 (Summer 2002): 86–98.

7. General Accounting Office, *Force Structure: Improved Strategic Planning Can Enhance DOD's Unmanned Aerial Vehicles Efforts* GAO-04-342 (Washington: GAO, March 2004), p. 4

8. Timothy Coffey and John A. Montgomery, "The Emergence of Mini UAVs for Military Applications," *Defense Horizons*, no. 22 (December 2002).

9. Vago Muradian, "USAF's New 'Black' Bird: Fast, Stealthy, Long-Endurance UAV Would Fill Satellite Gap," *Defense News*, August 2, 2004, p. 1.

10. The UAVs will also need the communications equipment to broadcast the data they acquire and the guidance and control systems that will allow them to fly, meaning that they will be packed full of sophisticated electronics.

11. Thomas K. Adams, "The Real Military Revolution," *Parameters* 30, no. 3 (Autumn 2000): 54–65.

12. Robert E. Armstrong and Jerry B. Warner, "Biology and the Battlefield," *Defense Horizons*, no. 25 (March 2003). Available at http://www.ndu.edu/inss/DefHor/DH25/DH_25.htm.

13. Russ Mitchell, "The Pilot, Gone. The Market, Huge," *New York Times*, March 31, 2002.

14. Cynthia di Pasquale, "Demo Proves One Pilot Can Simultaneously Fly Four Predator As," *Inside the Air Force*, April 8, 2005; "Boeing's J-UCAS Evade Simulated Targets in Latest Flight," *Defense Daily*, August 11, 2005.

15. National Academy of Sciences, Commission on Physical Sciences, Mathematics, and Applications, *Review of ONR's Uninhabited Combat Air Vehicles Program* (Washington: National Academies Press, 2000).

16. Dan Caterinicchiam, "Defense Dept. Studies Swarming," *Federal Computer Week*, July 29, 2003.

17. Bob Woodward, *Bush at War* (New York: Simon and Schuster, 2002), pp. 160, 163–64.

18. Ed Smith, Jr., "Network-Centric Warfare: What's the Point?" *Naval War College Review* (Winter 2001): 59–75.

19. Rich Tuttle, "C4ISR Speeded Combat in Iraq, Strained Bandwidth, Analysts Say," *Aerospace Daily*, April 30, 2003, p. 6.

20. Norman Friedman, "Maritime War in the 21st Century: The Medium and Small Navy Perspective," unpublished manuscript, 2002; Bone and Bolkcom, "Unmanned Aerial Vehicles," p. 18.

21. General Accounting Office, *Force Structure: Improved Strategic Planning Can Enhance DOD's Unmanned Vehicles Efforts*, GA-04–342 (Washington: General Accounting Office, 2004), p. 12.

22. John Birkler, Giles Smith, Glenn A. Kent, and Robert V. Johnson, *An Acquisition Strategy, Process, and Organization for Innovative Systems* (Santa Monica: RAND, 2000), pp. 8–9.

23. Eric Labs, *Options for Enhancing the Department of Defense's Aerial Vehicles Programs* (Washington: Congressional Budget Office, September 1998), table 1.

24. Thomas P. Erhard, *Unmanned Aerial Vehicles in the United States Armed Services: A Comparative Study of Weapon Innovation* (Ph.D. diss., The Johns Hopkins University, June 2000); Jon J. Rosenwasser, *Governance Structure and Weapon Innovation: The Case of Unmanned Aerial Vehicles* (Ph.D. diss., Tufts University, May 2004).

25. Ryan Aeronautical builds the Global Hawk and has systems development contracts for the Fire Scout and the Pegasus. General Atomics builds the Predator. AAI builds the Shadow.

26. Boeing and AeroVironment each are working on small, "over-the-hill" reconnaissance UAVs, among other projects; prototypes of Boeing's Scan-Eagle and AeroVironment's Dragon Eye have been used on a limited basis in Iraq. Guy Norris, "Dragon Eye UAV to be Improved," *Flight International,* August 24, 2004, p. 19.

27. This judgment is subject to dispute. Some engineers in the UAV business argue that current-generation UAVs represent an evolutionary step—either from manned to unmanned vehicles or from cruise missiles to unmanned vehicles. Under these interpretations, the UAV industry's antecedents lie with the aerospace and missile industries, respectively. Others suggest that antecedents of the UAV business extend all the way back to World War I, when target drones were first built. For our purposes, the most important point is that relatively large-scale production of UAVs did not begin until the late 1980s at the earliest; even then, production was fitful rather than sustained.

28. David A. Fulghum, "Gulfstream Plans UAV: Variants of the G550 Could Carry 10 Tons of Long-Range Sensors and, If Desired, Standoff Munitions," *Aviation Week,* July 14, 2003, pp. 28, 30.

29. Nick Johnson, "Analysts Say Boeing UAV Unit May Signify Change in Military Aerospace," *Aerospace Daily,* November 16, 2001.

30. George C. Wilson, "Pentagon Pushed to Purchase Unmanned Systems," *Government Executive,* December 4, 2001.

31. Frank Tiboni, "Border UAVs Take Off," *Federal Computer Week,* June 28, 2004; "Shadow UAV Passes 10,000 Flight Hours in Support of OIF," *Defense Daily,* September 7, 2004.

32. Data on European and Israeli UAV firms derived from Kenneth Munson, ed., *Jane's Unmanned Aerial Vehicles and Targets,* no. 17 (Coulsdon, Surrey, U.K., and Alexandria, VA: Jane's Information Group, Ltd., December 2001); Kenneth Munson, ed., *Jane's Unmanned Aerial Vehicles and Targets* (Surrey, U.K.: Jane's Information Group, 2005), p. [35].

33. "World Market for UAVs to Double by 2014, Study Says," *Aviation Week's Homeland Security and Defense,* August 11, 2004, p. 9.

34. Author interview with military officer, July 2001.

35. For example, Air Force Firebee drones flew more than 3,400 photoreconnaissance missions in Vietnam. Ed Moser, "US Military Developing Next Generation of Unmanned Air Vehicles (UAVs)," *Robotic Trends,* September 11, 2003.

36. Office of the Secretary of Defense, *Unmanned Aerial Vehicle Transformation Roadmap* (Washington: Department of Defense, April 2001), section 6.1.

37. General Accounting Office, *Force Structure: Improved Strategic Planning Can Enhance DOD's Unmanned Aerial Vehicles Efforts,* GAO-04–342 (Washington: General Accounting Office, March 2004), p. 12. Note, though, that DoD's metrics are not inconsistent with the broader ones discussed in this chapter.

38. David A. Fulgham, "Electronic Attack Targets Elusive Foes," *Aviation Week and Space Technology,* November 7, 2004.

39. "JSTARS provides ground situation information through communication

via secure data links with air force command posts, army mobile ground stations and centres of military analysis far from the point of conflict. JSTARS
provides a picture of the ground situation equivalent to that of the air situation provided by AWACS. JSTARS is capable of determining the direction,
speed and patterns of military activity of ground vehicles and helicopters."
Http://www.airforce-technology.com/projects/jstars/.

40. Mustin, "Future Employment of Unmanned Aerial Vehicles," p. 92; Erhard,
    "Unmanned Aerial Vehicles in the United States," p. 641.

41. Peter La Franchi, "US Study Recommends Self-Protection for UAVs,"
    Flight International, September 7, 2004, p. 24.

42. Antennas are large radar reflectors even when they are not broadcasting,
    and UAVs connected to their ground station by a datalink will constantly
    emit signals that can be intercepted by adversaries and used for tracking.
    UAV designers will of course use various strategies to reduce the probability
    that their transmissions will be intercepted and that their antennas will
    reflect enemy radar signals, but at some level they will be constrained by
    physics.

43. Office of the Secretary of Defense, *Unmanned Aerial Vehicle Roadmap,
    2000–2025*, section 6.3.

44. William M. Arkin, "Unmanned Planes Face Threats from Near and Far," *Los
    Angeles Times*, February 3, 2002; David A. Fulghum, "Unmanned Designs
    Expand Missions and Lower Costs," *Aviation Week and Space Technology*,
    July 29, 2002, p. 28.

45. Office of the Secretary of Defense, *Unmanned Aircraft Systems Roadmap,
    2005–2030* (Washington: Department of Defense, August 2005), p. F-2.
    The roadmap notes that the mishap rate seems to be dropping along the
    same track as followed by early manned aircraft, meaning that with enough
    flight experience, the rate should improve – and catch up to manned air-
    craft, since improvements in the mishap rate are subject to diminishing
    returns, meaning that manned aircraft are now improving far more slowly
    than unmanned aircraft. General Atomics executives claim that the Preda-
    tor is the only UAV that has demonstrated exceptional flight reliability.
    They further claim that the performance of the more advanced Predator B
    will be even better than the historical data on the early Predators suggest.
    Author interview with a defense industry representative, June 2002. Their
    claim is subject to interpretation: in the first months of Operation Enduring
    Freedom in Afghanistan, at least twenty-five Predators "crashed [due] to
    mechanical failure, weather, or operator [error]" or to enemy fire. See Project
    on Government Oversight, "Fighting with Failure Series: Case Studies of
    How the Pentagon Buys Weapons, Predator Unmanned Aerial Vehicle,"
    March 22, 2002, available at http://www.pogo.org/mici/failures/predator.
    htm. For a different take on the numbers lost, see Ron Laurenzo, "Combat
    Losses Account for Most Predators," *Defense Week*, May 28, 2002, p. 2.

46. Robert Wall, "Lock Step," *Aviation Week and Space Technology*, August 9,
    2004, p. 33.

47. Erhard, "Unmanned Aerial Vehicles in the United States Armed Services," p. 640.

48. Sandra I. Erwin, "Should Unmanned Aircraft Be Piloted Only by Fighter Pilots?" *National Defense*, 89, no. 612 (November 2004): 30.

49. James C. Hoffman and Charles Tustin Kamps, "At the Crossroads: Future 'Manning' for Unmanned Aerial Vehicles," *Air & Space Power Journal* 19, no. 1 (Spring 2005): 31–38.

50. Erhard, "Unmanned Aerial Vehicles in the United States Armed Services," p. 642.

51. Erhard, "Unmanned Aerial Vehicles in the United States Armed Services," p. 650.

52. Amy Butler, "Air Force to Propose $750 Million Cut to Global Hawk UAV in POM," *Inside the Air Force*, July 12, 2002, p. 1; Robert Wall, "Costs Spur Drive to Tweak Global Hawk," *Aviation Week and Space Technology*, June 17, 2002, p. 28. The details of how this figure was derived and how accurate it is are less important than the general point—that low-cost, potentially disposable UAVs show signs of becoming more expensive and less disposable.

53. Cahlin, "War of Machines."

54. Clayton M. Christensen and Michael E. Raynor, *The Innovator's Solution: Creating and Sustaining Successful Growth* (Boston: Harvard Business School Press, 2003), pp. 43–46.

55. Glenn W. Goodman Jr., "Manned Unmanned Synergy: US Army's UAV-Related Efforts Gain Momentum," *Armed Forces Journal International* (July 2002): 56–61.

56. Nathan Hodge, "Jumper: The Military Must Reorganize UAV Efforts," *Helicopter News*, May 3, 2005, p. 9.

57. Joshua Kucera, "US Seeks Drone That Can Avoid Collisions," *Jane's Defense Weekly*, August 18, 2004, p. 8.

58. Robert Wall, "Ducts in a Row," *Aviation Week & Space Technology*, August 16, 2004, p. 24.

59. Wall, "Lock Step," p. 33.

60. Lt. Col. Paul Waugh, Deputy Director for the X-47 System, "Challenges and Opportunities," Presentation at the DARPATech 2004 Symposium, March 9–11, 2004, Anaheim, California, http://www.darpa.mil/DARPAtech2004/proceedings.html.

61. For one of the more current iterations of this debate, see Hunter Keeter, "Pilot: EA-18, Not JSF Variant, Makes Stronger Case for EA-6B Replacement," *Defense Daily*, May 6, 2002.

62. Marshall L. Michel, III, *Clashes: Air Combat over North Vietnam 1965–1972* (Annapolis: Naval Institute Press, 1997).

63. Gene I. Rochlin, Todd R. La Porte, and Karlene H. Roberts, "The Self-Designing High-Reliability Organization: Aircraft Carrier Flight Operations at Sea," *Naval War College Review* 40, no. 4 (Autumn 1987): 76–90.

64. John M. Shalikashvili with Bruce Rember, Phil Her, and Thomas Longstreth, "Keeping the Edge in Joint Operations," in Aston B. Carter and

John P. White, eds., *Keeping the Edge: Managing Defense for the Future* (Cambridge: MIT Press, 2001), pp. 30–31.

65. William Matthews, "Triumph of Jointness," *Defense News*, April 14, 2003, p. 1.

66. David Talbot, "How Tech Failed in Iraq," *Technology Review* (November 2004): 40–41.

67. Defense Science Board, *Aerial Vehicles and Uninhabited Combat Aerial Vehicles*, pp. 25–26.

68. Erhard, "Unmanned Aerial Vehicles in the United States Armed Services," pp. 8–9, 53–54, 219.

69. Douglas A. Macgregor, *Breaking the Phalanx* (Westport: Praeger Publishers, 1997).

70. Friedman, "Maritime War"; Wayne Hughes, *Fleet Tactics and Coastal Combat*, 2nd edition (Annapolis: Naval Institute Press, 1999).

71. Jeremy Feiler, "Officials: UAV Lessons Among the Most Vital Gleaned in Iraq War," *Inside The Pentagon*, July 17, 2003, p. 1

72. Gopal Ratnam, "The Battle for UAV Dominance," *Defense News*, August 15, 2005, p. 17.

73. David A. Fulghum, "Predator's Progress: General Atomics Is Eying Production of New Lines of UAVs with Improved Speeds, Ranges and Payload-Carrying Capabilities," *Aviation Week & Space Technology*, March 3, 2003, p. 48

74. Author interview with a defense industry representative, June 2002.

75. Peter La Franchi and Guy Norris, "US Army Kicks Off UAV Contest," *Flight International*, August 10, 2004, p. 20.

76. "U.S. Grounds Hawk Spy Plane," *Washington Post*, July 11, 2002, p. 11.

77. Author interview with a defense industry representative, May 2002; Lisa Troshinsky, "FCS UAV Technology Will Be Ready When Funding Is, Official Says," *Aviation Now*, November 2, 2004. The Navy also renewed its interest in Fire Scout in FY2004 as a possible UAV to use with the Littoral Combat Ship. Jefferson Morris, "RQ-8A Fire Scout," *Aerospace Daily and Defense Report*, June 11, 2004, p. 6.

78. Marc Selinger, "Boeing Unveils New Push for Network-Centric Operations," *Aerospace Daily & Defense Report*, June 30, 2004.

79. Author interview with a defense industry representative, March, 2004. The other major defense prime contractors also have developed extensive computer simulation capabilities to model network-centric warfare, and they have similarly cooperated in military studies to contribute to requirements definition. Author interviews with defense industry representatives, July 2001, and December 2003.

80. Author interview with a defense industry representative, June 2002.

81. Northrop Grumman is also working on small contracts for trade studies and risk-reduction as part of DARPA and service programs. The government did not directly fund Northrop Grumman's direct competitor to the X-45, the Pegasus UAV, until a demonstration contract in 2004. Northrop Grumman's project has been as likely as Boeing's to help identify perfor-

mance metrics, but without government support, it was less likely to build an important customer–supplier relationship. "Boeing Wins Contract for Unmanned Aircraft," *Los Angeles Times*, October 13, 2004.

82. Author interview with a defense industry representative, May, 2002.

83. Nick Jonson, "UAV Market Expected to Total $10.6 Billion over Next Decade," *Aerospace Daily*, October 28, 2003.

84. Erhard, "Unmanned Aerial Vehicles in the United States Armed Services"; Fulgham, "Electronic Attack Targets Elusive Foes."

85. Geoff Fein, "US Will Remain Dominant Force in RDT&E Investment for UAVs Analyst Says," *Helicopter News*, May 3, 2005, p. 1.

86. George Wilson, "A Chairman Pushes Unmanned Warfare," *National Journal*, March 4, 2000.

87. Jefferson Morris, "A Third of Strike Aircraft Should Be UAVs, Weldon Says," *Aerospace Daily*, March 26, 2003.

88. Jospeh C. Anselmo, "Build It and They Will Come," *Aviation Week and Space Technology*, May 30, 2005, p. 50.

89. Erhard, "Unmanned Aerial Vehicles in the United States Armed Services," p. 56, suggests that an established lobbying relationship between UAV manufacturers and Congress will indicate, when it develops, that the UAV industry has "matured."

90. "Launch of Euro UAV Industry Consultation Body," *Uavworld*, August 6, 2004. Basic data on the various UAV associations can be found in Kenneth Munson, ed, *Jane's Unmanned Aerial Vehicles and Targets* (Surrey, U.K.: Jane's Information Group, LTD, 2005), p. 30.

91. Michael A. Dornheim, "Flying Well with Others," *Aviation Week and Space Technology*, August 2, 2004.

92. http://www.unite.aero/unite_custom/about.html, accessed September 28, 2005.

93. The Associated Press "Boeing, Insitu To Build Unmanned Plane," *Seattle Post-Intelligencer* (July 8, 2003).

94. Dominic Gates, "Tiny Plane Guides Troops in Battle," *Seattle Times*, November 13, 2004.

95. Fulghum, "Predator's Progress," p. 48.

96. Jason Ma, "DOD to Release Third Edition of UAV—Now UAS—Roadmap This Summer," *Inside the Navy*, July 18, 2005.

5. COMMUNICATIONS

1. United States Office of the Deputy Undersecretary of Defense (Industrial Policy), *Defense Industrial Base Capabilities Study: Command and Control*, June, 2004, pp. 2–3; Mattias Axelson and E. Anders Eriksson, *Towards an Industry for Network Based Defence? Creating Information Age Defence Systems*, Scientific Report of the Swedish Defence Research Agency, FOI-R-0490-SE, August 2002, p. 17.

2. David Talbot, "How Tech Failed in Iraq," *Technology Review* (November 2004): 36–44; Richard T. Cooper and Peter Pae, "Battle for Military's Future Unresolved," *Los Angeles Times*, April 12, 2003; U.S. General Accounting Office, *Military Operations: Recent Campaigns Benefited from Improved Communications and Technology, but Barriers to Continued Progress Remain*, June 2004.

3. U.S. Government Accountability Office, *Defense Acquisitions: The Global Information Grid and Challenges Facing Its Implementation*, GAO 04–858, July 2004, p. 1.

4. U.S. Government Accountability Office, *Defense Acquisitions: Assessments of Major Weapon Programs*, GAO 04–248, March 2004, p. 80.

5. U.S. GAO, *The Global Information Grid*, p. 26; Michael Brown, *Flying Blind: The Politics of the U.S. Strategic Bomber Program* (Ithaca: Cornell University Press, 1992), pp. 17–27, 337–42.

6. Stephen Trimble, "Joining the Dots," *Flight International*, September 7, 2004, p. 34.

7. "Consortium Forms to Standardize Government Communications," *Government Procurement Report* 2, no. 10 (October 1, 2004).

8. Quoted in Gail Kaufman, "U.S. to Reveal Plan for Data-Sharing Web," *Defense News*, June 14, 2004, p. 38.

9. Beyond actual warfighting, military transformation calls for at least one more type of investment in communications systems: in the interest of improving logistics, business practices, and routine communications among military personnel, the services have launched a series of other initiatives. For example, the U.S. Navy is currently implementing the Navy Marine Corps Internet (NMCI), a communications system that promises to "deliver a single integrated and coherent department-wide network for Navy and Marine Corps shore commands . . . [including] comprehensive, end-to-end information services for data, video and voice communications." http:// www.nmci.navy.mil/Secondary_Areas/FAQs/Index.htm#Q1. This chapter does not discuss this effort, because our focus is on the transformation of the combat forces.

10. Author interviews with FFRDC and defense industry representatives, April and May 2003.

11. This follows a well-established approach in networking theory that is widely taught in universities and is generally accepted within the defense industry. Author interviews with FFRDC and defense industry representatives, April 2003, and March 2004. The International Organization for Standardization (ISO) generalized the seven-layer model for computer networking. Defense Department users often refer to a compressed, four-layer version of the model. See http://en.wikipedia.org/wiki/OSI_model, accessed September 9, 2005.

12. Of course, defenders of the legacy systems point out that in many cases they can be adapted to the new networking style. Author interview with defense industry representative, March 2003. Moreover, legacy systems will remain in the force for many years during a phased transition as the new, network-

centric systems are acquired. Consequently, the new systems' requirements emphasize backward compatibility and provide a network interface for the legacy equipment. Trimble, "Joining the Dots"; Stephen Trimble, "JTRS Plan Takes New Shape as Bandwidth Target Soars," *Aerospace Daily*, March 7, 2003, p. 1.

13. Author interview with defense industry representative, March 2003. The legacy Link 16 system, for example, which is being installed in a wide range of Air Force, Navy, and allied aircraft, cannot send voice and data at the same time, has no video capability, and requires up to thirty-five minutes for a new node to sign on. Stephen Trimble and Graham Warwick, "Waveform Warfare," *Flight International*, September 7, 2004.

14. J.R. Wilson, "Military Communications: Technology Makes the Switch," *Military and Aerospace Electronics* (April 2002).

15. Stephen Trimble, "Pentagon Adds 'Network Router' to List of JTRS Missions," *Aerospace Daily*, April 17, 2003, p. 2.

16. Author interview with defense industry representative, May 2003.

17. Rear Adm. M.G. Mathis, USN, Col. H. Dutchyshyn, USAF, and Capt. Jeffery W. Wilson, USN, "Integrated Architecture Development," SIAP System Engineering Briefing (Rev. 12), March 26, 2003, slide 7. Note that at least the early phases of the SIAP SE project assumed that the underlying data link would be provided by the legacy Link 16, although the SIAP project was designed to be independent of the underlying "data shipping" implementation. The SIAP addresses the higher layers in the communications networking model. Author interview with military officer, April 2003.

18. For example, in the Navy's efforts to improve high-speed air defenses, at one point the Navy had decided to compete the Cooperative Engagement Capability (CEC) system's radio (the Distributed Data System) separately from the data fusion engine and battle management software (the Cooperative Engagement Processor). More recently, that block 2 competition was cancelled. Instead, plans call for incorporating the new round of CEC into the joint Single Integrated Air Picture to offer the "opportunity for greater competition at the component level," according to the Navy's Program Executive Officer for Integrated Warfare Systems. Rich Tuttle, "Move to Joint Battle Management C2 System Affects Navy's CEC," *Aerospace Daily*, January 27, 2004, p. 4.

19. Rich Tuttle, "Beyond BFT," *Aviation Week and Space Technology*, February 23, 2004, p. 84; Charles Dervarics, "Broadening Blue Force Tracking," *Defense News*, October 11, 2004, p. 30.

20. Lorenzo Cortes, "Industry Team Working on Architecture Interoperability of Services' C2 Constellations," *Defense Daily*, February 10, 2004; Lorenzo Cortes, "Navy Ponders 'Composable' FORCEnet Network," *C4I News*, November 27, 2003.

21. For a related review of national security space systems and transformation, see Eugene Gholz, "Military Transformation, Political Economy Pressures,

and the Future of Trans-Atlantic National Security Space Cooperation," *Astropolitics* 1, no. 2 (Fall 2003): 26–49.

22. "Industry Collaborates to Ensure Network Centricity," *Communications Daily*, September 29, 2004.

23. The NCOIC had grown to seventy-nine firms by September, 2005. Most of the industry's big players are included in the list of twenty-five "tier 1" members, who have voting rights at NCOIC meetings.

24. Boeing initially led the effort to organize the consortium. For a description, see Bradley C. Logan, "Technical Reference Model for Network-Centric Operations," *Crosstalk: The Journal of Defense Software Engineering* (August 2003).

25. Some firms, most notably Lockheed Martin, initially resisted the consortium idea, because they did not want to preempt the government's role in requirements definition, and they feared the implications of the consortium for proprietary technologies. Those problems have allegedly been settled now, and the holdouts have joined the project. See Renae Merle, "Contractors Form Standards Group," *Washington Post*, September 28, 2004, p. E5.

26. Mathis et al., "Integrated Architecture Development," slide 46; author interview with military officer, April 2003.

27. For example, a Lockheed Martin-led team that includes Boeing, IBM, L3 Communications, and Raytheon received a $3 million contract to use the Air Force's C2 Enterprise Integration Facility at Hanscom Air Force Base to develop a joint derivative of the Air Force's C2 Constellation for Time-Critical Targeting. Cortes, "Industry Team on Architecture Interoperability."

28. For example, Northrop Grumman Space Technology, a radio maker, is on Lockheed Martin's team competing for the JTRS Airborne and Maritime/ Fixed Station (AMF) Cluster, while its Northrop Grumman parent leads another team (and will be barred from making the radio component of JTRS if it wins the prime contract). Marc Selinger, "JTRS Combined Cluster Expected to Draw Three Competitors," *Aerospace Daily*, February 10, 2004, p. 1. Northrop Grumman Mission Systems also participates on the third team competing for the JTRS-AMF award. Marc Selinger, "Two More Firms Announce Teammates for JTRS Bid," *Aerospace Daily & Defense Report*, April 13, 2004, p. 5.

29. For the sake of efficiency and interoperability, requirements have been grouped into five "clusters" so that "similar requirements can be met with a single acquisition effort." There are currently five clusters, but in the future others may be developed for space, homeland security and other emerging DoD needs. JTRS Program Office, *JTRS Brochure*, http://jtrs.army.mil/documents/jtrs%2Bbrochure.pdf, accessed September 13, 2005.

30. Norman Friedman, "Maritime War in the 21st Century: The Medium and Small Navy Perspective," unpublished manuscript, 2002.

31. Norman Friedman, *Seapower and Space: From the Dawn of the Missile Age to Net-Centric Warfare* (Annapolis: Naval Institute Press, 2000).

32. Megan Scully, "Pocket Radio to Fill JTRS Gap for U.S. Army," *Defense News*, October 4, 2004, p. 13.

33. Alternatively, if every unit gets a complete set of the raw data and then does its own data fusion, there is no need to transmit the COP from a central processing node. The CEC works this way—by transmitting raw track data, or in recent updates to the software, transmitting semi-processed "tracklets" instead of full "tracks." Author interview with defense industry representative, May 2003.
34. Author interview with defense industry representative, April 2003; Friedman, "Maritime War."
35. Author interview with defense industry representative, March 2003.
36. Hunter Keeter, "Bandwidth Tops Short List of Fleets' Technology Priorities," *Defense Daily*, April 17, 2003, p. 9.
37. U.S. GAO, *The Global Information Grid*, p. 12.
38. Friedman, "Maritime War."
39. Author interview with FFRDC representative, April 2003.
40. Charlotte Adams, "Network Centric, Rush to Connect," *Aviation Today*, October 25, 2004; John Stenbit, the Assistant Secretary of Defense for C3I, Presentation at the Fourth Annual Conference on Implementing Network-Centric Warfare, Rosslyn, Virginia, April 7, 2003.
41. Author interview with FFRDC representative, April 2003.
42. The top ten list of technology priorities for the fleet asks for improvements in a number of areas besides bandwidth expansion that are related to data throughput: better antennas, dynamic bandwidth management, and other improvements to network hardware. Keeter, "Bandwidth Tops List."
43. Adams, "Rush to Connect."
44. This system is called structured time-division multiple-access (structured TDMA). Author interview with defense industry representative, March 2003. In one test that used Link 16 to develop a COP, the network's cycle time was twelve seconds; each node was polled to send or receive data so infrequently that the data transmission rate slowed dramatically. Sandra I. Erwin, "Joint 'Air Picture' Fractured by Long-Standing Rivalries," *National Defense*, December 2001.
45. Link 16 suppliers are working hard to mitigate these limitations in data flow—for example, by reallocating time slots on the fly from dormant nodes to nodes that have particularly important messages to send. Lorenzo Cortes, "ViaSat Working on a Variety of Emerging MIDS and Link 16 Solutions," *Defense Daily*, June 8, 2004.
46. John Stenbit, when he was Assistant Secretary of Defense for C3I and then Assistant Secretary of Defense for Networks and Information Integration, frequently distinguished the future network (the GIG, including JTRS) from the old "broadcast" system. Both JTRS and broadcast formats allow users to send data into the network without waiting for an allocated time slot. But JTRS does not force every node to listen whenever one node sends a packet; the packet is routed only to designated recipients. See, for example, Glenn W. Goodman Jr., "Interview with John P. Stenbit, Assistant Secretary of Defense for Networks and Information Integra-

tion," *Intelligence, Surveillance, and Reconnaissance Journal*, March 2004, p. 14.

47. Author interview with defense industry representative, March 2003.

48. Adams, "Rush to Connect."

49. Author interview with FFRDC representative, April 2003. A comparison to Link 16 messages gives a feel for the relative importance of this "header effect." Efforts to add IPv6 packets to the Link 16 library are severely limited, because sending just the IPv6 header almost fills the time slot allocated to a Link 16 terminal each time it gets a chance to broadcast. The result is that each packet includes only a trivial amount of data, and Internet Protocol messages sent over Link 16 take a very long time to send. Author interview with defense industry representative, March 2003.

50. Rockwell Collins has delivered prototype radios to the Navy that use bandwidth-efficient advanced modulation (BEAM) to transfer data five times as fast as conventional radios with the same waveform. "Rockwell Collins Delivers RT-1851 Next-Generation Radio to U.S. Navy," *RF Design*, August 2, 2002. Raytheon and Rockwell Collins each are working to apply similar technology for the Army's Future Combat Systems' communications needs. "DARPA, Army Announce Contracts for FCS Communications," *Aerospace Daily*, May 16, 2001, p. 6. The technology is also being incorporated into JTRS. Adams, "Rush to Connect."

51. Trimble, "Joining the Dots."

52. Loren Thompson, "Stay the Course with Revolutionary JTRS," *Defense News*, June 13, 2005, p. 60.

53. Boeing has announced long-term partnerships with IBM and Cisco for the explicit purpose of bringing their commercial Internet experience into the military environment. "Boeing, Cisco in Alliance for Network Centric Technologies," *Defense Daily*, June 9, 2005. Lockheed Martin has a similar deal with Hewlett Packard. Calvin Biesecker, "Lockheed Martin, HP Partner to Harness Systems Integration, IT Synergies," *C4I News*, November 11, 2004.

54. "DARPA Picks BAE, Raytheon, Rockwell Collins, TRW for FCS," *Defense Daily*, May 16, 2001.

55. Cortes, "Industry Team on Architecture Interoperability"; Trimble and Warwick, "Waveform Warfare."

56. Author interview with FFRDC representative, April 2003.

57. Author interview with defense industry representative, March 2003.

58. Amy Butler, "JTRS Program Seeks Savings, Unlikely to Merge Clusters 3, 4, Sources Say," *Defense Daily*, October 17, 2003.

59. Author interview with FFRDC representative, December 2000. Information for "situational awareness," which can tolerate some degree of latency, is generally good enough to provide the COP, specifically including the Single Integrated Air Picture. High-speed cruise missile defense, on the other hand, requires "fire control-quality tracking," which cannot tolerate latency. The SIAP can be transmitted over a Link 16 or a JTRS network; CEC needs faster transmissions.

60. Jam resistance and low probability of intercept are components of the "quality of service" metric and the "security" metric, respectively. Those metrics are discussed below.

61. Because each node does the same calculations using the same input data, all of the nodes find the same solutions and assign the same track numbers to the various incoming targets. More recent upgrades to the CEC software have reduced to some extent the amount of raw data that must be sent through the DDS, but the CEC system still requires high throughput and low latency. Author interviews with defense industry representatives, April 2003, and May 2003.

62. Author interview with defense industry representative, May 2002; Richard Mullen, "TCN Out to Wheel Past CEC," *Defense Week*, July 29, 2002.

63. Author interview with defense industry representative, April 2003.

64. Author interviews with defense industry representatives, May 2002, and April 2003; Sanda I. Erwin, "Companies Await Guidelines for Next Generation of CEC," *National Defense* (September 2002).

65. Author interview with military officer, April 2003.

66. Warren Citrin, the founder of Solipsys, was the lead engineer on CEC development for twelve of his eighteen years as an APL employee. When APL needed a radio supplier for the DDS, it found a company called ECI in St. Petersburg, Florida, which was later purchased by E Systems. When CEC entered later stages of development, the prime contract was given to E Systems. E Systems was then purchased by Raytheon, which is now building CEC systems for the Navy. Throughout the process, APL served as a "technology direction agent" for the CEC program. In the late 1990s, Citrin and forty-four other APL engineers decided that APL was too locked into CEC to support their idea for TCN, so they started Solipsys. In 2003, Raytheon bought Solipsys. TCN is now owned by a different division of Raytheon from the St. Petersburg operation that makes CEC. Raytheon has promised that the Solipsys team will be free to work with any prime contractor on future acquisition projects for the SIAP. The problems that these incestuous relationships in technology development pose will be considered in chapter 6 on systems integration.

67. Author interviews with defense industry representatives, May 2002, and April 2003.

68. Erwin, "Companies Await Guidelines."

69. CEC advocates also point out that the I-phone connection is not a very robust signal: it can be jammed relatively easily, and it is often disrupted by environmental interference (the weakness of the signal is suggested by commercial Iridium telephones' problems making calls from inside buildings). Author interview with defense industry representative, May 2003. On the other hand, TCN advocates argue that the latency in the I-phone transmission does not prevent them from achieving fire-control-quality tracking, given their software design. Author interview with defense industry representative, April 2003.

70. Clark A. Murdoch, lead investigator, *Beyond Goldwater-Nichols: Defense Reform for a New Strategic Era*, Phase 1 Report (Washington: Center for Strategic and International Studies, March 2004), pp. 14, 20, 47, 49.

71. Marc Selinger, "New Interoperability Rules Nearing Completion at DOD," *Aerospace Daily*, October 16, 2003, p. 3.

72. Victor A. DeMarines with David Lehman and John Quilty, "Exploiting the Internet Revolution," in Aston B. Carter and John P. White, eds., *Keeping the Edge: Managing Defense for the Future* (Cambridge: MIT Press, 2001), pp. 63–64.

73. Michael D. Doubler, *Closing with the Enemy: How GIs Fought the War in Europe, 1944–1945* (Lawrence: University of Kansas Press, 1994), pp. 65–75.

74. For various recent reports of the incident, see Lisa Sandberg, "Grenada: The Little Victory," *San Antonio Express-News*, November 2, 2003, p. 1A; John C. Wohlstetter, "Info-War Invades Iraq," *The American Spectator* (August–September 2003); Bridget Mintz Testa, "Redefining Radio with Software," *Electronic Business*, June 1, 2004, p. 58.

75. James R. Locher III, *Victory on the Potomac: The Goldwater-Nichols Act Unifies the Pentagon* (College Station: Texas A&M University Press, 2002), pp. 135, 219.

76. For similar observations about the technical implications of different operational needs for ground surveillance sensors, see Sanford L. Weiner, "Lessons from JSTARS," *Breakthroughs* 10, no. 1 (Spring 2001).

77. Butler, "JTRS Program Seeks Savings."

78. Author interview with defense industry representative, March 2003.

79. High-speed data links will still need dedicated networks that use gateways to transmit some of their processed data to the main network.

80. Author interview with FFRDC representative, April 2003.

81. Author interview with FFRDC representative, April 2003.

82. Wilson, "Military Communications."

83. John F. Jacobs, *The Sage Air Defense System: A Personal History* (Bedford: MITRE Corporation, 1986); Thomas P. Hughes, *Rescuing Prometheus: Four Monumental Projects that Changed the Modern World* (New York: Vintage Books, 1998).

84. Elizabeth Stanley-Mitchell, "Technology's Double-Edged Sword: The Case of U.S. Army Battlefield Digitization," *Defense Analysis* 17, no. 3 (December 2001): 267–88.

85. Friedman, "Maritime War."

86. Author interview with defense industry representative, May 2003.

87. Author interviews with defense industry representative, March 2002.

88. Amy Butler, "Bids Expected for Air Force, Navy JTRS as OSD Established New JPEO Oversight," *C4I News*, April 1, 2004.

89. Amy Butler, "Although RFP Delayed, DoD Nearing Resolution on JTRS Cost, Management," *Defense Daily*, December 10, 2003. In the summer of 2005, the Army reorganized its acquisition effort for the two JTRS clus-

ters that it controls, moving them up from management by a "program manager" to put them under the umbrella of a "project director" for Land-WarNet. LandWarNet also includes offices for multichannel satellite terminals, extremely high-frequency satellite systems, and the Warfare Information Network-Tactical (WIN-T). The additional centralization again was announced as an opportunity to "optimize cost, schedule and performance," and it again offers higher-level political support and coalition-building potential for the JTRS program. John Liang and Jen DiMascio, "Senior Boeing Official Confident JTRS Program 'Back on Track,' " *Inside the Army*, August 1, 2005.

90. Rich Tuttle, "New Organization to Stress Importance of Network Programs," *Aerospace Daily*, January 30, 2004, p. 5.

91. Murdoch, *Beyond Goldwater-Nichols*, pp. 33, 48–49.

92. For general discussion of cartel cooperation, see Simon J. Evenett, Margaret C. Levenstein, and Valerie Y. Suslow, "International Cartel Enforcement: Lessons from the 1990s," *The World Economy* 24, no. 9 (September 2001): 1221–45.

93. While centralization may help build political support for an agreed-upon vision of military innovation, it may come at the cost of problems managing programs' complexity. For development of this argument in reference to the military space program, see Eugene Gholz, "Czars and Company Men: The Wrong Way to Run National Security Space Acquisition," *Georgetown Journal of International Affairs* 5, no. 2 (Summer/Fall 2004): 11–19.

6. Systems Integration and Public–Private Partnership

1. Harvey M. Sapolsky, "Inventing Systems Integration," in Andrea Prencipe, Andrew Davies, and Michael Hobday, eds., *The Business of Systems Integration* (New York: Oxford University Press, 2003), pp. 15–34.

2. Amy Svitak, "Disjointed First Steps: U.S. Services' Transformation Plans Compete, Don't Cooperate," *Defense News*, August 19–25, 2002, p. 1.

3. Joseph S. Nye, Jr., and Admiral William A. Owens, "America's Information Edge," *Foreign Affairs* 75, no. 2 (March–April 1996): 4.

4. Other prime contractors perform a similar, product-specific kind of system integration for sensor equipment, propulsion equipment, and other major platform components.

5. Jen DiMascio, "DoD Needs to 'Do More with Less' in Coming Years, Acquisition Chief Says," *Inside the Army*, December 6, 2004.

6. Bruce L. R. Smith, *The RAND Corporation: Case Study of a Nonprofit Advisory Corporation* (Cambridge: Harvard University, 1966), pp. 13, 160–62.

7. Scott Tumpak, "Limit Super Primes," *Defense News*, July 15–21, 2002, p. 23; Andrew Chuter, "Honeywell Eyes FCS Systems Integration," *Defense News*, July 29–August 4, 2002, p. 4.

8. Harvey M. Sapolsky, Eugene Gholz, and Allen Kaufman, "Security Lessons from the Cold War," *Foreign Affairs* 78, no. 4 (July–August 1999): 77–89.
9. Author interview with civilian employee of the Navy, June 2002.
10. Hunter Keeter, "NAVSEA Makes 'Fundamental Changes,' Effective Nov. 1," *Defense Daily*, October 29, 2002.
11. James Q. Wilson, *Bureaucracy: What Government Agencies Do and Why They Do It* (New York: Basic Books, 1989), pp. 137–39.
12. For a related discussion of the tensions between operational Navy commanders and research scientists at the Office of Naval Research, see Harvey M. Sapolsky, *Science and the Navy: The History of the Office of Naval Research* (Princeton: Princeton University Press, 1990), pp. 86, 89, 96–98.
13. Author interviews with defense industry representative and FFRDC representatives, December 2000.
14. Author interview with civilian employees of the Navy, June 2002.
15. Of course, in-house military laboratories are not the only organizations that do extensive testing and prototype evaluation as part of system development. Private firms also test and evaluate; they just do not perform the final stage of customer acceptance tests. If in-house scientists are right that testing can help maintain technical skills and reveal important lines of evolutionary research, it might be desirable to sell the major testing facilities—the remnants of the unique intellectual and physical capital inside the military—to the organizations that can act as full system-of-systems integrators. The goal would be to leave the systems commands with enough technical competence to act as "smart buyers" that can react to technical advice and choose among systems integration proposals developed by outside organizations having the full range of facilities and skills at the system-of-systems level.
16. The defense business remains a political one, and it is unrealistic to believe that efficiency will ever be the only or even the paramount goal. Defense contracts impose certain social goals on the defense industry labor force, like cultivating small, minority-owned, or disadvantaged subcontractors.
17. Although this issue was recently highlighted by defense industry leaders' complaints about their firms' stock prices during the late-1990s technology bubble, it is actually a timeworn issue for high-end engineering workers in the defense sector. See, for example, Claude Baum, *The System Builders: The Story of SDC* (Santa Monica: System Development Corporation, 1981), pp. 129–31.
18. Private firms are sometimes accused of undervaluing research-staff continuity in the face of investor pressure for short-term earnings. It is not clear why investors should be expected to make systematic mistakes in valuing research teams; they can simply discount future payoffs of research investment back to a net present value for comparing investments. In the 1990s, as was generally the case, investors tended to overvalue the promise of technological progress in the defense industry (expectations for which were briefly confused with those for the "dot-com" companies). Eugene Gholz,

"Wall Street Lacks Realistic View of Defense Business," *Defense News*, December 20, 1999, p. 31.

19. Each of these sources of systems integration skill was cited in one or more interviews—usually in self-serving ways. Thus, a systems integration organization with close academic ties would emphasize the importance of access to basic scientific research to its work, while an organization with ties to a major defense production organization would emphasize production experience as a key underpinning of systems integration skill.

20. Paul Adams, "Defense Firm Alion Protests Pact's Switch to Rival ITT," *Baltimore Sun*, August 20, 2005.

21. Clayton M. Christensen and Michael E. Raynor, *The Innovator's Solution: Creating and Sustaining Successful Growth* (Boston: Harvard Business School Press, 2003), pp. 127–30.

22. Davis Dyer, *TRW: Pioneering Technology and Innovation since 1900* (Boston: Harvard Business School Press, 1998), pp. 225–39. Also, William L. Baldwin, *The Structure of the Defense Market 1955–1964* (Durham, N.C.: Duke University Press, 1967), pp. 45–46, 138–39. A similar situation led to the creation of MITRE. See John F. Jacobs, *The Sage Air Defense System: A Personal History* (Bedford, Mass.: MITRE Corporation, 1986), pp. 137–41.

23. Bruce L.R. Smith, *The Future of the Not-for-Profit Corporations*, P-3366 (Santa Monica: RAND, May 1966), p. 18. Smith predicted that the FFRDC role would fade as the military improved its in-house technical capabilities. But for the reasons discussed in the text—and because the FFRDCs' success, which Smith underlines in his report, reduced the demand for in-house systems integration capability—the military services never developed sufficient expertise to replace them. For-profit systems integration contractors (e.g., SAIC) have proven to be a bigger threat to the FFRDCs than resurgent government laboratories.

24. Johns Hopkins University Applied Physics Laboratory (APL) is not technically an FFRDC at present (it was until 1977), but it remains a nonprofit systems integration organization with a long-term contractual relationship with the U.S. Navy. Like an FFRDC, APL does not primarily engage in production, and it sometimes acts as the technical-direction agent on major naval systems contracts. For present purposes, APL can be grouped with MITRE and Aerospace as a systems integration FFRDC, although it also has a strong research program, analogous to that of Lincoln Laboratory.

25. U.S. General Accounting Office, *Strategic Defense Initiative Program: Experts' Views on DoD's Organizational Options and Plans for SDI Technical Support*, GAO/NSIAD-87-43 (Washington, D.C.: November 1986), p. 4

26. U.S. General Accounting Office, *Federally Funded R&D Centers: Issues Relating to the Management of DoD-Sponsored Centers*, GAO/NSIAD-96–112 (Washington, D.C.: August 1996), pp. 5–6; U.S. Congress, Office of Technology Assessment [hereafter OTA], *A History of the Department of Defense Federally Funded Research and Development Centers*, OTA-BP-ISS-157 (Washington, D.C.: U.S. Government Printing Office, June 1995), pp.

28–33. SAIC specifically acknowledges the technical skills of FFRDCs and actually tried to purchase Aerospace Corporation in 1996, claiming that it could maintain that organization's skills while its for-profit status would compel it to increase efficiency. Air Force resistance blocked this controversial move. Many scientists at Aerospace were also skeptical of the acquisition and now report that they would have considered leaving the company if the SAIC deal had gone though. See John Mintz, "Air Force Halts Merger of 2 Companies," *Washington Post*, November 16, 1996, p. D1.

27. Some involved in these Congressional decisions believe that the perceived high cost of FFRDCs was the crucial issue in establishing these limits; others see the effects of a lingering controversy over missile defense. The key rejected proposal would have established the Strategic Defense Initiative Institute to support the missile defense effort. In 2004, the Homeland Security Institute was created to support the Department of Homeland Security: the high level of perceived threat of terrorist attacks against the United States overcame Congressional reluctance. Calvin Biesecker, "New Homeland Security Institute Will Take Month to Ramp Up," *Defense Daily*, May 4, 2004.

28. SYNTEK, for example, has benefited by hiring a number of technical experts who worked in military laboratories in the 1960s and 1970s, when the labs had stronger roles in architecture definition. SYNTEK executives fear that their skills will be hard to maintain in future generations of technical staff. Author interviews with defense industry representatives, September 2000.

29. Author interview with defense industry representative, May 2003.

30. The SEI has begun to develop a new Capabilities Maturity Model to evaluate "Integration" skills: at the direction of OSD, they are trying to apply software systems engineering procedures to software–hardware integration. The goal is to develop best-practice methodologies for reducing the rate of failures in complex projects. Even this ongoing broadening of the SEI's research remains at a "lower" level than the overall system of systems integration that is the key, initial step in transformation.

31. Author interview with FFRDC representative, February 2003.

32. In interviews, several respondents noted that the CMM-I project was causing tension between the SEI and MITRE, as both clamored for the attention of key customers at the Air Force Electronic Systems Command at Hanscom Air Force Base.

33. Thomas P. Hughes, *Rescuing Prometheus: Four Monumental Projects That Changed the Modern World* (New York: Vintage Books, 1998).

34. Thomas L. McNaugher, *New Weapons, Old Politics: America's Military Procurement Muddle* (Washington, D.C.: Brookings Institution, 1989), pp. 3–12.

35. Harvey Sapolsky, "Myth and Reality in Project Planning and Control," in Frank Paul Davidson and C. Lawrence Meador, eds., *Macro-engineering and the Future: A Management Perspective* (Boulder, CO: Westview Press, 1982), pp. 173–82. On rare occasions, oversight officials or firms have been

known to falsify reports, but those cases are truly the exception rather than the rule. Robert Wall, "V-22 Support Fades Amid Accidents, Accusations, Probes," *Aviation Week and Space Technology*, January 29, 2001, p. 28.

36. Cindy Williams, "Holding the Line on Infrastructure Spending," in Cindy Williams, ed., *Holding the Line: U.S. Defense Alternatives for the 21st Century* (Cambridge: MIT Press, 2001), pp. 55–77.

37. Sapolsky, "Inventing Systems Integration," pp. 23–28.

38. Keith J. Costa, "Appropriators Approve Funding for Two More Littoral Combat Ships," *Inside the Pentagon*, June 9, 2005.

39. Geoff Fein, "First Mine Warfare Mission Package to be Ready before LCS Delivered," *Defense Daily*, June 30, 2005.

40. Harvey M. Sapolsky, *The Polaris System Development: Bureaucratic and Programmatic Success in Government* (Cambridge: Harvard University Press, 1972).

41. Sapolsky, "Inventing Systems Integration," pp. 20–21.

42. Conflicts among those tasks have been barriers to the successful application of the systems approach outside of the acquisition environment. Stephen P. Rosen, "Systems Analysis and the Quest for Rational Defense," *Public Interest*, no. 76 (Summer 1984): 3–17.

43. Thomas L. McNaugher, "Weapons Procurement: The Futility of Reform," in Michael Mandelbaum, ed., *America's Defense* (New York: Holmes and Meier, 1989), p. 72.

44. Jeffrey Pfeffer, "A Resource Dependence Perspective on Intercorporate Relations," in Mark S. Mizruchi and Michael Schwartz, eds., *Intercorporate Relations: The Structural Analysis of Business* (New York: Cambridge University Press, 1987).

45. William Rogerson, "Incentives in Defense Contracting," paper presented at the MIT Security Studies Program, October 1998.

46. Eugene Gholz and Harvey M. Sapolsky, "Restructuring the U.S. Defense Industry," *International Security* 24, no. 3 (Winter 1999–2000): 5–51.

47. Harvey M. Sapolsky, "Science and Politics of Defense Analysis," in Hamilton Cravens, ed., *The Social Sciences Go to Washington: The Politics of Knowledge in the Postmodern Age* (New Brunswick: Rutgers University Press, 2004), pp. 67–77.

48. Author interviews with FFRDC representatives and civilian employees of the Navy, May and June 2002.

49. Office of Technology Assessment, "History of FFRDCs."

50. In another recent example, a traditional technical adviser in the military communications sector, Alion Science and Technology Corporation (formerly known as IITRI), has protested the award of a contract for technical advice and testing services to ITT, a major producer of military communications systems, on conflict-of-interest grounds. Alion has for many years been the incumbent technical adviser to the military's Joint Spectrum Center. See Adams, "Defense Firm Alion Protests."

51. Author interview with defense industry representatives, May 2002.

52. Phil Balisle and Tom Bush, "CEC Provides Theater Air Dominance," U.S. Naval Institute *Proceedings* 128, no. 5 (May 2002): 60–62 and the responses in the July and August 2002 issues of *Proceedings*.

53. Jason Ma, "CEC Block II to be Redone as a Joint-Service Capability through OSD," *Inside the Navy*, January 19, 2004; "Raytheon's CLAWS Ends Development Testing with Direct Hit," *Defense Daily*, January 31, 2005.

54. McNaugher, "Weapons Procurement"; Ethan McKinney, Eugene Gholz, and Harvey M. Sapolsky, *Acquisition Reform*, MIT Lean Aircraft Initiative Policy Working Group, Working Paper 1, 1994.

55. Carl H. Builder, *The Masks of War* (Baltimore: Johns Hopkins University Press, 1989).

56. Peter J. Brown, "The Military Sector: Doing Business with the Decision-makers," *Via Satellite*, August 2, 2004.

57. OTA, *History of Department of Defense Federally Funded Research and Development Centers*, p. 5.

58. James Q. Wilson, *Bureaucracy*, pp. 91–101.

59. For example, Lockheed Martin has a large systems integration group in Valley Forge, Pennsylvania, with specific expertise in satellites and intelligence collection. Even Lockheed Martin's direct competitors acknowledge that this group has top-notch technical capability. Author interview with defense industry representative, March 2004. Lockheed Martin would need to keep some proprietary systems integration capability, even if it were clear that the military did not plan to delegate high-level systems integration/technical decision-making to the production prime contractors. In that scenario, each member of the production defense industrial base would have to make a business decision about what level of in-house funding to allot to SI, given that the main institutional home of that core competency would be outside the production industrial base.

60. That general support should be especially easy to arrange if systems integration organizations are paid for with a different part of the defense budget than the procurement accounts. Prime contractors naturally have the greatest interest and influence on procurement rather than infrastructure spending.

61. POET substantially outlived the particular "Phase One" referred to by its title. The reorganization of the BMDO into the Missile Defense Agency was accompanied by the creation of a "National Team" to provide technical support and systems integration for missile defense. The National Team involves prime contractors that produce platforms—specifically including platforms that will be deployed as part of the tiered missile-defense system of systems. Kerry Gildea, "First Increment of Missile Defense Command and Control Software Demonstrated," *C4I News*, May 1, 2003.

62. Author interview with civilian employee of the Ballistic Missile Defense Organization, August 2001.

63. Author interview with civilian employee of the Department of Defense, July 2002.

64. Jacobs, *The Sage Air Defense System*, p. 131; Hughes, *Rescuing Prometheus*, p. 62; Baum, *The System Builders*, pp. 38–39.

65. A similar idea was proposed to provide technical support to the missile-defense program—either personnel from established FFRDCs would have been reassigned to the new SDI Institute, or a new division of one of the established FFRDCs would have been created. This approach was rejected in favor of the POET, arguably because the new FFRDC approach was perceived as too slow to set up and too costly. Others suggest that the SDII proposal was blocked by political opponents of missile defense, who hoped to hamstring the effort by denying high-quality technical advice to the Strategic Defense Initiative Office. See Donald Baucom, "The Rise and Fall of the SDI Institute: A Case Study of the Management of the Strategic Defense Initiative," incomplete draft, August 1998.

7. MILITARY INNOVATION AND THE DEFENSE INDUSTRY

1. http://www.oft.osd.mil/

2. Lyle Goldstein and William Murray, "Undersea Dragons: China's Maturing Submarine Force," *International Security* 28, no. 4 (Spring 2004): 161–96.

3. Emily O. Goldman and Leslie C. Eliason, eds., *The Diffusion of Military Technology and Ideas* (Stanford: Stanford University Press, 2003); Emily Goldman, ed., *The Information Revolution in Military Affairs in Asia* (London: Palgrave Macmillan, 2004).

4. Barry R. Posen, *The Sources of Military Doctrine: France, Britain, and Germany Between the Wars* (Ithaca: Cornell University Press, 1984).

5. Clayton M. Christensen, *The Innovator's Dilemma: When New Technologies Cause Great Firms to Fail* (Boston: Harvard Business School Press, 1997).

6. Michael J. Lippitz, Sean O'Keefe, and John P. White, "Advancing the Revolution in Business Affairs," in Ashton Carter, ed., *Keeping the Edge: Managing Defense for the Future* (Cambridge: MIT Press, 2001), pp. 165–202.

7. Harvey M. Sapolsky, "Equipping the Armed Forces," in George Edwards and W. Earl Walker, eds., *National Security and the U.S. Constitution* (Baltimore: Johns Hopkins University Press, 1988), pp. 121–35.

8. Donald Rumsfeld, "21st Century Transformation," Remarks as Delivered by Secretary of Defense Donald Rumsfeld, National Defense University, Fort McNair, Washington, D.C., Thursday, January 31, 2002. Available at http://www.defenselink.mil/speeches/2002/s20020131-secdef.html.

9. Paul Bracken, "The Military after Next," *Washington Quarterly* 16, no. 4 (Autumn 1993): 157–74.

AAI, 64, 79, 141

Acquisition process, xi–xii, 19–21, 24–26, 28, 38, 52–54, 109–10, 111–17, 124–27, 133, 135, 139, 148

Advanced Concept Technology Demonstrations (ACTDs), 72, 139

Aerospace Corporation, 120, 123–24, 128

AeroVironment, 64, 82

Affordability, as a performance metric: for ships, 36, 44–46, 49

for UAVs, 61, 70–73, 74

Afghanistan, 13, 60, 62, 75, 78, 84–85, 136, 147

American Shipbuilding Association (ASA), 54, 81, 141

Analysis of Alternatives, 33, 111, 113, 117, 130

Antisubmarine Warfare (ASW), 35–36, 41, 47, 49

Applied Physics Laboratory (APL), 91, 101–2, 120, 123–24, 128, 129, 132

Arleigh Burke destroyers (DDG-51s), 40–41, 46, 47, 56

Association for Unmanned Vehicle Systems International (AUVSI), 81

Assured access, 11, 62

Austal USA, 37, 46, 56, 57, 141

BAe Systems, 90

Ballistic Missile Defense Organization (BMDO), 134–35

Bandwidth, 62, 95, 102

Bartlett, Rep. Roscoe (R-MD), 56

Bath Ironworks, 37, 39, 56, 114

Battle-group cooperation, as a performance metric: for ships, 43–44

Battlespace integration, as performance metric for UAVs, 73–75, 82

"Big Six" shipyards (see General Dynamics, Northrop Grumman)

Boeing, 24, 64, 72, 73, 80, 82–83, 90, 91, 112, 141

Bollinger Shipyards, 37, 56, 57, 141

Bureaucratic capture, 130–31

Capability-based planning, 6–7

Cebrowski, VADM Arthur, xii, 8, 12, 13, 14, 30–31, 55

Centralization, 109–10

Christensen, Clayton, 18, 27–28

Cisco Systems, xii, 31, 91

Civil service, 52, 117–18

Clark, ADM Vernon, 13, 40

Command and control, 75–77, 87, 106

Commercial information-technology industry, ix, 2, 30–31, 91, 98

Commercial Off-the-Shelf Technologies (COTS), xii, 52–53, 91

Common Operational Picture (COP), 9–10, 44, 61, 84, 86, 89, 90, 94–95, 98, 99, 101–2

Communications:
7-layer model (OSI), 87–90, 97
tactical v. reachback, 76, 86–87

Communications equipment, 5, 17, 84–85, 87–90, 103–4

Communications industry, 32, 84, 86, 92, 138–39, 142–43

Conflicts of interest, as performance metric for systems integration, 119–21, 126–29

Congress, 18, 22–23, 28, 54–56, 72, 81, 83, 86, 109–10, 127, 137–39, 142, 144, 146–48

Cooperative Engagement Capability (CEC), 44, 85, 92, 100–102, 107, 128

Core competency, 47, 53, 58, 111–12, 118, 122–23, 129, 139

"Cost as an Independent Variable," 45

Coté, Owen, 12, 13–14, 57

Customer-supplier relationship, 23–26, 27–28, 51–54, 78–80, 109, 145, 148

Customer understanding, 23–26, 28, 114, 118, 129–32
as performance metric for systems integration, 118, 129–32

Data Distribution System (DDS), 90, 100–101, 107

Data fusion, 61, 95, 98, 99–101

DD(X) destroyer, xiii, 36, 51, 148

Defense Advanced Research Projects Agency (DARPA), 30, 63, 73, 83, 123

Defense budget, 23, 34, 45, 81–82, 110, 129–30, 148

Defense industry (see also specific sectors), xii-xiii, 2, 19, 23–25, 30–31, 114–15, 133–34, 138–39

Department of Defense, ix, 12, 25, 109, 137–38, 147, 148

Dynamic allocation, as performance metric for communications, 89, 96, 101, 103, 105

Effects-based operations, 10–11, 62, 87

End-user control, as performance metric for UAVs, 61, 75–77

Endurance, as performance metric for UAVs, 61

England, Gordon (Secretary of the Navy), 56

Federally Funded Research and Development Centers (FFRDCs), 112, 114, 120–21, 127–28, 130, 134

Force protection, as performance metric for UAVs, 67–70

Force structure, 34–35, 59, 63–64, 81, 82–83, 109–10

FORCEnet, 90

Foreign suppliers, 52–53, 57, 64–65, 138

Future Combat Systems, 8, 79, 80, 98

General Atomics, 60, 64, 79, 82, 83, 141–42

General Dynamics, 37, 39, 41, 46, 53, 56, 64, 90, 147

Global Hawk UAV, 60, 62, 65, 72, 79, 142, 147

Global Information Grid, 76, 85–87, 95, 141

Gold plating, 40–41, 72

Halter Marine, 57

Information advantage, 8, 9, 106
Information Age, ix, xiv, 3, 4–6, 145
Information technology, 1, 5–6, 8, 38, 49, 125
Ingalls Shipyard, 39
Innovation:
    business school models of, 20–21
    defined, 2
    disruptive, 18, 27–28, 69–70, 72–73
    doctrinal, 2, 12–14, 17, 25, 137
    radical, 98
    sustaining, 18, 27, 69–70
    technological, 2, 26–29
Insitu, 82
Intelligence, Surveillance, and Reconnaissance (ISR), 10–11, 59, 61
Internet, 4–5, 17, 95, 98, 105–6, 123, 142
Internet Protocol version 6 (IPv6), 89, 96–97, 100, 106
Interoperability, 44, 75, 88, 91, 110, 111, 112, 117, 144
    as performance metric for communications, 102–5
Interservice rivalry, 13–14, 55, 57, 102–3, 130–31
Iraq, 13, 60, 73, 76, 78, 82, 84–85, 136, 147

Johns Hopkins University Applied Physics Laboratory (JHU-APL), see Applied Physics Laboratory (APL)
Joint Tactical Radio System (JTRS), 85, 90, 92, 96–98, 99, 104, 106, 109, 148
Joint ventures, 29, 39–40, 51, 57, 80, 82, 140–41
Joint Vision 2020, 8, 61

Kelly, Kevin (New Rules for a New Economy), 8

Latency, as performance metric for communications, 63, 98–102
Leadership, military, ix, xi, xiii, 7, 13–14, 21–23, 25–26, 40, 109, 145–47
Lewis, Rep. Jerry (R-CA), 81
Link 16, 96–98, 101, 105
Littoral Combat Ship (LCS), 36–37, 39, 40, 42, 125, 138, 140–41, 148
Lobbying, 18, 19–20, 23, 54–57, 81–83, 110, 142
Lockheed Martin, 37, 46, 56, 58, 64, 82, 83, 90, 91, 112, 114, 129

Manning, as a performance metric for ships, 50–51
Marinette Marine, 37, 56, 57, 141
Microsoft, 31
Military doctrine, xi, 7, 17, 25, 102, 114–15, 129, 137
Military expertise, 22, 24–25, 29, 37, 52, 80, 111, 114–18, 131–32
Military-industry relationship, xiii, 18, 19–21, 22–26, 52–54, 55, 78–80, 109, 116–18, 148
Military jargon, 8, 18, 24, 53, 80, 139
Military laboratories, 91, 114–18, 120, 134
Military services, 8–9, 13–14, 20, 22, 55, 77, 81, 102–3, 110, 111–12, 129–30, 137–38, 147
Missile Defense Agency (MDA), 134–35
MITRE, 91, 114, 120, 123, 132, 134
Modularity, as a performance metric for ships, 36, 49–50
Moore's Law, 8

Naval architecture, 41, 47–48, 49
Naval Sea Systems Command (NAVSEA), 52
Naval Surface Warfare Center—Dahlgren, 91, 114
Network Centric Operations Industry Consortium (NCOIC), 91, 110

Network-centric warfare:
    advantages, 7–8, 9–10, 35, 48
    contrast to platform-centric war-
        fare, 9, 48, 57, 135
    defined, xi, 3, 8, 9–12, 36, 113,
        123
Networks, xi, 9, 32, 89, 113
Nodes, 9, 32, 35, 61, 113
Nontraditional suppliers, xi–xiii, 2,
    24–25, 27–29, 30–31, 47, 51–53, 58,
    64–65, 105, 107, 138–39
Northrop Grumman, 21, 30, 39, 41, 53,
    60, 63, 72, 79, 82, 90, 91, 112, 113,
    141–42

Office of Force Transformation, x, 8, 14,
    135, 136
Organizational culture, 21, 29, 63, 77,
    116–17, 131, 134

Packet-switched networks, 96–97, 100,
    106
Patrick, Suzanne (Deputy Undersec-
    retary of Defense for Industrial
    Policy), 31
Perceived independence, as perfor-
    mance metric for systems integra-
    tion, 126–29
Performance metrics:
    defined, 27–28
    for communications, 93–108
    for ships, 36, 41–51, 140
    for systems integration 121–32
    for UAVs, 66–78
Phase One Evaluation Team (POET),
    134–35
Pork-barrel politics, 13, 22–23, 45, 56,
    83, 108–110, 127, 142
Posen, Barry, 12–13, 17
Precision weapons, 7, 10–11
Predator UAV, 60, 65, 79, 80, 142,
    147
Prime contractors, 28–29, 57–58,
    82–83, 90–91, 98, 112, 115, 118–19,
    132–34, 142

Profit motive, 20–21, 24, 120–21, 127,
    145
Project-management skill, as perfor-
    mance metric for systems integra-
    tion, 124–26
Public–private partnership, 82, 112,
    132, 146, 148
Public relations, 23, 55–56, 79

Quality of service, as performance
    metric for communications, 48, 96,
    105–6

Raytheon, 30, 58, 90, 91, 113, 128
Research and Development (R&D),
    20–21, 23, 81
Revolution in Military Affairs (RMA),
    1, 3–4, 6, 17, 30–31, 137–39, 145,
    147
"Revolving door," 24–25
Rosen, Stephen, 12, 13
Rumsfeld, Donald (Secretary of
    Defense), x, 12, 14, 136
Ryan Aeronautical, 63–64, 79

SAGE air defense system, 106, 134
ScanEagle UAV, 82
Science and Technology (S&T) spend-
    ing, 62
Science Applications International
    Corporation (SAIC), 91, 120–21,
    123
Sea Basing, 11, 35
Sea Power 21, 138
Security, as performance metric for
    communications, 106–7
Self-synchronization, 10, 43, 75–76
Shadow UAV, 64, 65, 79
Shipbuilding industry, 2, 32, 37, 38–39,
    41, 140–41
Single Integrated Air Picture (SIAP),
    89, 90, 91, 92, 101–2, 128
Single-purpose ships, as a performance
    metric for ships, 46–49
Situational awareness, 9, 61, 68–69, 74

Size, as a performance metric for ships, 41, 47–48

Small-unit initiative, 10, 17–18, 75–76

Software Engineering Institute (SEI), 91, 121–22, 123

Solipsys, 101–2, 128

Space and Naval Warfare Systems Center (SPAWAR), 30, 91

Speed, as a performance metric for ships, 36, 42–43

Startup firms, 28–30, 64, 80, 141

Stealth, as a performance metric for ships, 36, 43

Stevens, Sen. Ted (R-AK), 81

Streetfighter, 35, 45, 47

Subcontracting, 53–54, 58, 98, 114, 119, 125–26

Sun Microsystems, 31, 91

Swarming, 10, 35, 42, 43, 61, 74, 86

SYNTEK, 49, 121, 129

Systems engineering, 18, 100, 118

Systems integration, 32–33, 111–12, 133, 143–44
    architecture (see Systems integration, of systems of systems)
    definition, 111–15, 117, 133
    of components, 113–14, 119
    of platforms, 53–54, 57–58, 80, 83, 113–14, 118–19, 125–26
    of systems of systems, 86, 100, 111, 113–14, 119, 125–26, 131

Tactical Component Network (TCN), 101–2, 128

Technical awareness, as performance metric for systems integration, 114, 119, 122–24

Theory of military-technological innovation, 2, 17–19, 22, 26, 29–30, 137–38, 145–46

Threat-based planning, 7, 12–13

Throughput, as performance metric for communications, 62–63, 94–98, 99, 103

Transformation,
    defined, ix–xi, 6–9
    military, ix–xiv, 1–2, 6–9, 17–18, 29–30, 136–139

TRW Space Technology Laboratory, 120

UAV National Industry Team (UNITE), 82

University Applied Research Center (UARC), 120, 128

Unmanned Aerial Vehicles (UAVs), 32, 59–60, 63, 83, 93, 141–42, 147
    as communications relays, 62–63, 76, 106, 107
    communications links to pilots, 69, 74
    crash rate, 71
    for combat (UCAVs), 62, 72, 80
    maintenance, 71–72
    mean time between failures, 71
    personnel, 71
    stealth, 69, 74
    types, 60–62, 63–64

Unmanned Vehicle Systems International (UVSI), 81–82

Wal-Mart, xii, 8

Warfighter Information Network-Tactical (WIN-T), 85

Warner, Sen. John (R-VA), 81, 142

Weldon, Rep. Curt (R-PA), 81

World Wide Web, 9, 86

Young, John (Asst. Sec. of the Navy), 46

Young, Rep. C. W. (R-FL), 81

Edwards Brothers Inc.
Ann Arbor MI. USA
March 10, 2011